# THE CORRESPONDENCE OF HENRY JAMES AND THE HOUSE OF MACMILLAN, 1877–1914

# The Correspondence of Henry James and the House of Macmillan, 1877–1914

## 'All the Links in the Chain'

*Edited by*

Rayburn S. Moore

Louisiana State University Press
Baton Rouge

Printed in Hong Kong

First published in the United States of America 1993
by Louisiana State University Press

Library of Congress Cataloging-in-Publication Data

James, Henry, 1843–1916.
    The correspondence of Henry James and the house of Macmillan.
1877–1914 / edited by Rayburn S. Moore.
        p.    cm.
    Includes index.
    ISBN 0–8071–1834–6
    1. James, Henry, 1843–1916—Correspondence.    2. Macmillan
Publishing Company—Correspondence.    3. Publishers and publishing–
–United States—Correspondence.    4. Authors, American—19th century–
–Correspondence.    5. Authors, American—20th century–
–Correspondence.    6. Authors and publishers—United States—History.
I. Moore, Rayburn S., 1920–   .    II. Macmillan & Co.    III. Title.
PS2123.A46    1993
813'.4—dc20
[B]                                                                                    92–28962
                                                                                          CIP

The paper in this book meets the guidelines for permanence and
durability of the Committee on Production Guidelines for Book
Longevity of the Council on Library Resources. ∞

*For Margaret, again*

# Contents

A Note on Editorial Policy          viii

Acknowledgements          xi

List of Abbreviations          xiii

James Titles Published by Macmillan          xv

Introduction          xvii

**The Correspondence of Henry James and the House of Macmillan, 1877–1914**          1

Index          244

# A Note on Editorial Policy

This is an edition of the correspondence of Henry James and members of the firm of Macmillan and Company, 318 letters altogether. It includes all of James's letters to the firm in the Macmillan Archive, British Library, and a number that are available in other depositories, chiefly the New York Public Library, though it is clear from this correspondence that a few of his letters to both London and New York offices are missing for one reason or another and that at least one letter is incomplete. I have also omitted several letters – including one to Mrs Macmillan – that are mere receipts or brief social 'twaddle' and are impossible to date accurately. Despite company files in each headquarters, it should be added, copies of letters to James have in rare instances been misplaced and are not now included in letterbooks. Moreover, since James dealt chiefly with the London house, the correspondence focuses on James's exchange with that branch and with Frederick Macmillan in particular. It may be assumed, consequently, that those letters by James or by members of the firm whose locations are not given are in the Macmillan Archive; the locations of all others are mentioned in the notes.

In preparing these letters for print, I have tried, especially with James's letters (all manuscripts or signed typescripts in contrast to the company file copies) to provide a text based upon the letters in their earliest states and upon the collation of photocopy with manuscript or letterbook source. When the present text is based upon any other source, I have presented the appropriate information in the notes. Although some of the letters printed herein have appeared before in one form or another, I have, with a few exceptions, used the original or file copy as my text, acknowledged earlier printings in the annotation, and indicated, generally, differences between my texts and others. I have included previously published letters in order to offer in one place as complete a coverage as possible of the James–Macmillan correspondence and to provide texts consistently based upon fundamental materials.

I have tried throughout to follow James's epistolary practice with regard to a letter's content. I have retained his ampersands, reproduced *etc.* as &c, kept his punctuation within parentheses, maintained his dashes and in cases where they are used to indicate paragraphs have printed paragraphs accordingly, and, in short, have tried seriously to reproduce what James has written. On rare occasions I have silently completed a parenthesis or a dash, but in general I have refrained from correcting his spelling, his punctuation, and his syntax. When I have inserted something, I have indicated such additions by square brackets, and when I concluded that a Jamesian peculiarity might confuse the reader, I have used *sic*, but not often. Nor have I indicated titles of works (books, plays, or other literary productions) or foreign phrases by italics unless James has done so. (In the notes, of course, I follow the usual scholarly standards.) Fortunately, James makes few mistakes in spelling or grammar, and though he occasionally gets lost in the complexity of his syntax and dashes (especially as his style grows more complicated and ornate in his later period), he is normally in firm command of what he is writing, early or late, day or night, early phase or major phase. As for company correspondence, it is generally plainer and more direct, and I have followed the same standards of reproducing the text of these letters as well.

In regard to espistolary form itself, I have consistently placed addresses and dates in the upper right-hand corner, even when the address is printed top-centre on James's personal stationery. (This is the usual practice of both James and the firm, but James sometimes places this information after his signature and the company never includes its address on file copies.) I have retained the words and punctuation on such stationery even when I have regularised the address in regard to position or reduced the number of lines in order to save space. I have also attempted to reproduce James's and the company's underlining of *th* and *d* in dates, though I have omitted James's erratic underscoring of day, month, and year. I have followed James's inconsistent ways of indicating dates and have augmented the company practice of frequently supplying only the last digit of the year by giving the full complement of digits. I have also regularised the abbreviation of Junior to Jr with or without the comma and/or full stop as the case may be, but I have reproduced the inconsistencies of both James and the company correspondents in using upper or lower case, in separating the abbreviation from the name by a comma, and in indicating the abbreviation by a full stop.

Dates of James's letters are sometimes a problem. In a few instances he provides only a day for reference, and though dates may be provided by an unknown company hand, these may occasionally be inaccurate. All possible questions about dates – those in pencil and those provided by previous editors of James's letters – are discussed in the notes. As for salutations and closes, I have tried to follow the erratic practice of James and company correspondents. Salutations are frequently followed by a period, dash, or comma and in some instances by nothing at all. Complimentary closes, in James's case, are often incorporated in the last sentence of the text and only James's name is dropped below the last line – frequently with a flourish or a full stop that I have seen no need to include. Company closes are more standard in nature, and I have regularised them chiefly by bringing the phrases together in another effort to conserve space. It should be understood that all letters from James or the firm are signed or initialled by the writer (even company file copies) unless otherwise indicated.

My main intention is to offer a text that is as close to the original as possible but that is comprehensible to the printer, the scholar, and even, to borrow from Frederick Macmillan, 'that strange creature the "general reader"'. As I have indicated, I am aware of the problems of space, but I have always kept the centrality of the text in mind, even when I slightly modified form or convention.

Annotation is another matter. I have aimed primarily at an academic audience – scholar and student alike – and have tried to offer as much information and elucidation as will make the James–Macmillan correspondence accessible to readers of the present. I have provided much documentation and cross-reference in the conviction that readers who seek only one particular letter or another will use this edition as often as those who read it through from beginning to end. All readers, nevertheless, may consistently assume when annotation is not provided either that it is readily available in standard sources of reference or that I am, alas, not able to supply it.

A final word. James's handwriting, as is well known, is sometimes difficult to read and subject to varied interpretations. When words or passages are especially hard to make out, I have used question marks in the text or commented on them in the notes.

# Acknowledgements

It is a pleasure to record here the debts I have incurred in the preparation of this edition. I am particularly grateful to Alexander R. James, holder of the James family's copyrights, who has graciously permitted me to edit and publish the James letters in this edition; to T. M. Farmiloe, Editorial Director, and Macmillan Ltd, London, for giving me permission to include correspondence from the Macmillan Archive, the British Library, and to Agnes Fisher and Macmillan Publishing Company, New York, for permission to print from the firm's correspondence with James in the New York Public Library.

The letters in this edition are published with the permission also of the British Library; the New York Public Library (Rare Books and Manuscripts Division and the Berg Collection); the Houghton Library, Harvard University; the Library of Congress; and the Barrett Library, University of Virginia Library. These libraries and others have generously allowed me to use their holdings and have furnished photocopies of manuscripts, especially the Beinecke Rare Book and Manuscript Library, the Collection of American Literature, Yale University. The William R. Perkins Library, Duke University, and the National Library of Scotland, Edinburgh, have also been generous with their resources.

Among the many librarians who have been helpful, I should like to thank especially Julian Conway and his staff, Students' Reading Room, Department of Manuscripts, the British Library; Sally Brown, Keeper of Manuscripts, C. M. Hall, Higher Executive Officer, Department of Manuscripts, and Elizabeth James, English Language Collections, the British Library; Claire Columbo, Ilah Dunlap Little Library, University of Georgia; Rodney G. Dennis, Curator of Manuscripts, and Jennie Rathbun, Houghton Library, Harvard University; Ellen H. Belcher, New York Public Library; Michael Plunkett, Curator of Manuscripts, and Richard Lindemann, Barrett Library, University of Virginia Library; and Patricia C. Willis and Daria Ague, Beinecke Rare Book and Manuscript Library, Yale University.

Correspondence previously published in *Henry James Letters*, edited by Leon Edel, is reprinted by permission of Harvard University Press (B. K. Kinder) and is copyrighted 1975, 1980, 1984 by Alexander R. James. For permission to reprint letters published in *Letters to Macmillan*, I am pleased to thank Mr James and Macmillan Press Ltd.

For various scholarly courtesies, I am grateful to Alfred Bendixen, Leon Edel, Robert L. Gale, the late H. Montgomery Hyde, Margaret B. Moore, and Steven Ozment. Professor Gale deserves special mention for reading the manuscript so carefully and thoroughly yet promptly and for sharing his encyclopaedic knowledge of James so generously. For research assistance, I owe thanks to Walter Gordon and Hugh Ruppersburg who made it available and to Glenn Harris and Karen Radford who consistently supplied it.

I appreciate very much the support of Dean John J. Kozak, Franklin College of Arts and Sciences, University of Georgia, who made it possible for me to devote parts of each year to this project and who continued to encourage me even after the eleventh hour. My thanks also go to Coburn Freer, Head, Department of English, who scheduled released time and provided travel funds, and to Joe L. Key, Vice-President for Research, and Rita C. Richardson, for vital support.

For typing various drafts of the manuscript and for helping me to decipher James's scrawl as well as occasionally illegible handwritten company file copies, I am grateful to Florence Whitmire, who has also cheerfully put up with my own illegibility.

The editorial staff of Macmillan Ltd has been unfailingly helpful. Tim Farmiloe has encouraged me from the outset, John Handford has patiently answered queries about the firm, and Margaret Cannon and Valery Rose have worked diligently to prepare the manuscript for the press.

Last but not least, I am grateful to Linda Webster for indexing this edition with her usual competence.

# List of Abbreviations

| | |
|---|---|
| Anesko | Michael Anesko, *'Friction with the Market': Henry James and the Profession of Authorship* (New York: Oxford University Press, 1986). |
| BHJ | Leon Edel, Dan H. Laurence, and James Rambeau, *A Bibliography of Henry James*, 3rd edn (Oxford: Clarendon Press, 1982). |
| BL | British Library, London. |
| CN | Leon Edel and Lyall H. Powers (eds), *The Complete Notebooks of Henry James* (New York: Oxford University Press, 1987). |
| Edel | Leon Edel, *Henry James*, vol I: *The Untried Years, 1843–1870* (1953); vol. II: *The Conquest of London, 1870–1881* (1962); vol. III: *The Middle Years, 1882–1895* (1962); vol. IV: *The Treacherous Years, 1895–1901* (1969); vol. V: *The Master, 1901–1916* (1972). All volumes published by J. B. Lippincott & Co. in Philadelphia and by Rupert Hart-Davis in London. |
| Graves | Charles L. Graves, *Life and Letters of Alexander Macmillan* (London: Macmillan, 1910). |
| Harvard | Houghton Library, Harvard University. |
| HJEW | Lyall H. Powers (ed.), *Henry James and Edith Wharton: Letters, 1900–1915* (New York: Charles Scribner's Sons, 1990). |
| HJL | Leon Edel (ed.), *Henry James Letters*, 4 vols (Cambridge, Mass.: Harvard University Press, 1974, 1975, 1980, 1984). |
| HJ:SL | Leon Edel (ed.), *Henry James: Selected Letters* (Cambridge, Mass.: Harvard University Press, 1987). |
| LB | Letterbooks, Macmillan Archive, British Library; contains correspondence with James. |
| LC | Library of Congress. |
| LHJ | Percy Lubbock (ed.), *The Letters of Henry James*, 2 vols (New York: Charles Scribner's Sons, 1920; London: Macmillan, 1920). |
| LM | Simon Nowell-Smith (ed.), *Letters to Macmillan* (London: Macmillan, 1967; New York: St Martin's Press, 1967). |

MA   Macmillan Archive, British Library; contains Letter-books and James letters.

Morgan  Charles Morgan, *The House of Macmillan (1843–1943)* (New York: The Macmillan Company, 1944).

NYPL  New York Public Library. Rare Books and Manuscripts Division.

NYPLB  New York Public Library, Berg Collection.

*SL*   Leon Edel (ed.), *The Selected Letters of Henry James* (New York: Farrar, Straus & Giroux, 1955; repr. Garden City, N.Y.: Doubleday Anchor Books, 1960).

*SLHJEG* Rayburn S. Moore (ed.), *Selected Letters of Henry James to Edmund Gosse, 1882–1915: A Literary Friendship* (Baton Rouge: Louisiana State University Press, 1988).

TC   Typed copy.

TLS   Typed letter signed.

Virginia  Barrett Library, University of Virginia.

Yale   Beinecke Library, Yale University.

# James Titles Published by Macmillan

(This list includes neither cheap reprints nor those titles printed for copyright purposes only.)

| | | |
|---|---|---|
| 1. | *French Poets and Novelists.* <br> London only. | 1878 |
| 2. | *The Europeans.* <br> London only. | 1878 |
| 3. | *Daisy Miller: A Study. An International Episode.* <br> *Four Meetings.* <br> 2 volumes. London only. | 1879 |
| 4. | *The American.* <br> London only. | 1879 |
| 5. | *Roderick Hudson.* <br> 3 volumes. London only. | 1879 |
| 6. | *The Madonna of the Future and Other Tales.* <br> 2 volumes. London only. | 1879 |
| 7. | *Hawthorne.* <br> London only. | 1879 |
| 8. | *Washington Square. The Pension Beaurepas.* <br> *A Bundle of Letters.* <br> 2 volumes. London only. | 1881 |
| 9. | *The Portrait of a Lady.* <br> 3 volumes. London only. | 1881 |
| 10. | *Collective Edition.* <br> 14 volumes. London only. First collected edition <br> of James's work. | 1883 |
| 11. | *Portraits of Places.* <br> London only. | 1883 |
| 12. | *Tales of Three Cities.* <br> London only. | 1884 |
| 13. | *Stories Revived.* <br> 3 volumes. London only. | 1885 |

14. *The Bostonians.*                                                    1886
    3 volumes. London. 1 volume. New York.
15. *The Princess Casamassima.*                                          1886
    3 volumes. London and New York.
16. *Partial Portraits.*                                                 1888
    London and New York.
17. *The Reverberator.*                                                  1888
    2 volumes. London and New York.
18. *The Aspern Papers. Louisa Pallant. The Modern Warning.*             1888
    2 volumes. London and New York.
19. *A London Life. The Patagonia. The Liar. Mrs Temperly.*              1889
    2 volumes. London and New York.
20. *The Tragic Muse.*                                                   1890
    2 volumes. London only.
21. *The Lesson of the Master. The Marriages. The Pupil.*
    *Brooksmith. The Solution. Sir Edmund Orme.*                         1892
    New York and London.
22. *The Real Thing and Other Tales.*                                    1893
    New York and London.
23. *Embarrassments.*                                                    1896
    New York only.
24. *The Other House.*                                                   1896
    New York only.
25. *The Two Magics. The Turn of the Screw. Covering End.*               1898
    New York only.
26. *The Soft Side.*                                                     1900
    New York only.
27. *The Novels and Tales of Henry James.*                         1908–1909
    24 volumes. Edition de Luxe. London only.
28. *A Small Boy and Others.*                                           1913
    London only.
29. *Notes of a Son and Brother.*                                       1914
    London only.
30. *Letters.*                                                          1920
    2 volumes. London only.
31. *The Novels and Stories of Henry James.*                       1921–1923
    35 volumes. New and Complete Edition. London only.

# Introduction

On 7 August 1877 Henry James, recently settled in London with four books just out in America, wrote to Macmillan and Company, the publisher of Arnold, Kingsley, Pater, Lewis Carroll, and Christina Rossetti, among others, about the possibility of bringing out the first authorised printing in England of a new book, a collection of essays to be called *French Poets and Novelists*.[1] Frederick Macmillan, the son of the senior founding partner of the firm who was later destined to take charge of it, answered James the next day and invited him to send the essays and 'to call' at the company's Bedford Street office. James, accordingly, sent in the manuscript and may have visited the office to meet Macmillan. Within two weeks, despite an unfavourable reader's report (not mentioned to James in extant correspondence) and an awareness that 'volumes of reprinted Essays' seldom sold well, Macmillan agreed 'to take the risk of printing the book' on the basis of shared profits. Five days later on 27 August, James, who was out of town and had just received Macmillan's letter, acknowledged that he was 'glad' Macmillan was 'disposed to undertake [the] book' and promised 'to call upon [him] as soon as [he] return[ed] to London, which [he] expected to be tomorrow, to answer [his] observations touching details'. Macmillan had stipulated, for example, that the text be limited 'strictly to 350 pages' and had urged James to select 'those papers most likely to be interesting to that strange creature the "general reader"'. Though no memorandum of agreement was signed until 20 January 1879, James and Macmillan apparently agreed that the author could expand the manuscript by including three essays not originally listed and not necessarily calculated, one might add, to suit the taste of the 'general reader'.

James, then, revised the manuscript and it was put 'into the printer's hands' early in September, but he left England for the continent a few days later; and since he was not able to furnish the firm with a permanent address, did not see and correct proof until December. After his return home late in the month, he completed the task, the book was ready for the binder by the end of January, and it came out on 19 February.[2]

Thus Henry James first appeared officially before the British public as a writer of criticism, not as a fictionist, though both *Roderick Hudson* and *The American* had been sold in England in imported American editions before *French Poets and Novelists* appeared (*BHJ*, pp. 30, 32).

The professional tie between publisher and author now established, Macmillan sought to encourage a social relationship. After meeting in August, the two met in Paris following James's arrival in mid-September, and upon his return to London in late December, he was quickly invited to dinner at the Macmillan home in St John's Wood, where he soon became a frequent guest, not only as a result of Macmillan's interest in him and his work but because Mrs Macmillan, the former Georgiana Warrin of Newtown, Long Island, New York, took a liking to him and enjoyed his company. Moreover, Alexander Macmillan, the senior partner of the firm and Frederick's uncle, also invited James on occasion to dine at Knapdale, Upper Tooting, his home outside London, and by the summer of 1879 was so fond of him, James reported, that he 'physically *hugs* me'.[3]

Other members of the firm were also involved with James in one way or another. Maurice C. and George A. Macmillan, Frederick's brother and Alexander's son, respectively, both corresponded about various stages of proof and book production. George Lillie Craik, a partner in the company, wrote, too, on occasion. Business with *Macmillan's Magazine* and the *English Illustrated Magazine* was usually handled by one of the editors: George Grove, John Morley, Mowbray Morris, or Comyns Carr. In America, George E. Brett, the house's 'agent' in New York, usually took charge of its transactions with James, though after his death in 1890, his son and successor, George P. Brett, dealt more frequently with James.

From the beginning, however, James was primarily Frederick Macmillan's responsibility, and the junior partner conducted the firm's business affairs with James unless he was away from the office or out of town. With the first publication under production, Macmillan wasted no time in seeking another book from his new American author, and over the next twelve years he published fifteen titles by James, from *The Europeans* (1878) to *The Tragic Muse* (1890), including reprints of *The American* and *Roderick Hudson*, serial appearances in *Macmillan's Magazine* of *The Portrait of a Lady* (1881) and *The Reverberator* (1888), 'The Author of Beltraffio' (1884) in *English Illustrated Magazine*, and in 1883 the first collected edition of James's fiction, in fourteen volumes.

The only temporary break in the early relationship between the author and the firm occurred in 1879, when James, though pleased by his cordial social relations with 'the Macmillans', became concerned in the summer of that year about the 'conspicuous . . . absence' of the 'delicious ring of the sovereign'; and after receiving a disheartening account from the house of the sale of his books, offered the English book rights to his next novel *Confidence* to Chatto and Windus on 27 September for 'a royalty & a certain sum of money down', a ploy that led the rival company to offer to lease the English rights for three years for £100, a proposal James accepted.[4] Frederick Macmillan remonstrated with James on 12 November, noting that he thought 'it was understood that we were to publish' the book. Two days later he confessed that he 'did feel hurt' about James's handling of the novel, but he also apparently got the point about offering 'money down' on a manuscript.

> [W]e don't pretend to any claim over your work [he acknowledged], but as we have been your publishers hitherto [,] I am sorry you should have gone elsewhere merely because you wanted some ready money. If you had written to my Uncle [Frederick Macmillan himself had been out of town] proposing that we should advance you £100 on account of future profits, you would undoubtedly have received a cheque by return of post.

Acknowledging that 'the flavour' of James's work was 'too delicate to be at once appreciated by palates accustomed to coarser food', Macmillan urged James to 'trust us' and to consider '"the withdrawal of your confidence"' as 'only temporary', an entreaty to which James responded by continuing to publish with the firm until he became restive again a decade later.[5]

In the meantime, when James R. Osgood and Company failed in Boston in 1885 and left James in a real financial bind about the book publication in America of *The Bostonians*, James felt close enough to Frederick Macmillan to seek his help, and Macmillan came to the rescue with sound advice and action concerning James's situation *vis-à-vis* serial and book publication rights, despite George E. Brett's belated hint that the novel, though 'splendidly written', was 'so long'.[6] In an exchange of letters beginning on 5 May, James described his plight and supplied information about it, and Macmillan responded in detail from his own knowledge and that of the firm's solicitors. The outcome was that James lost the income from serial rights to the novel (for a flat sum of $4,000 never paid he had sold Osgood the serial and book rights that the publisher, in turn, had sold to others, received payment for, and spent the proceeds from without compensating James), but since Macmillan's firm was one of Osgood's creditors, he managed to retrieve the book rights for James and to publish both English and American issues of the novel, saving James in the end over half of what he would otherwise have lost by his arrangement with Osgood.

James, of course, was properly grateful and his relations with Macmillan and the firm developed without serious incident until *The Tragic Muse* came under consideration five years later, in 1890. When Macmillan wrote on 22 March to inquire abut the publication of the novel in England (James, he remarked, had 'not yet said anything . . . about this book'), James replied on 24 March that he had 'all along taken for granted . . . that in England you will still be glad to issue the book.' (Houghton, Mifflin and Company, Boston, was publishing it in America.) Macmillan, accordingly, proposed on 25 March that the firm bring out the novel in a three-volume format and that James receive '*two thirds* of whatever profits there may be'. On the next day James declined the offer of money 'in the future' and suggested instead 'a sum of money "down"' as a 'declaration of . . . alternative' and concluded: 'But I should be sorry to pursue this alternative without hearing from you again – though,' he admitted, 'I don't flatter myself that I hold the knife at your throat.' Macmillan answered promptly on the same day that his proposal had not been based upon any 'objection' to paying 'promptly' but upon a 'desire to guard against loss'. 'I am sorry to say,' he continued, 'that this caution arises from the fact that the commercial result of the last few books we have published for you has been anything but satisfactory.' Still, he acknowledged, 'we like to be your publishers and are anxious to fall in with your wishes about terms as far as we can prudently do so.' Consequently, he offered to 'pay "down"' a sum not 'less than £70', a total 'equal to two-thirds of the estimated profits of an edition of 500 copies'. James considered the proposal and on 28 March wrote his well-known 'farewell' letter to Macmillan. Noting that despite the 'poor success of my recent books' he wished to get a 'larger sum' than the £70 mentioned and was determined to take whatever steps were necessary, he granted that such action would 'carry me away from you'. ' . . . [I]t comes over me,' he continued, that that is after all better, even with a due & grateful recognition of the readiness you express to go on with me unprofitable as I am. I say it is "better" because I had far rather that in these circumstances you should *not* go on with me. I would rather not be published at all than be published & not pay – other people at least. . . . Unless [he concluded] I can put the matter on a more remunerative footing all round I shall give up my English "market" . . . & confine myself to my American. But I must experiment a bit first – & to experiment is of course to say farewell to you. Farewell, then, my dear Macmillan, with great regret – but with the sustaining cheer of all the links in the chain that remain still unbroken.[7]

James's farewell, however, was premature. He now turned the matter over to his recently acquired agent, A. P. Watt (he had come to terms with Watt in February 1888 concerning sales to English magazines, chiefly), and Watt proposed to Macmillan a five-year lease on the copyright of the novel for £250 'down'. Macmillan accepted these terms on 2 April, had the book 'all in type' early in May, and, despite the slowness of the printers, ready for publication on 7 July.[8]

Thus the possible break in the business relations between James and the firm was temporarily averted, and, despite Watt's role in the sale of *The Tragic Muse*, he seems to have had little to do with future negotiations between author and publisher. Moreover, James's decision to turn to drama and away from the novel did not prevent him from writing short stories and publishing collections of them with Macmillan in both London and New York.

By June 1893, however, despite James's view that it was a 'great convenience' to publish with Macmillan because of the firm's offices in England and America, his books began to appear with Harper and Brothers in New York and Osgood, McIlvaine and Company in London. In 1895, William Heinemann began to publish James's fiction in London, and in 1896, after an interim of three years, George P. Brett brought out two of James's books in New York only: *Embarrassments* (1896), a collection of tales, and *The Other House* (1896), a short novel.

When James returned seriously to the novel in 1897 with *The Spoils of Poynton* and *What Maisie Knew*, he continued to publish with Heinemann in London and various houses in New York. Subsequently, in 1898, James B. Pinker became James's literary agent, and although Macmillan and Company published in that year the American issue of *The Two Magics*, one of which 'magics', indeed, was 'The Turn of the Screw', and in 1900 the American edition of *The Soft Side*, a collection of stories, the firm did not bring out another James work until it acquired the English rights of the New York Edition in 1907. The reason for this hiatus, at least in part, was James's conviction that Brett was not paying him as well as other publishers and did not, on occasion, even pay promptly. The failure to settle accounts when due may have been based, unbeknownst to James, upon a lack of co-ordination between Brett and the London branch. Whatever the cause or lack of understanding, James decided in 1900 to 'terminate' relations with Brett.[9]

This decision did not involve the home office, and when, a few years later, Frederick Macmillan proposed a book on London and terms that appealed very much to James, he signed a contract in 1903 for a 20% royalty and an advance of £1,000 for a volume he tentatively called 'London Town'. Regrettably, the project came up during a period when James was involved with work on *The Golden Bowl*, *The American Scene*, and the selected edition of his novels and tales, and he never completed it, though he worked on it from time to time and the firm spent a considerable amount of money seeking to bring it to fruition, including £500 for illustrations by Joseph Pennell. As late as 5 April 1908, James bemoaned the 'long train of fatality and difficulty and practical deterrence' that had frustrated and delayed his performance of the project; still he maintained that he 'kept it constantly in view', had made a 'great deal of preparation for it', had 'read a great deal', and had 'roamed and poked and pried about in town' when he had had leisure to do so.[10]

As suggested, one of the chief reasons for the delay of 'London Town', according to James in the same letter, had been the time and energy he had spent on 'the publication of an elaborately revised and retouched and embellished and copiously prefaced and introduced Collective, and *selective*, Edition of my productions', a project Macmillan would accept in July and would begin publishing in England late in September.[11] More ironically still, however, was the tepid reaction of the public to this edition, as James confessed years later to Edmund Gosse. On 25 August 1915, seven months before his death, he informed his old friend:

That Edition has been, from the point of view of profit either to the publishers or to myself, practically a complete failure; vulgarly speaking, it doesn't sell – that is my annual report of what it does – the whole 25 vols. – in this country amounts to about £25 from the Macmillans; & the ditto from Scribners in the U.S. to very little more.[12]

Though the failure of 'London Town' to materialise apparently did not adversely affect James's relations with Frederick Macmillan, it may have led James and Pinker temporarily to seek to deal with other members of the firm. In 1910, for example, Pinker wrote to the house in an effort to sell English book rights to James's current (and last) collection of tales, *The Finer Grain*, and received a chilling reply from George B. Muir(?), a current member of the staff, on 6 April: 'We are afraid that we do not see our way to consider the question of the publication of the proposed volume of five stories by Mr Henry James; we feel sure that even in the most favourable circumstances the only terms we should now be able to propose for a book by Mr James would hardly be acceptable to him' (LB, MA).[13]

Despite this rejection, James published two more important titles with the firm, *A Small Boy and Others* and *Notes of a Son and Brother*, the first two volumes of his autobiography, in London in 1913 and 1914, respectively, and handled by Frederick Macmillan (Sir Frederick since 1909), with whom his relations continued to be cordial. Though many of the business details had been handled for years by Pinker, James and Macmillan still corresponded from time to time on such matters as proofs, illustrations, format, author's copies, reviews, and other aspects of publication, to say nothing of personal matters, greetings to each other and from Mrs Macmillan, and invitations to visit. The last letters of each regarding the newly published *Notes of a Son and Brother* suggest the nature of the relationship. On 16 March 1914, Macmillan wrote to James:

Very appreciative reviews of your book are coming in every day, but we are not forwarding them to you as I fancy you do not care to read newspaper criticism of your work. They are of course at your service if you care to see them. There is every sign that the book is going to "do."

James replied promptly on 17 March:

> Kindly permit me to thank you . . . for your interesting note about
> reviews etc. of my book just out. I am glad to hear of such friendly
> symptoms, but shall not trouble you to have them passed on – not
> from indifference to the reception of the work, but from prefer-
> ring, on the whole, to take the friendliness for granted and per-
> haps even hug a little the illusion of its being even more splendid
> than in fact. May it at any rate be splendid enough to give the
> book a lift; I am delighted to hear that there is such an appearance,
> and am yours all faithfully.[14]

Though *Notes of a Son and Brother* was the last book James published with the firm during his lifetime, he continued to visit Sir
Frederick and Lady Macmillan on occasion and dined with them on
18 May 1915, only six months before he suffered the first stroke of his
final illness on 2 December (*CN*, p. 422).

James died the following February, well over thirty-eight years
after penning his first letter to Macmillan and after arrangements
between artist and house had been initially settled. Based very much
upon friendly relations between author and publisher and upon
Frederick Macmillan's belief in James as a significant writer – 'all the
links in the chain', as James once characterised it – the relationship
was nevertheless concurrently concerned with the usual hardheaded
aspects of business – James's desire to get as much as possible for his
output and Macmillan's working premise that both author and firm
be served by the relationship.

In the end, both were served, though James had the best of it. The
firm, to be sure, lost over £120 on *The Tragic Muse* and well over
£500 on the 'London Town' project that James never completed. On
the other hand, the firm published twenty-seven titles by James and
four editions of his work (if the Lubbock edition of letters be included), more than any other publisher, American or British; enough,
one might say, to justify Macmillan's comments over the years regarding his wish to be James's publisher and 'to have the whole of
[his] books in a uniform edition'. In the Collective Edition of 1883,
the Edition de Luxe of 1908–1909 (the New York Edition in America),
the *Letters* of 1920, and the thirty-five-volume edition of 1921–1923,
Macmillan published virtually 'the whole' of James's work and more
than justified his faith in James's ability and promise, and served
James very well, indeed.[15]

## II

James's letters to the house of Macmillan have appeared chiefly in Simon Nowell-Smith's collection (1967) – six, including two in part – and in Leon Edel's edition (4 volumes, 1974–84) – seventeen, including two already published by Nowell-Smith – and some of James's correspondence and that of certain members of the firm are quoted from in Michael Anesko's '*Friction with the Market*' (1986), but the present edition prints in full over 290 previously unpublished letters by James and Frederick Macmillan and other writers representing the company in London and New York.

The letters, to be sure, discuss business matters primarily – terms for appearances in magazine and in book form, dates of publication, and format, type, and other technical matters – but the exchange between James and Frederick Macmillan usually includes greetings to and from Mrs Macmillan, invitations to dinner or to weekends at one Macmillan home or other, and from time to time bits of literary gossip about mutual friends or acquaintances.

The reader of these letters learns a good deal, particularly about Henry James and Frederick Macmillan, and about the literary and publishing worlds of this period. James's experience with the chief publisher of his books is clearly detailed, as is the gradual development of his awareness and knowledge of the business of getting his books to the market. In these ways the correspondence provides a fascinating insight into the relations between a major author and his publisher covering almost four decades of a fascinating time and illuminating especially the elements of commerce and friendship in the relationship. 'Solidity of specification', indeed, as James might have characterised it.

### Notes

1. The letters upon which this edition is based are chiefly in the MA, BL, London, and are cited with the permission of Mr Alexander R. James, holder of the James family copyrights, the Macmillan Press Ltd, and the BL. For a full listing of repositories and permissions, see letter 1, note 1.
2. All dates of publication of James's works are as given in *BHJ*, unless otherwise indicated.
3. For the Macmillans, see Graves, Morgan, *LM*, and *HJL*, III, 126. James's comment on Alexander Macmillan occurs in a letter of 15 June [1879?] to his brother William (Harvard).
4. Parts of James's letters are quoted in *BHJ*, p. 44, and in Anesko, p. 54. Ironically, less than two weeks earlier James had written to a friend that though he was

      'tolerably "in" with . . . the good Macmillans', one of the firm's 'strong points' was not to give authors a 'palpable sum of money in consequence' of publishing their books (*HJL*, ɪɪ, 255).

5.  'Confidence', indeed, was restored in 1883 when the novel was published by Macmillan in the Collective Edition of that year, the firm's first effort to publish a 'uniform edition', to use Macmillan's term, of James's fiction.

6.  George E. Brett to Frederick Macmillan, 18 May 1886 (LB, MA).

7.  This letter has been printed in *LM*, pp. 171–2 and in *HJL*, ɪɪɪ, 275.

8.  Some of these details are also available in *LM*, p. 172; *HJL*, ɪɪɪ, 276n; and in Anesko, pp. 129–30. Though *BHJ* proposes June as date of publication (p. 84), Macmillan's letter of 6 July (no. 208) clearly establishes 7 July as the correct date.

9.  See, below, letter 256, note 2, for James's remark to Pinker about his relations with Brett in a letter of 22 February 1900 (Yale).

10.  A year later James and Macmillan were still discussing the book. See *CN*, pp. 278, 309. For James's notes on 'London Town', see *CN*, pp. 273–80. See also Macmillan to Pennell, 10 April 1908 (LB, MA).

11.  See James's letters to Pinker of 12 June and 15 July 1908 (Yale) and *BHJ*, p. 138.

12.  *SLHJEG*, p. 313. James is wrong about the number of volumes. The edition appeared in 24 volumes, not 25. According to James's correspondence with Pinker in 1915, he acknowledged receiving £27.18.9 from Scribner on 4 January and £36.9.10 from Macmillan on 6 February (Yale).

13.  Though the initial M. is signed under the company rubric, the writer is presumably G.B.M. (George B. Muir?), an otherwise unidentified number of the firm during this period. I am grateful to Elizabeth James, British Library, for this information. For other correspondence by G.B.M., see letter 277, below.

14.  James's practice since the late 1880s had been to advise the firm not to send him copies of reviews and notices unless specifically requested.

15.  Still, after his death in 1916, James's books with the company were valued by the firm at only £75. See James Foster's letter to Pinker, 27 March 1916 (LB, MA). For Foster's service with the firm, see letter 293, note 2.

# The Correspondence of
# Henry James and the
# House of Macmillan
# 1877–1914

**1**

Messrs Macmillan & Co –
Dear Sirs:

It was mentioned to me some time since by my friend & country-man Mr. J. [*sic*] W. Smalley that you had inquired my address of him with some apparent intention of making a proposal to me with regard to the simultaneous issue here of a novel of mine lately published in Boston by Messrs. Osgood & Co. viz: "*The American*".[2] As, in fact, I did not hear from you, I supposed that you had sub-sequently decided otherwise: but the circumstance I mention gives me a certain ground for myself making you a proposal. I am dis-posed to collect into a volume a series of papers published during the last four or five years in American periodicals (the *N.A. Review*, the *Galaxy*, the *Nation* &c.) upon French writers. I should like to publish the book in England; I have taken & propose to take, no steps with regard to its appearing in America. It would consist of some 13 or 14 articles, of various lengths, & would make a volume, I should say, of about 325 (largely-printed) pages. It would treat of writers of the day, & I should call it "French Poets and Novelists". The table of contents would be about this:

Balzac's Novels.
Balzac's Letters.
George Sand.
Gustave Flaubert.
Alf. de Musset.
Théophile Gautier.
Ivan Tourguéneff.
Ch. Baudelaire.
Théâtre Français &c.[3]

Should you feel disposed to undertake the publication of such a volume as I speak of? I shall be glad to learn what your inclination may be.

I remain, dear Sirs,

Respectfully yours
Henry James Jr.

### Notes

1.  This is James's first letter in the letterbooks in the MA, BL, London. It has printed in *LM*, 168 (in part) and *HJL*, ɪɪ, 131–2 (in full). The present text differs in several substantive ways from these printings. All texts in this edition, unless otherwise indicated, are located in BL and are based, with a few exceptions, upon a comparison of photoduplications with James's original manuscripts and company file copies in BL and those that have been found elsewhere. All letters are printed here with the permission of Alexander R. James, present holder of the James family copyrights; The British Library; the Beinecke Library, Yale University; the Houghton Library, Harvard University; the Library of Congress; the New York Public Library; the Barrett Library, University of Virginia; and Macmillan Publishing Co., New York, and Macmillan Press Ltd, London.
2.  George Washburn Smalley (1833–1916) was the London correspondent of the New York *Tribune* (1867–95) and US correspondent of *The Times*, London (1895–1905). Smalley and his wife, Phoebe Garnaut, the adopted daughter of Wendell Phillips, both Americans, frequently entertained James in their London home and were well known in local social circles. *The American* had appeared in Boston in May 1877. Macmillan and Co. published the first authorised English edition of *The American* in March 1879. See letters 16 and 17.
3.  *French Poets and Novelists* was published 19 February 1878 and contained twelve essays, including the nine titles listed and three others: 'The Two Ampères', 'Madame de Sabran', and 'Mérimée's Letters'. See *BHJ*, pp. 34–5. All references to dates of James's books, unless otherwise indicated, are to this edition. For subsequent discussion of the publication of *French Poets*, see letters 3–12.

## 2

Aug: 8. 1877.

Dear Sir:

If you will kindly send us the papers to which you refer, or such of them as you happen to have by you we shall be glad to consider the question of publishing them in a volume.[1]

I was disappointed at not meeting you last Sunday when I lunched with our common friend Nadal, & I shall be very pleased to make your acquaintance if you can find time to call here any day between 11 and 5 o'clock – [2]

I am

Faithfully yours
Frederick Macmillan

H. James, Esq[3]

### Notes

1. The volume mentioned is *French Poets and Novelists*. See letter 1, note 3. For Macmillan's agreement to publish the book, see letter 3.
2. Ehrman Syme (usually E.S.) Nadal (1843–1916), a Virginian, was second secretary of the American legation in London (1877–84), and James had met him in July at the legation, though he had reviewed Nadal's *Impressions of London Social Life* (1875) for the *Nation* in 1875 (xxi, 7 October, 232–3).
3. Though James usually signed himself Junior until his father's death in 1882, he was not always addressed as such in correspondence.

## 3

Aug 22. 1877.

My dear Sir,

We have been carefully considering your proposed volume of Essays on "French Poets and Novelists", and though our previous experience of volumes of reprinted Essays has not been such as to make us very sanguine about the success of the venture we are willing to take the risk of printing the book, sharing with you any profit that may result from its publication.[1]

We propose to make a volume in form like Lord Albemarles [*sic*] autobiography a copy of which I send herewith (if you don't happen to have read it let me commend it to you as a most amusing book), and in order that it may not be too expensive we must limit you strictly to 350 pages.[2] I would also ask you to prepare the copy for press as carefully as you can before it goes to the printer; so that the book may not be weighted with a heavy charge for corrections.

In making arrangements with your American publisher, would you be kind enough to suggest that he should allow us to supply him with a set of stereotype plates from our type. Indeed if you will let me know who is to publish the volume in America, (is it Osgood?) I will write at once to him on the subject[.][3] By this arrangement which we frequently make, the original cost of composition is shared by both parties and the cost of the book is decreased for each. Of course anything that we get from America in this way will be put to the credit of the book and will be a direct benefit to you.

I expect you will hardly find room in the 350 pages for all the articles you mentioned in your letter: in making a selection it will be well to retain those papers most likely to be interesting to that strange creature the "general reader".[4]

I am,

Faithfully yours,
Frederick Macmillan

Henry James Jr., Esq.
3 Bolton Street
Piccadilly

### Notes

1.  See letter 1. Despite an unfavourable reading of the manuscript by John Morley, the firm's literary adviser, who characterised it as 'honest scribble work and no more' (Morgan, pp. 114–15), Frederick Macmillan apparently accepted James's book on the basis of his work and reputation in America, where, by this time, his fiction had appeared in the *Atlantic Monthly* and the *Galaxy* and his reviews and travel sketches in the *Nation* and the *North American Review*. Two novels, *Roderick Hudson* (1875) and *The American* (1877), had been published in book form, and the latter, though it had no authorised British publisher, had attracted Macmillan's attention (see letter 1) since the London firm of Trübner and Company had imported copies of the American edition for sale in June 1877. Moreover, by the time Macmillan had agreed to publish an English edition of *The American* in May 1878 (see letters 16 and 19), Ward, Lock and Company had pirated it in December 1877. See *BHJ*, pp, 32–3. Nevertheless, Macmillan's reference to the firm's previous experience with the small sale of collections of essays led him to offer no royalty payments and to suggest instead that 'any profit' be shared. Morley, it should be added, shortly afterwards overcame his objections to James's criticism and asked him to write the volume on Hawthorne in the English Men of Letters series. See letter 21.
2.  George Thomas Keppel, 6th Earl of Albemarle (1799–1891), *Fifty Years of My Life* (London: Macmillan, 1876). James's collection contained 440 pages when it was published in February 1878.
3.  The volume did not appear in a separate American edition. Bound copies of this edition were imported instead and first advertised in the New York *Tribune*, 2 March 1878 (*BHJ*, p. 34).
4.  Thus, even in the beginning of their relationship, Macmillan suggests that James consider a more 'general' audience, a point that he reiterates in the future.

**4**

The Spring,
Kenilworth.
Aug. 27th [1877]

My dear Mr. Macmillan

   I have just received your letter with regard to my projected volume – it not having been immediately forwarded to me from town.[1] I am glad you are disposed to undertake my book & I will call upon you as soon as I return to London, which I expect to be tomorrow, to answer your observations touching details. After that I think the affair may proceed as rapidly as you should desire.

Very truly yours<br>H. James Jr.

Fr. Macmillan Esq.

**Note**

1.   *French Poets and Novelists.* See letters 1–3. James apparently met Macmillan before he departed for France in early September.

**5**

Sep 7. 1877

Dear Mr. James

   In my cousin's absence I opened your note, & beg to acknowledge receipt of your revised ms. We have put it into the printers' hands, and shall be quite ready to send proofs to you at Paris in the course of next week. My cousin is now in Rouen & seems to be enjoying himself [.][1]

   I am

Yours very truly<br>George A. Macmillan

Henry James Esq Junr

**Note**

1.   The 'revised ms' is the copy for *French Poets and Novelists* (letters 1–4). The cousin
     referred to is Frederick O. Macmillan, James's contact with the firm from the
     beginning and the first cousin of George A. Macmillan, the author of this note. At
     this time both were junior partners in the firm.

## 6

Sep. 13. 1877

Dear Mr. James

Many thanks for your second note. We hope to send you proofs
early next week.[1]

My cousin Fred. Macmillan is in Paris just now, at the Hotel de
l'Amirante, 55 Rue Neuve St Augustin.[2] I conclude that bad weather
has driven him from Normandy.

Yours very truly<br>
George A. Macmillan

Henry James Esq Junr

**Notes**

1.   James's 'second note' is not in the LB, MA. The 'proofs' are of *French Poets and
     Novelists*.
2.   See letter 5.

## 7

Sept 21. 1877

Dear Mr. James

Today we send you the first sheet of proof of your Essays, and
hope to keep up a regular supply, if you will kindly return the proofs
for press with as little delay as possible.[1]

I am

Yours very truly<br>
George A. Macmillan

Henry James Esq Junr

**Note**

1.   See, especially, letters 5–6.

**8**

> 51 Rue Neuve
> St. Augustin [Paris]
> Nov. 8*th* [1877]

Dear Mr. Macmillan.

I have something of a bad conscience in writing to you again about my proofs. I hoped to have been able to send you from Italy an address which would have put it in your power to forward me there such proofs as might present themselves – but I was so constantly moving about & so uncertain in my movements – so likely too to be back in Paris at any moment – that I thought it better to wait. I hope the delay has not incommoded you. Here I am back in Paris & ready to read & return directly any thing which may be sent to the above address. I am here but for two or three weeks, after which I return to London, where the proof-reading process may go on as rapidly as is necessary.[1]

Paris is not as charming as when you were here in that lovely September weather, & after six weeks in Italy it seems very prosaic. I hanker for Piccadilly.[2]

I hope Mrs. Macmillan is well, & getting toughened to the trials of English life. Pray give her my kind regards.[3] Do you ever see Nadal?[4] Do ask him why he doesn't answer my letters.

Perhaps you will prefer the proofs should wait till I get back to London; but I shall be very willing to make up for arrears here.[5] Yours very truly –

> H. James Jr

**Notes**

1.   The firm had apparently sent the proof of *French Poets and Novelists* (see letter 7) to James's London address, a not uncommon practice that James requested when he was moving about on the continent.
2.   Frederick Macmillan had returned from his trip to France in October (see letters 5 and 6), and James presumably had seen him in Paris in September. James's London flat was in Piccadilly.

3.   Georgiana Elizabeth Warrin, of Newtown, Long Island, New York, and Frederick
     Macmillan were married in 1874, while he was working at the company branch
     in New York City. This is the first of many references to Mrs Macmillan in the
     correspondence. As fellow expatriates, James and Mrs Macmillan were friends
     until his death in 1916.
4.   For E. S. Nadal, see letter 2, note 2.
5.   Macmillan took James at his word and sent proofs of *French Poets and Novelists* to
     Paris. See letter 9.


**9**

Dec 10*th*. 1877.

Dear Mr. James,

We are sending you today a batch of proofs of your "Essays" and
can now go on quickly until the book is finished.[1]

We shall be very glad to see you in London again though I cant
promise you any particularly fine weather, but I dont think even a
London fog is either so black or so brown as it is painted.[2]

I see that a new story of James is promised in the "Atlantic" for
1878. Is it to appear early or late in the year? If you were willing to
submit any of it to us beforehand we should be very glad to consider
the possibility of publishing it simultaneously in "Macmillan's Magazine". But of course you will understand that it must depend greatly
upon how it would fall in with our other arrangements.[3]

> Believe me,
> Very truly yours
> Frederick Macmillan

Henry James Jr, Esq.
51 Rue Neuve
St Augustin
Paris.


**Notes**

1.   See letter 8. The book appeared the following February (*BHJ*, p. 34).
2.   From the beginning of their professional relationship, Macmillan had tried to
     establish a social tie with James, and through his wife and frequent offers of
     hospitality, soon succeeded in making friends with his new author. For James's
     response, see his letter to Alice James of 29 December [1877] (*HJL*, ɪɪ, 148).
3.   The story referred to is presumably *The Europeans*, a short novel that appeared in
     the *Atlantic Monthly* from July to October 1878, and in book form in September
     1878. Macmillan published the English edition, but the novel was not serialised
     in *Macmillan's Magazine*. See letter 10.

**10**

> 51 Rue Neuve.
> St. Augustin.
> Dec. 12*th* [1877]

Dear Mr. Macmillan –

Many thanks for the proofs, which I have revised & returned directly to the printer's.[1] I shall do the same as fast as they come along.

As regards my story in the *Atlantic* it is to appear some four or five months hence; but I am rather afraid that for various reasons it will be difficult for you to arrange putting it into Macmillan's, even should your own circumstances permit.[2] I thank you very much, however, for the offer. I wish this might be, and perhaps it may. I shall know more definitely a month hence, & by that time I shall probably have seen you.

> Very truly yours
> H. James Jr.

Frederick Macmillan Esq

**Notes**

1.   *French Poets and Novelists*. See letter 9.
2.   *The Europeans*, the 'story' referred to, did not appear in Macmillan's, for the *Atlantic's* owners – Houghton, Osgood – opposed the practice of concurrent publication at this time. See Anesko, pp. 212–13.

**11**

> Paris. Dec. 17 [1877]

Dear Mr. Macmillan –

Please cause all further proofs to be sent to 3 *Bolton St. Piccadilly.* I return there immediately, & shall soon give myself the pleasure of seeing you.[1]

> Yours very truly
> H. James Jr.

**Note**

1.   James returned to his Bolton Street flat before Christmas, continued working on the proofs of *French Poets and Novelists*, and 'dined the other day' with Macmillan. See his letter to Alice James of 29 December [1877] in *HJL*, II, 148.

**12**

Jan$^y$, 29, 1878

My dear James,

Your book will be ready for the binder at the end of this week or the beginning of next, & we may as well decide on a cover. We had a specimen copy done up some time ago which I now send you. If you like it we will do the rest of it in the same style.[1]

With kind regards,
Yours very truly,
Frederick Macmillan

Henry James, Esq

**Note**

1.  The book is *French Poets and Novelists*. See letters 1–11 for other discussion of the publication of this title. Throughout their long business relationship, Macmillan often consulted James on matters of the format, print, paper, and type planned for his books. See letters 279–80, for example.

**13**

3 Bolton St. W.
March 27*th* [1878]

My dear Macmillan –

You have kindly sent me notice that there is a review of my book in the Non *conformist* [*sic*] of Mch. 20th.[1] I find the paper is not to be had at the newspaper-stalls & should be much obliged if you would ask that it be sent me. If need be I will return it.

Faithfully yours
H. James Jr

**Note**

1.  A review of *French Poets and Novelists* appeared in the *Nonconformist*, 20 March 1878, 273. See letter 14. The 'notice' referred to is not included in LB, MA.

**14**

March 27. 1878

My dear James,

Here is the review.[1] We generally preserve such things but if you have the least desire to keep it yourself we can easily get another copy.

Yours most truly,
Frederick Macmillan

H. James Jr. Esq

**Note**

1. *French Poets and Novelists.* See letter 13.

**15**

3 Bolton St.
Mch. 28*th* [1878]

Dear Macmillan

Since you give me leave to keep the article from the NonConformist [*sic*] I will take the liberty of doing so; as I amuse myself with sending all the notices of my book to my sister, in the U.S.[1]

I send you the enclosed, which explain themselves. If you will please to send me the book in question (Joubert's *Thoughts*) I will comply with Garrison's request to notice it for the *Nation*.[2]

Very truly yours
H. James Jr.

**Notes**

1. The reference is to a review of *French Poets and Novelists.* See letters 13 and 14. Later in his career, James instructs Macmillan *not* to send copies of reviews. See letter 304, for example.
2. James reviewed the *Pensées of Joubert,* selected by Henry Attwell (London: Macmillan, 1877) in *Nation,* xxvi (2 June 1878), 423–4. W. P. Garrison (1840–1907) was a member of the journal's staff and subsequently edited it from 1881 to 1906.

**16**

3 Bolton St.

April 5*th* [1878]

Dear Macmillan –

I have no volume of the *American*; but have laid my hands on a copy of the odious reprint, which I send you by post. You might tell Mr. Grove – to impress the editorial imagination – that the book has been twice translated into German.[1]

Very truly yrs.

H. James Jr.

**Note**

1. James had suggested that the firm bring out an English edition of *The American*, but George Grove (1820–1900), editor of *Macmillan's Magazine*, had informed Frederick Macmillan that he could not finish the book and had reservations about it. See letter 17. Nevertheless, Macmillan later agreed to publish the book in England. See letter 27. The "odious reprint" refers to the pirated edition of the novel by Ward, Lock & Co. of December 1877. See *BHJ*, p. 32.

**17**

Ventnor

Isle of Wight.

April 24*th* [1878][1]

Mr dear Mr. Grove –

Your note has just been forwarded to me here.[2] I shall be very happy to come and see you on Monday next, & give you what information I can about my projected novel, of which Frederick Macmillan spoke to you. I say "what information I can", for I have not got the MS. in any state to show. I can, however, tell you definitely what the thing is about & show you some of it some time hence.[3] But I confess frankly that if you broke down in the middle of the *American* I fear there is a danger of the present story finding little more favour with you. Still, I hasten to add, that I think I may claim for it that it is a stronger work than the *American*. As regards the latter I venture to recommend you, since you express a disposition to do so, to have, as they say, another "try" at it. Perhaps it will go more smoothly.[4] At any rate I will, gladly, call on you on Monday. Very truly yours

Henry James Jr.

**Notes**

1.  This letter has previously been printed in *LM*, p. 169, but my text differs in both accidental and substantive particulars.
2.  Grove's 'note' is not included in LB, MA. James and Grove had met a week earlier at a dinner hosted by Frederick Macmillan on 17 April. See *HJL*, ɪɪ, 167–8.
3.  Though Simon Nowell-Smith maintains that the 'projected novel' is *The Europeans*, James's description of the 'state' of the project suggests that it is more likely *The Portrait of a Lady*, a view also expressed by Anesko, p. 211.
4.  For Grove's difficulties with *The American*, see also letter 16, but compare James's comment on Grove's 'great delight' with the novel in a letter to his father of 19 April [1878] in *HJL*, ɪɪ, 168.

## 18

July 31. 1878.

My dear James,

We shall be glad to publish "The Europeans" on the terms I mentioned yesterday, that is, we will assume the entire risk of the undertaking, and share with you any profits that may arise. I hope the British public may take to the book in such a way as to make these same profits enormous.[1]

In order to secure a copyright we must publish our Edition before the appearance of the last part in America, i.e. before Sept 15th [.][2] No time therefore must be lost in getting it done and I have today sent the two first parts down to the printers. We shall be glad to have the remainder as soon as possible.

Yours most truly,
Frederick Macmillan

Henry James Jr Esq

**Notes**

1.  These are the terms proposed by Macmillan for James's first four books. See the Memorandum of Agreement dated 20 January 1879 on *Daisy Miller*, *The Europeans*, *The American*, and *French Poets and Novelists*, all of which were to be published at the firm's expense with James to receive '¹/₂ profits'. The contract is printed below following letter 32. In his reply, James picks up some of Macmillan's language. See letter 19.
2.  The novel was actually published in London on 18 September 1878, almost a month before the American edition appeared on 12 October (*BHJ*, 37–8). The novel completed its serial run in the *Atlantic Monthly* for October 1878.

## 19

[August 1, 1878][1]

Dear Macmillan –

I meant to have written you yesterday that I am very glad you undertake the book.[2] As regards the profits I am afraid there is not much danger of their being "enormous," exactly; but even if they are only moderate, it will be a beginning of my appearance before the British public as a novelist – as *the* novelist of the future, destined to extract from the B.P. eventually (both for himself & his publishers) a colossal fortune![3] You shall have the rest of the copy the moment it arrives & proofsheets shall receive the promptest attention.[4] Kind regards in St John's Wood, & a *bon voyage* for Etretat.[5]

Yours very truly
H. James Jr.

### Notes

1. James did not date this letter, and though it is printed in *LM*, pp. 169–70, as having been written in May 1878, the date is in error, for the letter is an obvious response to Macmillan's of 31 July (no. 18). Anesko suggests a date of 1 August, a reasonable assumption (p. 213).
2. *The Europeans.* See letter 18.
3. The novel went through three printings of 250 each in the fall of 1878, a one-volume six-shilling edition of 1,000 copies came out in the following April, and it was eventually remaindered by The Times Book Club. See *BHJ*, 37–8, 386–7.
4. James was receiving copy of the novel from the *Atlantic Monthly* (July–October 1878).
5. James often completes a letter with a greeting or reference to Mrs Macmillan either directly or indirectly. At this time the Macmillans had a home in St John's Wood.

## 20

Gillesbie,
Lockerbie. N.B.
Sept. 26*th* [1878]

Dear Macmillan –

I see my book is out, & I suppose some copies of it have been sent to Bolton St.[1] I shall not get at them until I get home, which will not be till Oct. 1*st*; & I should like you meanwhile to have three or four sent according to the list I enclose.[2] I have been spending three weeks in Scotland, with extraordinary pleasure, thanks in a great measure to glorious weather. I have taken a great fancy to the whole place & think of settling in Edinburgh.[3] But I will relate my impressions on my return. I hope the days have gone well with you. With kind regards in St. John's Wood,[4] Faithfully yours

H. James Jr.

### Notes

1.    *The Europeans* appeared in London on 18 September. James lived at 3 Bolton Street from 1876 to 1883.
2.    The list is not in LB, MA.
3.    James had been visiting friends in 'bonnie Scotland', as he characterised it in a letter to his sister Alice on 15 September [1878] (*HJL*, ii, 184–7).
4.    See letter 19, note 5.

## 21

4, Chesham Place.
Brighton.
Oct. 9. 1878.[1]

My dear Sir;

You may possibly remember that I once had the pleasure of meeting you at Lord Houghton's some time ago, and I hope you will allow that to be a sufficient introduction to warrant me in writing to you.[2]

As you may have seen, I am editing a series of short books on English Men of Letters, and it has occurred to us that there is no reason why we should not for the purposes of literature consider Americans as English. If so, I think that a short book on Washington Irving, or on Hawthorne would be a proper and an attractive feature in our scheme. Would you be inclined to undertake such a book?[3] The task, as you may know, is no inordinately lengthy one. We require about 180 or 190 smallish pages (say 300 words each) – and extracts from letters or from the books – the latter of course in moderation – are a welcome rather than an unwelcome feature. I may refer you to the books already published – and *especially* the "Shelley" *wh* will be out next week – for a specimen of what it is that I seek.[4]

May I hope that you will consider the proposal? If you will, and come to a favourable decision, I shall think myself fortunate.

> Yours very faithfully,
> John Morley.

### Notes

1. The present text is based upon the original at Harvard.
2. Richard Monckton Milnes (1809–85), first Baron Houghton, whom James had known since February 1877 (*HJL*, II, 99). Morley (1838–1923), the author of books on Burke (1867), Voltaire (1872), and Rousseau (1873), among others, was editor of the *Fortnightly Review* (1867–82) and an advisor to Macmillan and Company. By this time, apparently, Morley had overcome his objections to James's criticism. See letter 3, note 1.
3. See letter 22. After some irresolution, James finally wrote the book on Hawthorne, and it was published by Macmillan in London on 12 December 1879, and by Harper in New York on 15 January 1880 (*BHJ*, pp. 46–7).
4. The first edition consisted of 184 pages sized $7\,^1/_4 \times 4\,^7/_8$. The EML volume on Shelley (1878) was written by John Addington Symonds (1840–93).

## 22

> 3 Bolton St. W.
> Oct. 11*th* [1878]

My dear Macmillan

Thank you for Sir C. Dilke's letter – so long as he got the book it is no matter whom *he* thanks.[1]

I have heard from Morley in regard to *Hawthorne*; & have written to him assenting to his proposal. But the letter written, I have left it on my table, hesitating to send it. I shall, however, probably do so.[2]

I intended to ask you the last time I saw you to please send *one* copy of the "Europeans" to America, for my father. I desire to send him one, & with the present beastly U.S. postal arrangements can't do so by post. The book [s] are stopped or returned. Will you send one in your box to your New York people, & ask them to forward it by post to –

*Henry James esq*
*Cambridge*
*Mass. ?*
I shall be greatly obliged.

> Very truly yours
> H. James Jr.

**Notes**

1. Apparently Sir Charles W. Dilke (1810–69) had been on James's list of those to
   whom author's copies of *The Europeans* were to be sent. See letter 20. Dilke was
   a member of Parliament and a good friend to James. He supported James for
   membership in the Reform Club, for example. See *HJL*, II, 175.
2. See letter 21 and note 3.


## 23

Oct 23. 1878

My dear James,

I am sending a copy of the "Europeans" to Baron Tauchnitz.
Please tell him that it has been copyrighted in England, and that his
reprint can only be sold on the Continent. I mention this because as
you are an American he might not think of it.[1]

There is an advertisement on the back page of *this* evenings [*sic*]
Pall Mall which ought to raise your drooping spirits [.][2]

Yours ever

Frederick Macmillan

H. James Jr. Esq

**Notes**

1. Baron Christian Bernhard von Tauchnitz (1816–95), founder of the well-known
   reprint house in Leipzig, had already reprinted *The American* (1878) in his 'Collection of British and American Authors'. *The Europeans* appeared later in 1878.
   See *BHJ*, p. 384.
2. For the firm's promotion of *The Europeans*, see the *Pall Mall Gazette*, 23 October
   1878, 12.


## 24

3 Bolton St.

Oct. 27*th* [1878]

Dear Macmillan –

I suppose you have heard of, if you don't know, Mrs. Julia Ward
Howe, of Boston. She, being now here, has asked me to exert myself
with you to the effect that you should look at the MS. of a small
volume on *Brittany*, which she desires to publish here. She has been

there this summer, & has written her book, & wishes much to bring it out, & even to publish some fragments of it in *Macmillan*, first, or elsewhere.[1] I have not seen the book, & don't know what manner of thing it is; I only know the lady is clever, & should suppose it would be worth your looking at. I promised her to speak to you thus (& I called in Bedford St. to day [*sic*] – but you were absent) – & you see that I zealously keep my promise. She is to be here (at present) only a week longer, so that if she can submit the MS. will you let me know?

What a very *amusing*, (as well as flattering) notice of *The Europeans* that was in the *Spectator*. It was too deliciously characteristic of the Journal.[2] Ever yours

H. James Jr.

**Notes**

1.  Julia Ward Howe (1819–1910), author of the 'Battle Hymn of the Republic' and supporter of many social causes in America. James had known Mrs Howe and her family for years and subsequently used her as the model for the central character of 'The Beldonald Holbein' (1901). Her volume on Brittany was published neither by the firm nor the magazine.
2.  *Spectator*, LI (26 October 1878), 1334–36. The review, by R. H. Hutton, acknowledges the 'slight novelette's' faults – 'slender materials', lack of plot and story – but compliments the author on his 'genuine and brilliant creative power of the dramatic kind' (1334). James, consequently, may be expressing an ironic view of the notice. Certainly, less than a year later in a letter to his mother of 6 July 1879, he characterised Hutton's review of *Roderick Hudson* (*Spectator*, LII, 5 July 1879, 854–55) as '*inane*', essentially unintelligent, and extremely narrow (*HJL*, II, 249–50).

## 25

Oct 30. 1878

My dear James,

I met Mrs. Howe some five or six years ago but I dont suppose she remembers me at all. But we shall be very glad to look at her mss [*sic*] and give it careful consideration: more than that I cant say.[1]

I am sorry not to have answered your letter before but I have only just returned from Liverpool whither I went to see Miss Warrin off.[2]

Yours very truly
Frederick Macmillan

H. James Jr

**Notes**

1. Macmillan had represented the firm in New York from 1871 to 1876 and had apparently met Mrs Howe during that period. See letter 24.
2. Miss Warrin was Mrs Macmillan's sister from New York.


# 26

Sunday a.m.
[November 17?, 1878][1]

Dear Macmillan –

Many thanks to your uncle, to Pater & to you. I am very grateful to the exquisite P. for his compliment & to you for transmitting it.[2]

Yes, I think you may now announce my name for *Hawthorne*. I shall write, formally, to Morley.[3]

Within a few days past I have become conscious of a deepening interest, fostered by my acute desire to make next year as much money as possible in the matter of the republication of the "American." Even if it should not sell very largely, a small profit would be welcome; & I cannot but think that it would have a tolerable sale. (Excuse my slovenly haste.) Have you thought any more about it? – and will you let me know? I don't suppose Osgood's selling you the plates would mean that he alone would profit by the operation. Or is the thing a matter between me & him. *Je n'y comprends rien*; I only should be very glad to give the book a chance here.[4] Yours ever

H. James Jr.

**Notes**

1. James does not give a date for this letter, but internal evidence suggests that though James had backed and filled on the Hawthorne book (see letter 22, above, and his letter to Henry James, Sr, 18 October 1878, quoted in Anesko, p. 63), he had already decided to undertake the project, perhaps even as another means of persuading Macmillan to 'republish' *The American*. If so, the ploy succeeded, as letter 27 indicates.
2. Walter Pater (1839–94), author of *Studies in the History of the Renaissance*, a Macmillan title of 1873, apparently praised *The Europeans* to Alexander Macmillan, who, in turn, passed on the compliment to Frederick Macmillan, who 'transmitted' it to James.
3. James is formally accepting the assignment to write the Hawthorne volume in the English Men of Letters series. See letters 21 and 22.
4. James and Macmillan had apparently discussed the possibility of 'republishing' *The American* in England in April 1878. See letter 16, and James's letter to his father of 19 April (*HJL*, ii, 167–8). For Macmillan's favourable response, see letter 27.

**27**

Nov: 18/1878

Dear James,

We shall be very glad to republish "The American" and I am writing to America to day to find out whether Osgood will sell us a set of duplicate plates at a reasonable price. If he won't we will set the book up here.[1]

Yours very sincerely
Frederick Macmillan

H James Jr. Esq

**Note**

1.    The authorised English edition of *The American* was set up by the firm and was published 11 March 1879. See letter 30 and *BHJ*, p. 33.

**28**

Dec 3. 1878.

My dear James,

I have much pleasure in sending you a cheque for £50 which represents as nearly as I can get it, what we should owe you if accounts between us were to be made up now – as you know, we only balance our books formally once a year.[1]

Please sign & return the enclosed receipt & believe me

Yours very truly,
Frederick Macmillan

Henry James Jr. Esq

**Note**

1.    James had apparently requested a statement of his account (not in LB, MA), and Macmillan's response suggests something of the informality of arrangements between them. There was as yet, for example, no contract between author and firm (James would not sign a memorandum of agreement until 20 January 1879 – see letter 32), and the firm's deliberate method of settling accounts (they were usually drawn up in June, authors were notified of a year's sale in October, and then paid the following January) led James to dun Macmillan on occasion for some part of his royalty.

**29**

> 3 Bolton St.
> Piccadilly
> Dec. 8*th* [1878]

Dear Macmillan –

Have you any objection to sending me a copy of the Memoirs of Fr. Hodgson – Byron's friend, of which I incline to write a notice? It will go into the *Nation* & perhaps be of some use to the book in America.[1]

> Faithfully yours
> H. James Jr.

**Note**

1.  Macmillan sent James a copy of the *Memoir of the Rev. Francis Hodgson, B.D.* (1878). Since the *Nation* had already published a review when James's manuscript arrived, James's notice was sent to the *North American Review*, where it appeared in CXXVIII (April 1979), 388–92. For James's annoyance with the *NAR* for printing his 'little book-notice . . . as a signed article', see his letter to his mother of 8 April [1879] (*HJL*, II, 229).

**30**

> Dec 30/1878

Dear James,

Will you please look through *The American* and mark any changes you wish to make before we begin setting it up.[1]

> Yours ever truly,
> Frederick Macmillan

H. James Jr Esq

**Note**

1.  See letters 16 and 27.

**31**

3, Bolton Street.
Piccadilly, W.
Jan. 19*th* [1879]

My dear Macmillan –

I ought long since to have returned you Chas. de Kay's poor little tale, which I read as soon as it arrived, but which subsequently got shoved out of sight, & out of mind, beneath some papers.[1] There is not much to be said about it – it strikes me as almost painfully, pitifully, feeble & crude. What an odd thing that a practical editor, like Gilder, should get agog about it![2] I am sorry young New York hasn't something better to show – for one can't make out what C. de Kay has been "after," at all. It reads like a thing he might have written at a tender age. But I hope he will do better next time.

Since writing this ½ an hour ago, I have been turning over the "Bohemian" again. There is a certain sort of picturesque, poetic intention about it – one sees he has meant something; but nevertheless it is very immature & weak. Such at least is my impression. I was yesterday at Bedford St., to see Grove, with whom I had a pleasant talk – & I was sorry to learn you were at home, unwell.[3] I hope it is nothing serious & that this will find you *rétabli*. Yours ever

H.J. Jr.

**Notes**

1. Macmillan had asked James to read Charles De Kay's *The Bohemian* and James has readily obliged. See also letter 32.
2. Richard Watson Gilder (1844–1909), managing editor of *Scribner's Monthly* (1870–81) and subsequently editor of *The Century* (1881–1909), was also the brother-in-law of De Kay (1848–1935). Since James knew the Gilders and Katherine De Kay Bronson, another of De Kay's sisters, he surely knew of the relationship between Gilder and De Kay. The book had been published by Scribner in 1878.
3. George Grove, editor of *Macmillan's Magazine*, had been a bit reluctant about James's work in the beginning. See letters 16 and 17. Bedford Street was the location of the firm's main office at the time.

**32**

Jan 20th 1879

Dear James

I was sorry not to be here on Saturday when you called.[1] Many thanks for your opinion on "The Bohemian" which assures me that I have not ignorantly refused a great work of genius![2]

By the way I find that although we settled between us the terms on which your books were to be published, we have no written memorandum of the arrangement. We find it convenient always to have something of the kind. I shall be much obliged therefore if you will sign the enclosed papers and return one of them to me.[3] Believe me,

Yours very truly<br>Frederick Macmillan

H. James Jr.

I hope the printers are keeping you well supplied with proof.[4]

**Notes**

1. James had called at the company office on 18 January. See letter 31.
2. For James's opinion of Charles De Kay's *The Bohemian*, see letter 31.
3. This is the first reference to the need for a written contract between publisher and author. James signed the memorandum of agreement on 20 January. It is printed following letter 32.
4. *The American* is being printed for its first authorised English edition; it appeared on 11 March 1879 (*BHJ*, p. 33).

## Memorandum of Agreement

*Dated* Jan 20 1879

BETWEEN

Henry James Esq.

AND

MACMILLAN AND CO.

FOR THE PUBLICATION OF

"Daisy Miller", "The Europeans", "The American", & "French Poets"

$1/2$ Profits

**Memorandum of Agreement** made this 20th day of January 1879, between Henry James Jun[r] Esq. on the one part, and Messrs. MACMILLAN and Co. on the other part

It is Agreed that the said Messrs. MACMILLAN and Co. shall publish at their own risk and expense "Daisy Miller" and other stories, the copyright of which shall be the joint property of Henry James Jun[r] Esq. and Messrs. MACMILLAN and Co. in the proportions stated below, and after deducting from the produce of the sale thereof all the expenses of printing, paper, boarding, advertising, trade allowances, and other incidental expenses, the profits remaining of every edition that may be printed of the work during the term of legal copyright are to be divided into two equal parts, one part to be paid to the said Henry James Jun[r] Esq. and the other to belong to Messrs. MACMILLAN and Co.

The books to be accounted for at the trade-sale price, twenty-five as twenty-four, unless it be thought advisable to dispose of copies or of the remainder at a lower price, which is left to the discretion of Messrs. MACMILLAN and Co.

Accounts to be made up annually to Midsummer, delivered on or before October 1, and settled by cash in the ensuing January.

It is further agreed that "French Poets & Novelists", "The Europeans" and "The Americans" shall be published on the above terms.

Macmillan & Co.

James's signature

# 33

3, Bolton Street.
Piccadilly. W.
[January 21?, 1879][1]

My dear Macmillan –

I return one of the agreements, signed.[2]

Yes, the proof is coming in very well.[3]

No, I don't think I could have said anything else about the "Bohemian".[4]

Yours ever
H. J. Jr.

**Notes**

1. This note is not dated, but since James and Macmillan often wrote each other and responded to letters on the same day and since James signed the inclosed agreement on 20 January, the date could as readily be 20 January.
2. The memorandum of agreement is printed following letter 32.
3. For the proof of *The American*, see letter 32, note 4.
4. See letters 31 and 32.

## 34

Jan 22. 1879.

My dear James,

We have received a letter from Harpers who wish you to sign an Agreement assigning to them the copyright of your book on *Hawthorne* for a royalty of 10% on the selling price.

In the case of the other authors who have written for this Series we have paid £100 for the copyright which has been understood to include whatever we could get from America. Of course they had no legal rights in the U.S. and you have and your book may be worth more there on that account. We of course wish to make an arrangement which you will consider fair and to give you the full benefit of the honour that you have in your own country. We therefore propose an alternative agreement – Either we will pay you £100 to cover all rights, or we will pay only £75 and hand over to you the American profits. Which would you prefer?[1]

Yours very truly
Frederick Macmillan

H. James Jr Esq

**Note**

1. James decided to accept a flat sum of £100 for *Hawthorne* and, accordingly, received no royalties from the Harper firm. See letter 35.

## 35

3 Bolton St. W
Jan 22*d* [1879][1]

My dear Macmillan

I have just rec'd. your note in regard to the Harpers' proposal.[2] The amount of the profit of my "Hawthorne" being uncertain, & the convenience to me of receiving a round sum, down, on the completion of the book, being considerable, I prefer, of your two alternatives, the 1ˢᵗ: viz: the £100, covering everything. I shall content myself with a disinterested observation of the sale, whatever it is, that the book may have in the Harpers' hands. Thank you for the choice.[3]

I have had a little correspondence with Julian Hawthorne, whom I shall go some day to Hastings to interrogate, & who writes me that his wife has just had a little girl.[4]

Yours ever
H. James Jr.

**Notes**

1.   Since this is obviously a response to Macmillan's 'note' of 22 January, it follows letter 34.
2.   See letter 34.
3.   Though James accepted the 'round sum, down', he was hardly a 'disinterested' observer of the sales. When he heard from his family that the book was selling well in America, he wrote Henry James, Sr that he would receive 'none of the profit of it' and therefore not 'to glory [in the sale of the book], but repine' (17 January 1880, quoted in *BHJ*, p. 47). A copy of the memorandum of agreement dated 20 January 1879 that Harper proposed and James declined is in LB, MA.
4.   James had known Hawthorne (1846–1934) since his brothers Wilky and Bob had been his schoolmates in Concord, and he had reviewed Hawthorne's *Saxon Studies* unfavourably in the *Nation* (xxɪɪ, 30 March 1876, 214–15). See Hawthorne's *Memoirs* (New York: The Macmillan Co., 1938), pp. 120–8, and Maurice Bassan, *Hawthorne's Son* (Columbus: Ohio State University Press, 1970), pp. 111–13. In a letter of 15 January 1879 James expressed his gratitude to Hawthorne for his 'kind allusions to hospitality' (Bancroft Library, University of California, Berkeley), but since Mrs Hawthorne was about to have a baby, he delayed his visit until February 28. See letter 41 and note 3.

## 36

3, Bolton Street.
Piccadilly. W.
Feb. 16*th* [1879]

My dear Grove – [1]

I have returned the sheets of the little tale I gave you the other day (& which Fredr. Macmillan made over to me) to the printers with the request that they send me a revise which I shall despatch to America for simultaneous publication in a magazine there – & I have asked that this be done as soon as possible – as in such a case time is valuable. Will you please therefore let me know when it would be convenient that the tale should appear in Macmillan – so that I may fix this point for my American editor? Would the *July* Macmillan suit you?[2] Of course I should bargain that it appears over there not a day *before* its publication here.

Yours faithfully
H. James Jr.

**Notes**

1.  For George Grove, editor of *Macmillan's Magazine*, see letters 16 and 17.
2.  'The Diary of a Man of Fifty' appeared, concurrently, in *Harper's New Monthly Magazine*, LIX (July 1879), 282–97, and *Macmillan's Magazine*, XL (July 1879), 205–23. The remarks on dates of publication are relevant to the protection of copyrights in both countries.

**37**

Feb 17 [1879]

My dear James,

Thanks for your note. I will put the tale into the July No. of the Magazine, and therefore according to an abstruse calculation of Fred's it ought to appear in the *August no.* of the *American* magazine.[1]

Did Fred tell you how much I liked it?

Yours ever truly
G. Grove

Henry James Esq

**Note**

1.  See letter 36, note 2, and letter 38, note 6. Frederick Macmillan's 'calculation' notwithstanding, the 'Diary of a Man of Fifty' appeared in the July number of *Harper's New Monthly Magazine*.

**38**

> 3, Bolton Street.
> Piccadilly. W.
> Monday a.m.
> [Feb 17? 1879][1]

My dear Macmillan –

Thank you for the sheets, with regard to which I have written to Grove.[2] Also for my two volumes, which are extremely pretty.[3] I don't see how all the world can keep from reading them. I enclose you a rather long list, as usual, of people to whom I should like "Daisy Miller" sent.[4] Will you kindly see that the copy for *Henley* (the 1*st*) goes *immediately*? He is an admirable reviewer to whom I promised an early one.[5]

I have proposed to Grove, in order that both he & Harpers should have plenty of time, that my little tale should not come out till (say) *July*.[6] If it is within your convenience I should take it kindly that you send me a cheque for the same without waiting for the rather remote date of publication.[7] I should rather appreciate its arrival.

> Yours very truly
> H. James Jr.

My poor madman has not turned up again – but I fear I must expect him. I have written to Oxford.[8]

**Notes**

1. 'Feb. 17' is written lightly in a hand other than James's, but since he had written Grove on 16 February and *Daisy Miller* had appeared on 15 February and since Macmillan responded on 18 February and James refers on 18 February to a 'list' he had forgotten 'yesterday', this date is obviously correct.
2. See letter 36.
3. The first English edition of *Daisy Miller: A Study* had appeared in two volumes on 15 February 1879. See *BHJ*, pp. 34–40.
4. The list is not presently included with the letter in LB, MA.
5. William Ernest Henley (1849–1903), poet, critic, and friend of Robert Louis Stevenson, reviewed several of James's book during this time, including *Roderick Hudson* (1879) and *Washington Square* (1881).
6. 'The Diary of a Man of Fifty' was published concurrently in July in both *Harper's* and *Macmillan's*. See letter 36, note 2.
7. James had already formed the habit of asking for payment after a work was in the process of publication and before it appeared. Macmillan usually humoured him. See, for example, letter 39.
8. The 'poor madman' (not identified) did indeed turn up in Oxford. See letter 40.

**39**

Feb 18. 1879.

My dear James,

July will suit Grove very well.[1] I enclose a cheque for the story and hope that I may always be able to oblige you as easily.[2]

Believe me

Yours very truly,
Frederick Macmillan

H James Jr. Esq

**Notes**

1.  See letter 38, note 6.
2.  The cheque was for £35; a receipt dated 18 February 1879 is in LB, MA. Anesko indicates James received $170 from Macmillan and $125 from Harper (p. 188). For James's response, see letter 40.

**40**

3, Bolton Street.
Piccadilly. W.
Feb 18*th* [1879]

My dear Macmillan

Many thanks for the cheque, which is very good, and a service.[1]

I returned the sheets you sent me to the printers, with a request for a revise, if possible, in pages as for the magazine, & as immediately as may be.[2] I suppose they will give me them without urgency [*sic*] from you. –

I have just heard from Oxford that my poor friend is returned there very mad & is supposed to have gone to Egypt![3]

Yours ever truly
H James Jr.

P.S.   I enclose a short supplementary list, for "Daisy Miller," of people whom I forgot yesterday.[4]

**Notes**

1.  The cheque is for 'The Diary of a Man of Fifty'. See letter 39.
2.  James was reading, revising, and preparing copy of 'The Diary' for *Macmillan's* and *Harper's Monthly*. See letter 36, note 2.

3.    James's 'poor madman' (not identified) had been mentioned in letter 38.
4.    Another list of friends James wished to receive author's copies of *Daisy Miller* (not in LB, MA). See letter 38.

## 41

> 3, Bolton Street.
> Piccadilly. W.
> Feb. 28*th* [1879][1]

Dear Macmillan –

Will you kindly have these three or four names more, which I enclose, supplied with "Daisy Miller"?[2]

I go down to Hastings this p.m. to stop till Friday, & I will give you news of my adventures.[3]

> Yours ever
> H. James Jr.

Ash Wednesday.

### Notes

1.    Since James refers at the end of the letter to this day as 'Ash Wednesday', the date must be 26 February 1879; 28 February occurred on Friday in 1879.
2.    See letter 40. These names are not included with the letter in LB, MA. Over the years Macmillan was generous in the matter of author's copies. See, for example, letter 44.
3.    In January James had been invited by Julian Hawthorne to visit him in order to discuss the forthcoming volume on his father in the English Men of Letters series. See letter 35. On 4 March James reported on his 'talk' with Hawthorne in a letter to his brother William. 'He gave me little satisfaction or information about his father; but I enjoyed my day by the sea, and also got on very well with him' (*HJL*, ii, 216).

## 42

> Mch 17*th* [1879]

Dear Macmillan.

I shall bother you with one more very ultimate request.

Will you send an author's copy of *D.M.* as enclosed, & greatly oblige (till to-morrow) yours very faithfully

H. James Jr.

Please send *Daisy Miller* from the author to:
Mrs. Frank Mathews[1]
8 Boundary Road
St. Johns [*sic*] Wood N.W.

**Note**

1.  Mrs Mathews was a daughter of Dr J. J. Garth Wilkinson, an old friend of Henry James, Sr, and the wife of a London solicitor. See *HJL*, II, 169–70, 378–9. During his early years in London, James visited her in St John's Wood and put her on his lists for author's copies. Macmillan had published the English edition of *Daisy Miller: A Study* on 15 February 1879 (*BHJ*, p. 40).

## 43

3, Bolton Street.
Piccadilly. W.
June 18*th* [1879]

Dear Macmillan –

"Roderick H." makes a very pretty figure indeed – & I hope he will justify this further on the ground of "handsome is that handsome *does*."[1] They have sent me three copies of him but I shld. like you to send 2 or 3 more.

One to my amiable critic  W. E. Henley esq.[2]
36 Loftus Road
Shepherd's Bush
W.

One please to *Matthew Arnold*, to whom I promised it.[3]
One to my sister –
Miss James
20 Quincy St.
Cambridge, Mass.
U.S.A.

In sending the latter to your people in N.Y. to be forwarded, will you please send with it, for the same address a copy of "The American," & one of the cheap edition of the "Europeans"? I want her to have all my English editions.

> Yours ever
> H. James Jr.

**Notes**

1.  *Roderick Hudson* had just appeared in its first English edition on 11 June (*BHJ*, p. 31).
2.  W. E. Henley had also received a review copy of *Daisy Miller*. See letter 38.
3.  James had met Arnold, a boyhood idol, in Rome in 1873 and had been a bit disappointed in him, but liked him better when he met him again in London in the late 1870s. See Edel, ɪɪ, 122–5, 321–2. After reading the novel, Arnold wrote James to congratulate him on it (Edel, ɪɪ, 394).

## 44

June 27. 1879

My dear James,

A copy of "Daisy Miller" is going to Mrs. George Howard.[1]

By the way I find that a bill has been sent you for certain copies of "French Poets & Novelists" which were sent to different people at your request. We will make you a present of these if you will allow us so if you have the bill still by you please destroy it, as it won't be rendered to you again.[2]

It was a capital notice of Roderick Hudson in the P.M.G.[3]

> Yours very truly
> Frederick Macmillan

**Notes**

1.  Mrs Howard, the wife of George James Howard (1843–1911), MP, painter, and eventually Earl of Carlisle (1889–1911), presumably was one of those mentioned by James on a list for author's copies. See letters 38, 40, 41, and 42.

2.   Macmillan made a practice of providing James with author's copies *gratis*. The only exception to this occurred with the Edition de Luxe (New York Edition) of James's novels and tales. Since the firm was buying the text from Charles Scribner's Sons, Frederick Macmillan charged James for each copy what the company paid Scribner's. See James's postcard to J. B. Pinker, 13 October 1908 (Yale) and letter 281, note 1.

3.   *Roderick Hudson* had been reprinted by Macmillan on 11 June and was reviewed in the *Pall Mall Gazette*, 26 June 1879, 12. See also letter 43.

## 45

3, Bolton Street.
Piccadilly. W.
July 14*th* [1879][1]

Dear Macmillan –

I meant to say to you to day [*sic*], but lost the opportunity, that if there is any money to my credit in consequence of the various publications of the last months I should take it kindly that you should give me some palpable symbol of it before you leave town. You intimated to me the other day that the proceeds of these publications were the reverse of copious – but I don't know whether you meant that they were nil. I prefer not to believe it at any rate without a definite assurance; & the fact of their being small would not prevent me from accepting them.[2]

Another thing I meant to say is that if the copy for the "M. of the F." should prove scanty for *two* volumes, I have 1 or 2 tales which I could easily add.[3] Yours ever, in haste –

H. James Jr.

### Notes

1.   Previously printed in *HJL*, ɪɪ, 250–1. The present text differs chiefly in accidentals.

2.   James consistently seeks payment on his royalties or for magazine contributions before Macmillan (or any other firm) normally considered accounts were due. See, for example, letter 38, note 7, and Macmillan's effort at compromise in letter 46. For some months prior to the letter, James had been trying to pay off a debt to his father, a fact that may have led to some importunity. See *HJL*, ɪɪ, 236.

3.   *The Madonna of the Future and Other Tales* appeared in two volumes on 16 October 1879 and included five stories in addition to the titlepiece. This edition was not issued in America. See *BHJ*, pp. 42–3.

## 46

July 15, 1879

My dear James,

It is impossible to say just yet how the books will turn out. The accounts are in the process of being made up but are not yet finished. I therefore send you £50 on account of the *Hawthorne* volume for which we agreed to give you £100 on publication. I hope this will be satisfactory.[1]

Believe me,

Yours very truly,
Frederick Macmillan

Henry James Jr Esq

**Note**

1.   Macmillan's willingness to send money, even if not in direct response to James's actual request, is characteristic of a consistent effort on his part to reply as positively and promptly as possible to James's suggestions about payment for his work. *Hawthorne* did not appear until the following December (*BHJ*, pp. 46–7).

## 47

3, Bolton Street.
Piccadilly. W.
July 15*th* [1879]

Dear Macmillan –

I didn't know how it would be about the accounts; I thought you might have mysterious ways of judging. But if they are being looked into, let it stand by all means till the results are known.[1] Thank you meanwhile for the £50 for *Hawthorne*. I have as a general thing a lively aversion to receiving money in anticipation for work not delivered & I think that if you had proposed this yesterday I should have said *No*, for the present. But I should feel ungracious in returning the cheque – so I keep it, with many acknowledgements.[2] Till Saturday – Yours very truly

H. James Jr.

**Notes**

1.  At this time James was not completely familiar with the firm's habit of paying royalty accounts once a year. In letter 45, he had asked for 'some palpable symbol' of any money to his credit for work already received, and Macmillan's response in letter 46 momentarily satisfied him.
2.  James had not yet delivered the manuscript of *Hawthorne* to the firm. The volume was published later in the year on 12 December. A receipt by James for £50 is dated 15 July 1879 and included in LB, MA.

## 48

July 21st 1879

My dear James,

I have no wish to press you about the story for our magazine but it would be a help to us in making our arrangements if we could foresee when it is likely to come. We have as I told you a story by Mrs. Oliphant which is to begin in November 1879 and which will go on until October 1880. If you thought that you could promise us the beginning of your story about November 1880 it would just suit us but if you dont think that would be giving yourself time enough we would then make arrangements for still another story to fill up the gap. I hope you will not think me importunate and a nuisance for attempting to fix a date on you in this way, but as you can easily understand, it is important for us to have arrangements for the magazine stories concluded some time ahead. It so happens that we have the offer of a story which would do for a stop gap if we needed it so that it would be convenient for us to know pretty soon. I need not say that we would all rather have your novel than any other.[1]

If you can answer my question off hand, a note will catch me if addressed to the care of Samuel Lord Esq, Oakleigh, Ashton-on-Mersey-Cheshire & if you have to think about it for a day or two, perhaps you would see my Uncle about it.[2] Believe me

Yours very truly
Frederick Macmillan

H James Jr., Esq.

**Notes**

1.  *The Portrait of a Lady* actually began to appear in *Macmillan's Magazine* in October 1880, and was brought out by Macmillan in book form on 8 November 1881. See *BHJ*, pp. 52–3.

2.    On the next day James suggested to Frederick Macmillan that November 1880 would be too soon unless 'simultaneity' of publication could be arranged with the *Atlantic Monthly* (letter 49).

## 49

Reform Club.
Pall Mall. S.W.
July 22*d* [1879]

My dear Macmillan

I write you a line to day [*sic*], in hopes it may catch you in Cheshire.[1] I think that *November 1880* would be too early a date for me to attempt to begin a novel in *Macmillan*, & that January of the following year is the first moment at which I ought to undertake it. If you have a story for the gap after the termination of Mrs. O. [Oliphant], I will undertake to begin in *January 1881* – *unless* you are disposed to assent to a scheme which occurred to me this morning. I am to furnish Howells a story for the last half of 1880, & the *Atlantic* has always objected to "simultaneity" with the English magazines.[2] But as he has, (as I told you,) just written to me to propose simultaneity with *Macmillan* or the *Cornhill* for his own forthcoming novel, I suppose he wouldn't raise his prohibition as to mine.[3] In that case you would of course be welcome to begin my story at the same time he does – I suppose at midsummer. If you don't like this, & prefer an *exclusive* novel, then, as I say I will begin in January of the following year. The latter scheme I think I like as well as the former, & if you will let me know your disposition I will abide by what you say. Let me know when you write whether you have any American regular address. Of course – I forgot – your N.Y. house! Bon voyage again, & a happy return.[4] All good wishes to your wife.[5] Yours ever

H. James Jr.

### Notes

1.    Macmillan was visiting Ashton-on-Mersey, Cheshire. See letter 48.
2.    *The Portrait of a Lady* eventually appeared in *Macmillan's*, October 1880– November 1881 and in the *Atlantic Monthly*, November 1880–December 1881.
3.    William Dean Howells's *The Undiscovered Country* appeared in the *Atlantic Monthly* from January to July 1880, and failed to achieve 'simultaneity' with either English magazine.
4.    Macmillan and his wife were planning a visit to America, a trip that lasted until late October. See letter 59. His uncle, Alexander Macmillan, the senior partner of

the firm at the time, had considered establishing a 'house' in America as early as 1867, but contented himself with sending Frederick as a 'direct agent' in 1871. By the 1890s, however, a branch was set up in New York. See Graves, pp. 275–6.

5. James frequently included a greeting to Mrs Macmillan at the end of a letter, a habit began as early as 8 November [1877] (letter 8).

# 50

Henry James Esquire
The Reform Club
Pall Mall

July 25. 1879.

My dear Mr James,

Fred sends me your letter about your Magazine story, with your alternatives. We certainly would prefer that you should begin early, say June next year! The Atlantic loses nothing by this & we and you gain prior publication and thereby to your copyright.[1]

We are willing to pay you £250 for Magazine use and half profits for book-form.[2]

When can you come to see me & talk over the matter? I am almost desolate next Sunday. You know our midday meal hour. The train from Victoria at 1–20 to Balham brings you in time. My wife & one daughter will be at table. Come if you can.[3]

We are practically committed to your following Mrs. Oliphant. I have been telling many people you were going to.[4]

Yours ever
Alex. Macmillan.

## Notes

1. During Frederick Macmillan's absence in America, negotiations on *The Portrait of a Lady* were handled by Alexander Macmillan, the senior partner. See letters 49 and 50, 52, 54, 55, 57. The novel actually began to appear in *Macmillan's* in October 1880 and in the *Atlantic* the following month.

2. James eventually received £326 for the serial appearance of the novel in *Macmillan's* when it turned out to be longer than James had anticipated and $3,500 for its publication in the *Atlantic Monthly*. See Anesko, p. 188.

3. James was not able to accept Macmillan's invitation to Sunday dinner at Knapdale, Upper Tooting, on this occasion. See letter 51.

4. Mrs Margaret Oliphant's *He That Will Not When He May* completed its run in October 1880, and James's *Portrait* began in the same number (XLII, 401–27) and continued until XLV (November 1881), 1–19.

**51**

> 3, Bolton Street.
> Piccadilly. W.
> July 26*th* [1879]

Dear Mr. Macmillan

Many thanks for your note – & let me say at once, that I have the ill-fortune that I have once or twice had before with regard to your invitations. Tomorrow is a very occupied day with me in town, as all my days have been for the last several weeks. I have an engagement to lunch, & ½ a dozen others in the afternoon; so that I shall be unable to get down to Tooting.[1] Many thanks & regrets.

As regards the story I shall be very glad to begin in Macmillan toward the middle of next year, if I hear definitely from Howells, of the *Atlantic* [,] that he will not object to simultaneity of publication. I think on the whole that he will consent to it & as soon as I do hear, as I expect to do soon, I will let you know.[2] The £250 in that case will suit me very well. I don't envy at the present moment those two young sea-farers![3] Yours very truly

> H James Jr.

**Notes**

1. See letter 50, note 3.
2. *The Portrait of a Lady* began in October 1880 in Macmillan's *Magazine* and in November in the *Atlantic*.
3. Since the novel turned out to be longer than James had anticipated, he eventually received £326 for it. See letter 50, note 2. The 'sea-farers' are Frederick and Georgiana Macmillan, who are sailing to America.

**52**

> 42 Rue de Luxembourg
> Paris
> (Sept 14*th*.) [1879]

Dear Mr. Macmillan –

When the "Madonna of the Future" appears, as I suppose she is liable to do just now at any time – will you please send me a single copy by book-post, to the above address, without sending any, as you have usually done, to my London address? When the book is out, I will send you a list of a few people to whom I shld. like it despatched.[1] I am in Paris for the greater part of the autumn, & suppose I shall hardly get back to London before the New Year. I hope you are spending a comfortable September & making up a little for the melancholy English summer. Also that you get good news from nephew & his wife.[2] I am just sending Morley my long-delayed *Hawthorne* which is, however, all the better for my having been long about it.[3] My kind regards to Mrs. Macmillan[4] & your daughters – Yours very truly –

H. James Jr.

### Notes

1. *The Madonna of the Future and Other Tales* was published 16 October 1879 (*BHJ*, p. 42). James received a copy on 18 October in Paris and enclosed his list in letter 55, though the list itself is no longer available.
2. Frederick and Georgiana Macmillan were in America. See letter 49, note 4.
3. John Morley was editor of the English Men of Letters series, for which James prepared his study of Hawthorne. See letters 21 and 22.
4. The reference is to Alexander Macmillan's second wife, Emma Pignatel Macmillan.

## 53

Sept 16. 1879

Dear Mr. James

My father was away when your letter came so I answer it. The Madonna is nearly ready & a copy shall be sent to you the moment she is.[1]

We are delighted to hear that Hawthorne is ready & are all anxious to read it.[2]

We hear good news of Fred who seems to like the other side as much as ever.[3] I am occupying his house meanwhile [.]

Believe me

Yours very truly<br>George A. Macmillan[4]

Henry James Esq Junr

**Notes**

1.   James received a copy of the *Madonna* on 18 October. See letter 52, note 1.
2.   James had mentioned posting the manuscript of *Hawthorne* in letter 52.
3.   Frederick Macmillan had represented the firm in America 1871–6 and had married an American woman. See letter 8, note 3.
4.   George A. Macmillan (1855–1936) was the second son of Alexander Macmillan and a junior partner in the firm.


**54**

> Paris.
> 42 Rue Cambon.
> 28*th* September [1879][1]

Dear Mr. Macmillan

In answering your note in regard to the proposed serial for next year in the Magazine, just before I left London, about a month ago, I promised you that I would let you know definitively about the matter as soon as I shld. have heard from the *Atlantic Monthly*, in which my plan was to publish the novel simultaneously with *Macmillan*. I have only just heard; but apparently the project can be carried out. There is a point which differs from your proposal, but I imagine that you will be able to accede to it: viz: that the novel begin in *July* rather than in *June*. This would be more convenient both to the *Atlantic* & to me. I should also mention that the monthly parts are to be pretty long – 24 or 25 pages – ; there will be, I suppose, *about eight* of them. I don't think there will be less than eight, and there may be *nine*. I wrote to you that your terms – £250 – were agreeable to me, & if these details are not inconvenient to you, I suppose we may consider the matter settled.[2] My novel is *probably* to be called "The Portrait of a Lady"; but upon this I observe the Silence of death! –

I received yesterday my account of the Sales of my books, from your people. The results are not brilliant – on the contrary – & I grieve that the books should not do better. It seems to me an anomaly that they don't, as they have been on the whole largely & favourably noticed, & apparently a good deal talked about. I hope better things for the serial – & also, if possible, for the "Madonna", which I suppose is about appearing, though I haven't yet received her.[3] I am happy to say that I at last, some days since, consigned my *Hawthorne* to Morley.[4] Very truly yours

> H. James Jr.

**Notes**

1. Previously printed in *HJL*, II, 256–7. The present text differs both in substantives and accidentals; moreover, this letter is addressed to Alexander Macmillan – not to Frederick Macmillan as Edel ascribes it – who was handling James's work while his nephew was in America. See letters 49 and 50.
2. See letters 50 and 51. The serial actually began in the October 1880 number and there were fourteen instalments instead of the eight or nine mentioned or the twelve parts eventually contracted for. Despite his acceptance of Macmillan's offer of £250, James received £326 for the novel. See letter 50, note 2.
3. For James's unhappiness with the 'anomaly' of his sales, see his letter of 11 October [1879] to his father (*HJL*, II, 259–60). For the *Madonna of the Future*, see letters 52, 53, and 55.
4. See letters 52 and 53.

# 55

Paris,
Rue Cambon 42.
Oct. 19*th* [1879]

Dear Mr. Macmillan –

I received yesterday the copy of the "Madonna" which you sent me by post, and which makes a very comely appearance. I wish the book all possible success – more than that of its but scantily prosperous predecessors. I enclose a list of the few persons to whom I should like copies sent.[1]

I wrote to you some month ago with regard to the subject of the letter you wrote me at the end of the summer – the time of publication of my serial for next year in *Macmillan*, which I have had to settle with the *Atlantic*. Receiving no answer from you I have taken for granted that *July* suits you, & have written to the Atlantic accordingly.[2]

Morley writes me that he is much pleased with my *Hawthorne* & that "it will certainly be one of the most attractive of the whole series" – which I am glad to hear.[3]

In relation to this I should be greatly obliged to you if you would send me a cheque, without further delay, for the remainder of the amount I am to receive for the Hawthorne – the 1st half of which your nephew sent me before he went to America.[4] Excuse my appearance of dunning you – but I am rather in want of the money. The same motive leads me to add that I shld. take it very kindly if you would include in the same cheque whatever money is owing me on the account of sales of my books, sent me the other day. This sum is apparently very small – your nephew having advanced me £50 in December (or January) last; but such as it is it will be a convenience to me to have it – & not an inconvenience to you, I hope, to send it, though I believe your regular way is not to settle those matters till somewhat later.[5]

I hope you continue to get good news from your nephew – isn't it time he should turn up?[6]

> Very truly yours
> H. James Jr.

### Notes

1.  *The Madonna of the Future*, according to the firm, had been published 16 October (*BHJ*, p. 42). The list is not in LB, MA.
2.  See letters 48–51.
3.  James had mentioned sending Morley the manuscript of *Hawthorne* in letters 52 and 54.
4.  See letter 46.
5.  James was no more backward in seeking payment for his work from the senior partner than he was in 'dunning' it from Frederick Macmillan, and Alexander Macmillan responded promptly with a cheque. See letters 56 and 57. Nevertheless, James was not happy with the sales of his book and planned to leave the 'unremunerative Macmillans' 'for [his] next novel at least', as he had informed his father a week earlier on 11 October (*HJL*, ii, 259).
6.  Frederick Macmillan was scheduled to return from America Saturday, 25 October. See also letter 57, note 1.

## 56

Henry James Jun Esqr.
Rue Cambon 42
Paris

> Oct. 20. 1879.

Dear Mr James,

I took for granted that your last letter was simply an answer and not a rejection of mine. The details of time &c I wished Grove to answer but he was abroad when your letter arrived. But they also will be gradually settled. He will write you himself. In the meantime I enclose cheque for the amount due according to statement. Would it were larger for your sake – and ours.[1]

Fred comes home on Saturday I hope. When do you return to our little village here?[2]

Yours very truly
A Macmillan

**Notes**

1. For earlier discussion of the terms of publication of 'The Portrait of a Lady' in *Macmillan's Magazine*, see letters 48–51, 54. The first paragraph of this letter is so blotted and blurred that it may not be accurately recorded. From the context, Macmillan is apparently referring to James's letter of 28 September, not the one of 19 October.
2. Frederick Macmillan was due to return 25 October, and Alexander Macmillan renewed his invitation of 25 July (letter 50) for James to visit him at Knapdale, Upper Tooting.

## 57

Paris.
42 Rue Cambon.
Oct. 21*st* [1879]

Dear Mr. Macmillan

I am much obliged to you for your prompt response to my letter, & I enclose the two receipts of the cheque. I am afraid I am not likely to get back to London for another six or eight weeks, as I shall probably go for a month to Italy. Give your nephew & his wife my welcome on his arrival.[1]

Very truly yours
H. James Jr.

**Note**

1. For the cheque, see letter 56 and receipt in LB, MA for £50 for final payment on copyright of *Hawthorne*. James returned to London 11 December 1879 (see his letter to Grace Norton of 21 December 1879 in *HJL*, ɪɪ, 261). Frederick Macmillan and his wife returned from America Saturday, 25 October.

**58**

Nov. 1. 1879

Dear James,

I did not answer your note of last week because I gathered from it that you were on your way home. Today I receive yours of yesterday and hasten now to thank you for them both and also to utter a devout word of gratitude to Providence for having brought things about so exactly to my mind.[1]

August 1880 then is to see the beginning of your novel in Macmillan.[2]

I had no holiday (as you so kindly ask about it,), but I had to run to Berlin & Leipsic to look at the *Archiv* of the Mendelssohns and as I was successful and made some excellent new friends, though only away a fortnight, I must take that as a holiday.[3]

I shall hope to see you very soon after your return [.]

Yours very truly
G. Grove

F. Macmillan is back & looking very well.[4]
Henry James Esq
Rue Cambon 42
Paris.

**Notes**

1.  Neither of James's notes to George Grove is in LB, MA.
2.  *The Portrait of a Lady* began appearing in *Macmillan's* in the October issue, not in the August number.
3.  Grove was also editing a *Dictionary of Music and Musicians* (4 volumes, 1878–89).
4.  See letter 57, note 1.

**59**

Nov: 10. 1879

My dear James,

We have been back for a fortnight but I have been so busy getting into my work again that I have not until today been able to find time to write to you. This morning a document came from Harper & Brothers to be forwarded to you for your signature & just serves to turn what had been a matter of inclination into a necessity.[1]

We had a most delightful holiday in America. I only hope you enjoyed your summer half as much. We were in the United States for 10 weeks during which time we only had *two* rainy days. The thermometer stood at 90 deg. in the shade the day we landed and 85 deg. when we left on October 18. That kind of temperature with nothing to do is to me the height of luxury. I must confess that I began to tire of my ease a week or two before it was time to return, & that I was far from sorry when the time came for going "back again" to fog and work.

I am glad to find that the "Madonna of the Future" is doing so well. We have already sold 250 copies which is only 35 copies less than the whole sale of Daisy Miller. What about *Confidence*? It ought to appear in England before it is all published in "Scribner" so that there may be no question about copyright. Will you be able to get early proofs for us to print from?[2]

Will you be so kind as to sign & return the enclosed agreement & I will forward it to Harpers.

I suppose you will be in London again by the New Year, & we shall then hope to see a great deal of you at Elm Tree Road. My wife asked me to send you her regards when I wrote. She is very well & 10 lbs heavier than when she left England! of which she is very proud.[3]

Believe me my dear James,

Yours most truly,
Frederick Macmillan

H James Jr Esq

### Notes

1. The Harper document was a memorandum of agreement for the publication of *Hawthorne* in America. Though Macmillan had given James an opportunity to take £75 outright for English rights and to receive 10% royalty from Harper on sales in America (see letter 34), James took a flat £100 for the book and Macmillan received the American royalties (see letter 35). For James's response to the successful sale of *Hawthorne* in America, see his letter of 17 January 1880 to his father, in which he urges the family not to 'glory' in the book's sale since the money 'will all flow into the over-gorged coffers of Bedford St' (*BHJ*, p. 47).

2. *The Madonna of the Future* had appeared on 16 October (*BHJ*, p. 42). As for *Confidence*, Chatto and Windus had offered James better terms (£100 down on publication) than he inferred that Macmillan would offer, so he closed with Chatto and Windus, to Macmillan's chagrin. Letters 60–63 also deal with this matter. For James's dissatisfaction with his royalties from the sales of his first books with Macmillan, see his letter to his father of 11 October [1879] (*HJL*, II, 259–60).

3.   The usual greetings in Macmillan's letters from Mrs Macmillan to James are often followed by a reference to her erratic health. During the 1880s in particular she apparently needed frequent changes of scene from London to Brighton or Cheshire or to the Continent.

## 60

Nov: 12. 1879

My dear James,

Your letter received this morning has crossed one that I wrote you & sent to Rue de Cambon the address which we had. As the letter contained an enclosure I hope it will have been forwarded to you.[1]

We are sending for a copy of the "Athenaeum" and will continue to send you any reviews of the "Madonna" that may appear: if you go to Italy or change your address please send word.[2]

I am very sorry to hear that "Confidence" is to appear under another imprint than ours, especially as I thought when you told me about the story in the summer it was understood that we were to publish it. We always hoped to have the whole of your books in a uniform edition, and it was rather for the sake of completeness than in the expectation of a remunerative sale that we undertook to print *The American* in the face of the two-shilling piracy. If your going elsewhere was a question of terms, if for instance you wished to sell the book outright, or to be paid something on publication on account of future profits I wish you had mentioned it to me first for we have every wish to deal liberally with you and would have tried to meet your wishes about any matter of the kind.[3]

My wife is very well thank you. She was much annoyed at finding when we left New York that maple sugar was out of season & unobtainable but I believe she made arrangements for the importation of a small cargo which will be ready for you when you get back to London – [4]

Believe me

Yours very truly
Frederick Macmillan

Hawthorne is to be published early next month.[5]

## Notes

1.   See letter 59. James's letter is not in the James correspondence in LB, MA.

2. A review of *The Madonna of the Future and Other Tales* had appeared in the *Athenaeum*, 2715 (8 November 1879), 593–4. James, indeed, went to Italy and returned to London on 11 December 1879. See letter 57, note 1.
3. Macmillan's explanation of his plans for publishing and paying James satisfied him, and he returned to the firm for another decade. Thereafter he published with it more erratically.
4. Such favours illustrate the growing friendship between Mrs Macmillan and James.
5. *Hawthorne* was published in London on 12 December 1879 (*BHJ*, p. 46).


# 61

Nov: 14. 1879

My dear James,

I can't understand why my letter was not in the same envelope with Harper's Memorandum of Agreement. However it does not matter. It was only a friendly epistle announcing our return from America, and asking you to sign and send back Harper's Memorandum.[1]

I confess that I did feel hurt about "Confidence." Of course we don't pretend to any claim over your work, but as we have been your publishers hitherto I am sorry you should have gone elsewhere merely because you wanted some ready money. If you had written to my Uncle proposing that we should advance you £100 on account of future profits, you would undoubtedly have received a cheque by return of post.[2] Certainly the money result last year was not very encouraging, but you must remember it was the result of your first year before the British public as a writer of fiction. No doubt the flavour of your work is too delicate to be at once appreciated by palates accustomed to coarser food, but I believe that the cordial recognition your books have received from the critical papers & reviews will in time have its effect on the sales, indeed I think this is already evident as each new book seems to do better than the last. It is somewhat up-hill work in the meanwhile, but if you will only trust us I think we shall be able to give you as much help on the road as our neighbours.[3] Hoping therefore that "the withdrawal of your Confidence" is only temporary, I am

Yours very truly,
Frederick Macmillan

Henry James Jr Esq
51 Rue Neuve/St. Augustin [,] Paris

**Notes**

1.   See letters 59–60. Another of James's letters, apparently, is not included with his correspondence in LB, MA.
2.   These additional remarks about *Confidence* and about payment for James's work in general led eventually to the payment of advances that James's sales could not sustain, but Macmillan tried seriously and consistently to pay James as well as his prospects allowed.
3.   James returned to the fold, and when Macmillan brought out the first 'collective edition' of his work in 1883, *Confidence*, having run its three-year course with Chatto and Windus, appeared as volume 10 (*BHJ*, p. 59).

## 62

17*th* Nov: 1879

Dear Mr. James,

Your letter comes to Frederick today when he happens to be confined to the house with a cold. I am not sure that I quite understand the position of authors, but if £100 is of any importance to you take this amt. I enclose.[1] We are glad to send it & I hope you will always tell us when we can be any convenience to you in this way.

Yours ever truly
Geo. Lillie Craik

Henry James Jun Esq

**Note**

1.   Since Frederick Macmillan was absent, George Lillie Craik, a member of the firm since 1865 and husband of the novelist Dinah Mulock Craik, wrote on his behalf and in accordance with what he knew of Macmillan's correspondence with James (see letter 61, for example), sent a cheque promptly. James's letter is not contained in LB, MA.

## 63

Nov: 19. 1879

My dear James,

I have been laid up since Saturday with my first cold this season & was therefore away when your last letter arrived. It was opened by Mr. Craik who was not very clear as to the subject of our recent correspondence, but gathering from your note that you had not yet received the money you expected from C & W. thought that £100 on account would not be unacceptable to you & therefore sent it. It can of course be put against what we shall have to pay you at our next settlement.[1]

Julian Hawthorne has just called. He has grown tired of Hastings and is as usual employed in moving himself & his belongings.[2]

Believe me

> Yours very truly,
> Frederick Macmillan

H. James Jr. Esq

### Notes

1. Though James's letter is not available, he apparently requested an advance in the context of Macmillan's letter (no. 61), a suggestion Macmillan proposed that Craik misunderstood; nevertheless, he (Macmillan) agreed that it should be related to the 'next settlement'. C & W refers to Chatto & Windus (see letter 59, note 2).
2. James had visited Hawthorne in Hastings the previous winter. See his letter of 22 January [1879] to Hawthorne (Virginia), and his comment on the man and the visit in a letter to William James of 4 March [1879] (*HJL*, II, 216–17). See letter 41, note 3.

## 64

Jan 8: 1880

My dear James,

I am sending you a copy of the cheap edition of "Daisy Miller" which comes out today, and which I think looks very nice. If you would like to give any away, please let me know.[1]

> Yours ever,
> Frederick Macmillan

H. James Jr. Esq

### Note

1. *BHJ* dates this one-volume edition as 'January 1880' (p. 40). As usual Macmillan offers James an unspecified number of author's copies.

## 65

Sept 17 1880

Mr dear James,

I enclose a batch of accounts, the net result of which is that there is £110 to put to your credit. This is not so much as I hope we shall have to pay you in future years, but it might be worse. I am glad to see that the six Shilling Editions of the older books e.g. "The American" have a steady sale, and look as if they intended to bring something in one of these days.[1]

Will you not soon have material enough for a new collection of short stories? "The Packet of Letters" [sic], "Washington Square," xc. I think it will be a good plan to make up 3 volumes next time instead of two, if you can manage it. A three volume book is more profitable in proportion than a two volume one.[2] I am pleased to think that we shall have you in the magazine for some time forward from next month. Grove tells me that you are giving him good big instalments.[3]

I called the other day at Bolton Street but found that you like everybody else were out of town. I hope you will let me know as soon as you come back. We had a very pleasant holiday first in America and then in Normandy.

> Believe me
> Yours very truly,
> Frederick Macmillan

Henry James Jr Esq

### Notes

1. At this time Macmillan and Co. had published six-shilling editions of *The American*, *The Europeans*, *Daisy Miller*, and *The Madonna of the Future and Other Tales*. None of these issues sold as well as Macmillan had hoped. See letter 83.
2. 'A Bundle of Letters' (not 'The Packet of Letters') appeared in two volumes with *Washington Square* and 'The Pension Beaurepas' in January 1881. See *BHJ*, p. 51. James's next novel, *The Portrait of a Lady*, did indeed appear in three volumes.
3. The first episode of 'The Portrait of a Lady' appeared in *Macmillan's Magazine* in October 1880.

## 66

Reform Club.
Pall Mall. S.W.
Sept. 20*th* 1880

Dear Macmillan,

I found your note, with the statement of account, on Saturday, on my return from the seaside, but had immediately to leave town again, until this morning. I am glad to find my profits show some signs of extending – & that the amount set down to my credit covers the £100 advanced to me by Mr. Craik last autumn.[1]

I am *probably* back in town permanently – save for an occasional short absence – & I shall take an early day, or rather evening, for coming up to St. John's Wood & talking with you of your own adventures. (I shall probably take my chance of finding you some evening this week.) I will then speak to you of the book of three tales – which, I suppose ought to come out about Dec. 1*st*.[2]

I hope your wife is well & that London seems as pleasant again to both of you as it does to *my* incurable cockneyship.

Yours very truly
H. James Jr.

**Notes**

1. See letter 62. With the advance deducted, James was owed £10 for almost a year's royalties.
2. *Washington Square* and the two short stories mentioned in letter 65, note 2.

## 67

Sept 30 1880

My dear James,

I have much pleasure in enclosing a cheque for the October instalment of your story.[1]

Believe me

Yours very truly,
Frederick Macmillan

H. James Jr Esq

Note

1.  Although Alexander Macmillan had promised £250 for English magazine rights
    to the novel (see letter 50, note 2), James was paid by the instalment, and when
    he added several to the original number, he was paid at a rate that eventually
    brought him £326 for the serial. See Anesko, p. 188.


## 68

Oct 4. 1880

My dear James,
   One Grädener of Hamburg who publishes "Ashers Collection of
English Authors" has written to say that he would like to buy the
right to print 'The Portrait of a Lady'.[1] I fancy however that your
books are published by Tauchnitz and will tell him so if you like. I
hope the Baron pays you well – If the stories you heard in Florence
about the enormous sale of the 'Madonna of the Future' are true he
ought to send you something reasonable.[2]

Yours very truly,<br>Frederick Macmillan

Henry James Jr. Esq


Notes

1.  For James's refusal to allow Karl Grädener to reprint *The Portrait of a Lady*, see
    letter 69.
2.  James had spent much of the previous spring in Florence, the setting of the story.
    In his 'Collection of British Authors', Tauchnitz had published volume one of the
    Macmillan edition of *The Madonna of the Future and Other Tales* as volume 1881
    and volume two as volume 1888. See LeRoy Phillips, *A Bibliography of the Writ-
    ings of Henry James*, revised edition, 1930 (New York: Burt Franklin, 1968), pp.
    16–17, and *BHJ*, p. 384.


## 69

3, Bolton Street.<br>Piccadilly. W.<br>Oct. 8th [1880]

Dear Macmillan,
   Excuse my levity in not having sooner answered your note about
Karl Grädener.[1] I laid it out for this purpose, but it got pushed out of

sight before I took it up again, & then, having vanished from sight, vanish'ed also from mind.

Please say to Mr. G. that I have standing engagements with another publisher which prevent my entertaining his kind proposal.

This is the case. I do as well with Tauchnitz as I should do with him, & in Tauchnitz one is better placed.[2] Grädener wrote me a general proposal some time since, to which I returned a definite negative.

I spent 3 days at St. Leonard's – & then fled before the howling blast.

I am going to walk up N.W. one of these evenings.[3]

> Yours very truly
> H. James Jr

### Notes

1. See letter 68 for Macmillan's reference to Grädener's interest in *The Portrait of a Lady*.
2. Tauchnitz published the novel in his 'Collection of British Authors' in 1882 (*BHJ*, p. 384).
3. James apparently meant to walk to Elm Tree Road, St John's Wood, the site of Macmillan's home.

## 70

> Nov: 3*rd* 1880.

My dear James,

Many thanks for the copy of your new volume.[1] It shall be put in hand immediately.

> Yours very truly,
> Frederick Macmillan

H. James Jr. Esq

### Note

1. The 'copy' received, presumably, is for *Washington Square, Pension Beaurepas, A Bundle of Letters*, the first printing of which appeared the following January. *BHJ*, pp. 51–2.

## 71

Dec 21. 1880.

My dear James,

There is a word on page 295 which is evidently a misprint. Will you kindly correct it and return the page. [*sic*][1]

I suppose you are just leaving town. You take with you the best Christmas wishes of

Yours very truly,
Frederick Macmillan

H. James Jr. Esq.

### Note

1.   Apparently a reference to a page in the July instalment of *Washington Square* in *Harper's New Monthly* (LX, 287–301), the basis for the Macmillan text in book form. Macmillan may be referring to a lower-case 'a' in 'aunt Penniman'.

## 72

Dec 22 1880.

My dear James,

I have just discovered to my annoyance that we omitted to send you a cheque for the December instalment of "The Portrait of a Lady." I therefore enclose one now which covers both December & January numbers.[1] Believe me

Yours very truly,
Frederick Macmillan

H. James Jr. Esq.

### Note

1.   See letter 67, note 1. Though the firm had offered and James had accepted £250 for the serial, Macmillan was paying by instalment.

## 73

Dec 22. 1880

Dear James,

I think it is not too late to put the printers right about beginning the sections with simple numerals instead of the word *Chapter*. I have written to them about it.

My letter with cheque for Dec: & Jan: magazine crossed yours.[1]

Believe me

Yours very truly,

Frederick Macmillan

H. James Jr. Esq.

### Note

1.　See letter 72. James's letter is not included in LB, MA. The comment on numerals and chapters refers to *Washington Square/The Pension Beaurepas/A Bundle of Letters*.

## 74

Kerris Vean,

Falmouth.

Dec. 28*th* [1880]

Dear Macmillan.

I have just received a letter from Houghton & Mifflin which I enclose to you on account of the paragraph about the arrival of *Macmillan* in the U.S. It appears that it is devoured in the American papers before my story appears in the *Atlantic*. This must in fact be rather a disadvantage, & even danger. Is it not possible to delay the departure of the magazine for America, so as to give the *Atlantic* a better chance? For what you can do in this way I should be very grateful.[1]

Behold me in the depths of Cornwall, with an Atlantic gale howling about the house, & the rain lashing the windows. I am wofully homesick for Piccadilly – & appalled by the prospect of being dragged through the storm to the Land's End. I prefer the Land's Centre, – i.e. Bolton St.[2] Yours ever, in haste

H. James Jr.

### Notes

1.　Since *Macmillan's Magazine* had published the first instalment of 'The Portrait of a Lady' a month before the *Atlantic Monthly*, the arrival and sale of *Macmillan's* before the appearance of the *Atlantic* posed a real problem to the American magazine. Macmillan, however, could do very little about the matter (see letter 75).

2.　James's flat was located at 3 Bolton Street, Piccadilly.

**75**

Dec 30 1880

My dear James,

I return Messrs Houghton & Co's letter, but I do not quite see how to avoid the difficulty they complain of. It arises from the habit prevailing among American publishers of issuing their magazines a fortnight before the proper time. The December "*Atlantic*" was published on the 15*th* of November while the December *Macmillan* is published at what seems to me the more reasonable date of December 1*st*. If therefore our Dec magazine contained the same chapters of your story as the December *Atlantic* the English copyright – which depends on first publication, would be lost.[1]

I should be very glad to delay the departure of the copies of the magazine which we send out if it would do any good, but only a minority of the number of copies which go to America are sent through our Agency – and of course once the Magazine is out we have no control over its distribution.

The only thing I can propose is that the *Atlantic* should be issued on the 10*th* instead of the 15*th* of the month. It would then be in the hands of the readers before *Macmillan*. A still better plan would be for them to publish on the first of the month which gives its name to the number – but this I suppose is too great a change.

There is no danger as far as copyright is concerned. The English copyright depends upon the book being published first in British Dominions but the American law only demands registration, which Houghton & Co. can easily arrange. Believe me, with best wishes for the New Year,

Yours very truly,
Frederick Macmillan

H. James Jr. Esq

**Note**

1.    See James's request in letter 74.

## 76

Jan 25./1881

My dear James,
   Will you kindly send me the names of any persons to whom you wish presentation copies of *Washington Square* to go. [sic][1]

Yours very truly,
Frederick Macmillan

H. James Jr. Esq.

**Note**

1.    *Washington Square* was published in London on 26 January 1881 (*BHJ*, p. 52). See also letter 77.

## 77

Jan 26/1881

My dear James,
   We will send out the presentation copies of "Washington Square" today. I am happy to be able to tell you that the trade has subscribed more liberally for this than for any of your previous books. Mudie and Smith & Son have each of them bought 100 copies and the rest of the London booksellers 80 between them, so that with the country orders we start off with a sale of 300 copies.[1]

   As those two charming sketches in the second volume are both quite new to the English public,[2] I can't help thinking that the book will be a success. Believe me

Yours very sincerely
Frederick Macmillan

H. James Jr Esq^re

**Notes**

1.    C. E. Mudie's Circulating Library and W. H. Smith's bookstalls were usually among the firm's best customers. The advance sale led to the printing of a second impression in March, a total of 750 copies. In August a one-volume edition of 500 copies appeared, and in November 1883, the novel appeared in Macmillan's 'Collective Edition' in an issue of 5,000 copies, putting a respectable total of 6,250 copies before the public in less than three years. See *BHJ*, pp. 51–2, 58–9. James's list of those he wished to receive presentation copies is not in LB, MA.
2.    'The Pension Beaurepas' and 'A Bundle of Letters'.

**78**

Feb 2. 1881.

My dear James,

I have the pleasure to enclose a cheque for your February number.[1]

Yours very truly,

Frederick Macmillan

H James Jr. Esq

**Note**

1.  Payment for the fifth instalment of 'The Portrait of a Lady' in *Macmillan's Magazine*.

**79**

Hotel de Londres
San Remo
Feb. 27*th* [1881]

Dear Macmillan.

From the Mediterranean shore, face to face with a sea which ought to be blue, but is actually the colour of a London fog, & amid orange groves that ought to be golden, but are no more so than the fruit which blooms in Piccadilly – from the midst of such scenes I write you a hasty appeal. Will you, if you have not already sent it to Bolton St, send me the *March* Macmillan directly to the above address? Or rather, even if you have, will you still send me another? I have been despatching the magazine, since my story has been coming out, to several people, & I should like it continued while I am away – if you wd kindly give orders to this effect, I will write the names on another paper.[1]

I spent about a fortnight in Paris after leaving London & then came almost directly here – via Avignon, Marseilles & Nice; having had designs of staying a little at the last named place, but finding it so crowded & loathsome that I was glad to flee to this less sophisticated shore, where I shall probably remain for a week or two – or even longer, if I find the rain is not perpetual. I shall probably go from here directly to Venice, where I shall spend as much as possible of the time I am absent from London – my most earnest wish being for the repose of foreign scenes & not for the agitation of travel.

Meanwhile what has happened to you all in London? What did

poor Dr. Max Schlesinger die of? – I was extremely shocked to learn the event.[2] Though I find it good to get away for a while from London, I find it even better (while away) to make the chains that fasten me to it occasionally vibrate, & am therefore always thankful for any news that isn't *too* interesting. In the latter case the rope pulls rather too hard. Have there been any (noticeable) notices of my book?[3] Perhaps you have sent two or three to Bolton St. I should be glad to see the few that appear in the important papers: for the others I don't care.

I read about *Snow* in London, & am really almost ashamed, for I have been *transpiring* as they say in French, for the last week. I have only time to catch the post, & to add kind remembrances for your wife.

Yours ever, faithfully
H. James Jr.

### Notes

1. The March issue of *Macmillan's Magazine* contained the sixth instalment of 'The Portrait of a Lady'. The list James refers to is not included with his letter in the LB, MA.
2. Max Schlesinger, London correspondent of the *Cologne Gazette*, died in his '59th year' on 10 February 1881 (*Times*, 14 February 1881, p. 11). See also letter 80.
3. In letter 80, Macmillan mentions a notice of *Washington Square* in the *Pall Mall Gazette*, 4 March 1881, 11–12. Others had appeared in the *Spectator*, LIV (5 February 1881), 185–6 and *Athenaeum*, 2791 (12 February 1881), 228, and another subsequently in the *Saturday Review*, LI (19 March 1881), 372–3.

## 80

March 4 1881.

My dear James,

I was very glad to receive your letter and to learn from it that you are flourishing and in good spirits. The mere fact of having heard from you renders me at once an object of interest, perhaps of envy to a multitude of your friends and admirers, one of whom by the way, Mrs. Procter – who was at our house last night – bid me say that she is about to write to you herself to express her delight at your last number, & to tell you the news.[1] I cautioned her against making the letter too interesting.

There have been several good reviews of "Washington Square"; there is one only this afternoon in the "Pall Mall Gazette".[2] I am having them collected and sent on to you, and we will forward anything of interest that appears in them hereafter. Let me know when you change your address.

The sales are very satisfactory. We have already actually sold 450 copies which is as many as were sold altogether of the 2 volume edition of the "Madonna".[3]

Poor Max Schlesinger died quite suddenly of fatty [?] degeneration of the heart. He was in the Garrick Club up to 5 o'clock in the afternoon and on going home complained of a pain in his side which he attributed to indigestion. All at once he said "Oh this pain is dreadful!" and died then [one word torn] at about 7 o'c p.m. It was a very shocking event. Somehow or other he was a man that one did not expect to die for a long while.[4]

I suppose you have at one time or another seen pictures by W. M. Hunt of Boston. His widow has brought a number of them over and has opened an exhibition in Bond St. for the purpose of establishing a posthumous European reputation for her husband. I don't know whether she will succeed, but I should be inclined to doubt it. The pictures certainly have quality, but people who know say they are wanting in technical skill.[5]

There is to be a wonderful contribution of histrionic talent at the Lyceum in May. Irving & Booth are to play Othello & Iago, but I hope you will be back in London again before that comes off.[6]

The weather – but I wont say anything about that lest it should influence you in fixing a date for your return.

With kind regards in which my wife joins me, I am

Yours truly truly,
Frederick Macmillan

H. James Jr Esq
Hotel de Londres
San Remo

**Notes**

1.　Anne Benson Skepper Procter (1798–1888), wife of Bryan Waller Procter, 'Barry Cornwall' (1787–1874), and a good friend to James since 1877. See *HJL*, II, 113, 199, 201, 208, 417–18.
2.　See letter 79, note 3.
3.　Macmillan is referring to the two-volume edition of *Washington Square* in the context of the sale of *The Madonna of the Future and Other Tales*. Since only 500

copies had been printed in January, a second impression was now necessary (*BHJ*, pp. 51–2).
4. James had asked about Schlesinger in letter 79.
5. This exhibition of the paintings of William Morris Hunt (1824–79) is mentioned in *The Times*, 26 February 1881, p. 1. Macmillan, obviously, did not know that James had often visited Hunt's studio in Newport, R.I. in 1860–61, when his brother William was taking lessons from Hunt. See Edel, I, 156, 160–62.
6. Henry Irving (1838–1905) and Edwin Booth (1833–93) began their production of *Othello* at the Lyceum on 2 May (Ellen Terry, 1848–1928, played Desdemona): *The Times*, 2 May 1881, p. 10. The last performance took place on 15 June. James missed this theatrical event, for he did not return from the Continent until 12 July. See *HJL*, II, 356.

# 81

(3 Bolton St W.)
Aug. 21*st* [1881]

Dear Macmillan.

I should have sent you before (though probably the printer has not yet needed them) the remainder of all the revised copy that I have for the plates of my book. As I don't know who is making them will you kindly forward these sheets, which I send by this post.[1]

And will you, speaking with the voice of authority, do me these favours? 1. Direct that Mrs. [*sic*] Clay & Taylor send me the advance sheets of the *October Macmillan*, that I may revise that portion of my tale & let the printers have it without delay.[2]

2*d*. Direct the same firm to send me as *soon as possible* the proof of the concluding (November) instalment of the serial, that I may also immediately put it into the hands of the platemakers. If left to themselves C & T. may not send me proof for some little time.[3] I leave town from one day to another, but everything is forwarded from Bolton St.

I hope you keep a good fire at Walton?[4]

Yours ever
H. James Jr.

**Notes**

1. James was revising the instalments of 'The Portrait of a Lady' for publication in book form.
2. Clay and Taylor printed the monthly episodes of the novel for *Macmillan's Magazine*.
3. For Macmillan's positive reply to James's request, see letter 82.
4. By this time the Frederick Macmillans had taken a house in Walton-on-Thames, where James visited them. See *HJL*, II, 327.

**82**

Aug 31. 1881.

My dear James,

Many thanks for the revised copy. I am telling Clays [*sic*] to send you proofs of the October and November nos of 'The Portrait of a Lady' at once.[1] Believe me

Yours ever truly,
Frederick Macmillan

H James Jr. Esq

**Note**

1.    This is Macmillan's response to James's request in letter 81.

**83**

Sept 30 1881.

My dear James,

I enclose our yearly statement of accounts. I am sorry to see that the 1 volume editions of the old books have not yet begun to yield any profit, but the sale keeps up fairly well and another year will see one of them at all events (The American) turn the corner.[1] You will notice that the advertising of the six shilling Editions is very costly. This is because they are always advertised with our "Series of Six Shilling Novels" and as much is spent on them as on some other books which have a far larger sale. It was extravagant to spend so much on advertisements when the returns are so moderate but I think it would be a pity to take them out of the sales.

As it may be a convenience to you to have this money before you start for America I am paying it in to Brown Shipley & Co's [*sic*] with what is due to you for the October number of our magazine.[2]

We came back from Walton yesterday.[3] I hope you will propose to come to Elm Tree Road some evening before you sail.

Believe me

Yours very truly,
Frederick Macmillan

H. James Jr Esq^re

**Notes**

1.  Macmillan had published a six-shilling one-volume edition of *The American* in March 1879 and another of *Roderick Hudson* in May 1880. See *BHJ*, 31, 33. The 'statement of accounts' is not in LB, MA.
2.  James was leaving for America on 20 October 1881, and Macmillan wished to make the best of a disappointing royalty account by paying up promptly on the serial before he embarked and by including an advance on *Portrait of a Lady* in book form, a total of £88, as indicated in separate figures written on the top of letter 84.
3.  See letter 81, note 4.

## 84

3 Bolton St. W.
Oct. 14th a.m. [1881]

Dear Macmillan

On second thought I *won't* refuse your offer of an advance on my new book, & shall be thankful for anything you may send to B. S. & Co. in that character.[1] It will add to my sense of greatness in returning to the U.S. – which I trust I shall not have to do before the wind goes down! What a night! If it is possible along with the sheets of Macmillan, &c before I go, to send me also a set of sheets of the book though it be not yet bound, I shall also be grateful.[2] If I shouldn't have time to see you again, farewell till the next time.

Ever yours
H. James Jr.

**Notes**

1.  See letter 83. According to figures written on the top of page 1 of this letter, £38 was presumably paid for the October episode of the novel and £50 for an advance on its appearance in book form. James subsequently requested an advance ('money down') on new books.
2.  James obviously meant sheets of the concluding instalment of 'The Portrait of a Lady' (November) in *Macmillan's Magazine*.

## 85

Adelphi Hotel,
Liverpool,
Oct. 20*th* 1881[1]

Dear Macmillan.

I embark in ½ an hour; but I am literary to the last! I meant to have sent you before I left London a list of people to whom I should like author's copies of my book sent. As I had already made it out, I enclose it herewith.[2] Please to make 'em send *me* a copy – but I will write it on the list.

It is blowing stiffly, but bright, & I have just performed the religious rite of buying a sea-chair from that horribly dirty old woman opposite the hotel. Pray for me, & don't let my fame die out. Many thanks for the draft.[3] Be well & happy (both of you) – & sell, you in particular, 5000 copies of my works. I see them in *all* the shop windows (booksellers' of course) here; which makes me feel as if I had not only started but arrived. A tender farewell again to Mrs. Macmillan.

Yours ever, qualmishly,
H. James[4]

**Notes**

1. Previously printed in *HJL*, ii, 360–61. The present text differs in several substantive matters.
2. The list is no longer with the letter in LB, MA. For one name on this list, see letter 86.
3. The payment referred to in letters 83 and 84, note 1.
4. For once prior to his father's death, James failed to include 'Junior' in his signature.

## 86

Cambridge, Mass.,
Dec. 27*th* [1881]

My dear Macmillan.

Will you kindly inquire what mistake there was regarding the sending out one of my *Portraits*, according to my list? I was notified a few days since that the copy to be addressed – "Countess of Rosebery, Mentmore, Leighton Buzzard," had not, up to Dec. 1*st*, reached the *destinataire*. But hold: I may have given another address; i.e. *Dalmeny, Edinburgh*! Will you at any rate please ask whether to one or other of these addresses a copy of my novel was sent? I fondly hope that the others went out in order.[1]

I wrote to you (from here) a few days after my arrival in these climes, & though there was nothing particular in my letter to answer have had ever since a sort of yearning to hear from you.[2] Like the

German woman of letters mentioned by Heine, who always wrote with one eye fixed on her MS & the other on some man – I too pass my life in a sort of divergent squint. One of my orbs of vision rests (complacently enough) on the scenes that surround me here; the other constantly wanders away to the shores of Old England; & takes the train for Euston as soon as it arrives.

I wrote to you from Cambridge, but I have not been here ever since then. I have spent a month, most agreeably, in New York (staying, the whole time with E. L. Godkin, a most genial host,) & came on here to pass Xmas in the bosom of my family.[3] I have done so, very pleasantly, and tomorrow I return to N.Y. & to further adventures. My winter, thus far, has gone on very happily, though I cannot say it has been devoted to literary composition. No, I have only been seeing American life; from about 9 o'clock a.m. daily, to considerably past midnight. I have seen a great deal & been charmingly treated; but I begin to long, powerfully, for a studious seclusion which I am afraid is till distant. If I can't, before long, obtain it otherwise, I shall return to Europe for it. New York is a big place, & is rapidly becoming an interesting one. I am struck, throughout, with the rapid & general increase of the *agreeable* in American life, & the development of material civilization. As we are having moreover a winter at once extraordinarily mild & charmingly bright, my impressions are decidedly genial. Also my book is selling – largely, for one of mine.[4] I hope it is doing something of the kind *chez vous*. I have seen a good many English notices, & appear to myself to have got off on the whole very well. Look, if you can put your hand on it, at a Review in the *Tribune* for Dec. 25*th* – very glowing, & well-written.[5] Write me – something, anything, provided it speak to me of London! I hear you are having a "fine" winter, & I am sorry; for I love, as they say here, to think of the dear old dingy air. Keep some pleasant evening in May clear for me to dine with you. I send *mille tendresses* to Mrs. Macmillan & remain with all good wishes very faithfully yours

H. James Jr.

**Notes**

1.  James had visited Lord and Lady Rosebery at both stately homes. The copy of *The Portrait of a Lady*, as James indicates in letter 87, had been sent to Dalmeny.
2.  This letter is not in LB, MA. James had arrived in Cambridge 1 November (*HJL*, II, 361).

3.  Edwin Lawrence Godkin (1831–1902) founded the *Nation* in 1865, a journal James had contributed to from the beginning.
4.  *The Portrait of a Lady* had been published in Boston on 16 November and already was selling well enough to prompt the printing of 5,000 copies in less than a year (*BHJ*, p. 54).
5.  *New-York Daily Tribune*, 25 December 1881, p. 8. The reviewer – John Hay, former secretary to Abraham Lincoln and a friend – summed up: 'Of the importance of this volume there can be no question. It will certainly remain one of the notable books of the time. It is properly to be compared, not with the light and ephemeral literature of amusement, but with the gravest and most serious works of imagination which have been devoted to the study of the social conditions of the age and the moral aspects of our civilization' (p. 8). For more on James and Hay, see George Monteiro, *Henry James and John Hay: The Record of a Friendship* (Providence, Rhode Island: Brown University Press, 1965).

## 87

Westminster Hotel
New York.
Dec. 30*th* [1881]

My dear Macmillan.

Don't bother about the Rosebery *Portrait*. It is all right – having gone to Dalmeny & been inexcusably delayed at that place.[1] Meanwhile your letter of the 15*th* ult. has come & been welcomed, the day after I wrote to you last.[2] Thank you for your London news, as well as for your cautions with regard to taking root in this patriot soil. The latter have an almost ironical sound. I am desperately homesick here & I am *not* homesick in London. The natural inference would seem to be that London is my home.[3] I came hither two days since from Cambridge, but am here only *in transition*. It poured with rain yesterday, & I stopped in doors [*sic*] till eve – a degree of confinement which the much-abused climate of Bolton St. never renders necessary. Then I went to the Madison Lyceum Theatre to see a highly successful play by Mrs. Hodgson Burnett – which, though the theatre is very aesthetic, made one blush for the human mind.[4] Your account of Hawthorne's mysteries reminds me that when I first came to New York a month ago I received a note from Mrs. H., earnestly requesting me to call on her. I did so – in some trepidation, & found her residing in a gorgeous "up-town" mansion, in black brocade, & with a footman to wait upon her! She wished me to "sympathise with her about America," which, strange to say, under the circumstances, she appeared to find unsatisfactory; but to this hour I don't know where she was or what she was "up to."[5] Give my love to every one, without exception, & be careful of that evening in May. My tender remembrances to Miss Warrin as well as to Mrs. Macmillan.[6] Ever yours

H. James Jr

### Notes

1. See letter 86.
2. Macmillan's letter is not in LB, MA.
3. A year earlier James had written from Falmouth (letter 74): 'I am wofully home-sick for Piccadilly. . . . I prefer the Land's Centre, – i.e. Bolton St. [to the Land's End.]'
4. Frances Hodgson Burnett's *Esmeralda* is mentioned in the *New York Times*, 30 December 1881, 7. When James settled at Lamb House, Rye, in 1898, he and 'Fluffy' Burnett (1849–1924) became neighbours. See *SLHJEG*, pp. 138, 163.
5. May Albertina Amelung Hawthorne (1848–1925) had married Julian Hawthorne in 1870, and they had spent much of their married life in Europe. See Maurice Bassan, *Hawthorne's Son*, facing p. 14, passim. For James's proposed visit to Hawthorne in Hastings, see letter 35.
6. Miss Warrin is presumbaly Mrs Georgiana Warrin Macmillan's sister.

## 88

June 21. 1882.[1]

Dear James,

I enclose the card of a person who does copying with a typewriter and who is said to be very accurate & reliable. His charge is $1^{1}/_{2}$ (three halfpence) per folio of 72 words.[2]

I am<br>Yours ever,<br>Frederick Macmillan.

H James Jr. Esq

### Notes

1. James had returned from America to London on 22 May 1882. See his letter of 25 May to Grace Norton in *HJL*, ii, 382 and Edel, iii, 44.
2. This may be James's earliest effort to find a typist, though there is no evidence that he hired the person whose card was enclosed but is now no longer available.

**89**

Reform Club.
Pall Mall. S.W.
July 12*th* [1882]

Dear Macmillan.

Would you kindly give the printers a push about my *Point of View* (the tale they were to set up) which they have had since Monday week.[1] The time has passed since I was to have sent it to America, & I am somewhat discomfited. They haven't sent me, either, the batch of *Daisy Millers* – but that doesn't particularly matter.[2] I shall come & see you – after the 20*th*![3] Have you a correspondent at Alexandria?

Yours ever
H. James, Jr

**Notes**

1. This tale was being privately printed for James at his own expense for copyright protection (*BHJ*, pp. 54–5). According to Macmillan (letter 90), it was to be ready 14 July. The story later appeared in the *Century Magazine*, xxv (December 1882), 248–68.
2. *Daisy Miller: A Comedy* was also printed by Macmillan in a pre-publication copyright edition in July, though the first published edition was brought out in Boston by James R. Osgood Company in September 1883 (*BHJ*, pp. 55–6).
3. This date left Macmillan a bit confused. See letter 90.

**90**

July 13. 1882.

My dear James,

I am sorry you have been kept waiting so long for your proof. The printers promise to let me have it tomorrow morning which will be in time for Saturdays [*sic*] mail to America.[1]

I do not understand your mysterious allusion to *the 20th*! but shall be delighted to see you before or after that date.[2]

We have been away for a few days to the very unaristocratic, but healthy [,] town of Margate. Believe me

Yours ever,
Frederick Macmillan.

H James Jr. Esq.

**Notes**

1. Presumably the proof referred to is that of 'The Point of View' (letter 89).
2. Macmillan is not clear about James's reference to 'the 20*th*' in letter 89.

## 91

July 28. 1882.

My dear James,

Perhaps when you are writing to Houghton it would be as well to name a definite price for the plates of the dramatized D.M. I think you might say £20. This with the duty would bring it up to £25 which is I fancy about what it would cost him to make them afresh. Even if it is a little more it will be worth his while to pay it in order to become the publisher of your play.[1]

Believe me

Yours ever,
Frederick Macmillan.

H. James Esq.
3 Bolton Street [,] W.

**Note**

1. Since Macmillan had prepared the plates for a pre-publication copyright edition of *Daisy Miller: A Comedy*, he is suggesting that James indicate to his American publisher (as it happens, Osgood *not* Houghton) that they can be bought for £25. Osgood published the play with new plates in September 1883 (*BHJ*, pp. 55–6).

## 92

Boston,
131 Mount Vernon St.
Dec. 26*th* [1882]

My dear Macmillan.

I reached America on Thursday 21*st* after a surprisingly quick & prosperous, though to me, as always, most detestable, voyage.[1] I arrived too late, however; my poor father had not only passed away, but had been laid that morning in the earth. This, as you may imagine, has made it a sorrowful home-coming & a dreary Xmas – the more so that I have been ill ever since my return; though to-day I am much mended. They gave me your note on the Werra just as she was leaving Southampton. I don't know as yet what I shall do – I have not had time to look about me, more than to see that it is well I have come over, as I have several duties to perform.[2] It is too soon for me to measure my stay here, which will now depend much (or mainly) upon my sister, who is very unwell; & it is not of that just now I wish to write. Rather, of a little matter of business which I should like you to attend to at your earliest convenience. You owe me some money, I believe – the remainder due on your last acct. of my sales after certain subtractions have been made. Please make those subtractions – that of £50 advanced to me a year ago & that of the amount of your printer's bill for my two pamphlets in June last. Please then send the remainder in the form of a cheque to the order of Thomas W. Cook, on my behalf, to the said T. W. Cook, No. 8 Clifford St., Bond St. He is my tailor, I owe him some money, & this will be a convenient way to pay him. I hope you will be able to see that this is done without trouble, & I shall be much obliged. I should like to know the amount of the cheque sent to Cook.[3]

I am able to add little more. The suddenness of my jump from London to Boston has left me in a sort of daze – & I look out of my window into the hard bright light which makes me feel as if I could touch the red brick house, opposite, with my pen-point, & wonder for the moment what has come over Bolton St. After I have been here two or three weeks I shall know pretty well where I am, & perhaps how long I shall be here.[4] When you write me tell me what is happening.

With love to your wife [*sic*] ever yours, faithfully

H. James[5]

**Notes**

1.  James had unexpectedly returned to America because of his father's serious illness, but, as he indicates, his father died before he arrived.
2.  James's principal duties were to serve as the executor of his father's estate and to see that his invalid sister Alice received proper care.
3.  James's relations with Macmillan have reached such a state of familiarity that he could ask his publisher to serve as an agent in such a non-literary affair. The 'two pamphlets' referred to are the two works Macmillan had prepared pre-publication copies for – 'A Point of View' and *Daisy Miller: A Comedy* – in July (letters 89 and 90).

4. James remained in America until August 1883, and when he returned to England, he stayed there for twenty-one years, apart from vacations on the Continent, before going back to the United States.
5. With the death of his father, James dropped, with at least one immediate exception (see letter 94), the 'Junior' in his name both in his correspondence and on his books. See letter 96, note 11.

## 93

131 Mount Vernon St.
Boston
Jan 27*th* [1883]

My dear Macmillan

I learn, by a note from my Tailor, that you were so good as to send him the cheque (for £84,) which I asked you to transmit. £84 is more than I owed him, I think; but I can draw upon him, by clothes, for the balance! Receive my thanks accordingly.[1] Let me now ask you to do something else for me.

I think you must have on hand two or three copies of *French Poets & Novelists*. Will you please transmit one of them by book-post to *Baron Tauchnitz, Leipzig*? There is some little question of his republishing it, & I have promised to send it to him, though he may not do so.[2] I have under under my hand here only one or two copies, which contain valuable autographs & which I therefore wish not to sacrifice. So much for business.

I feel strangely settled here for the present, & shall probably remain for the summer. But after that – open thy bosom, London of my soul! This is very tolerable, though, as I have plenty of occupation, & moreover, I feel as if it were a kind of wind-up. My sister & I make an harmonious little *menage*, & I feel a good deal as if I were married: almost as *you* must feel.[3] We have even the counterpart of Tiny – in the shape of a gross & shaggy quadruped.[4] It would be vain however to deny that I am homesick; & I am simply purchasing my future liberty![5] I have just come back from a journey to the West – Wisconsin in January! – where I encountered one of the famous "blizzards" or arctic waves – a moving wall of icy air.[6] The thermometer at Milwaukee was at 20° below zero, & you may imagine how I enjoyed the noble accident. It had one merit, however; it made Boston seem Italian. Boston is to Chicago what Florence is to Boston!

How, among all these comparisons, is London? Give me some news – & give news *of* me. I send my love to your wife & remain ever yours

H. James

### Notes

1. See letter 92 for James's request concerning the transmission of the cheque to his tailor.
2. Tauchnitz published a 'specially revised edition' of *French Poets and Novelists* in 1883 (*BHJ*, p. 384).
3. James and his sister Alice (1848–92) were quite close, but after she followed him to England in 1884, she became even more an invalid, and they lived apart, though James took the responsibility for certain of her affairs.
4. James normally kept dogs as pets throughout his life in England.
5. Working vigorously to get his father's affairs in such condition that his brother William (1842–1910) could handle routine matters, James was able to leave the following August and not return for twenty-one years: 'future liberty', indeed.
6. Garth Wilkinson (Wilky) James (1845–83), one of James's younger brothers, lived in Milwaukee with his family and was the cause of his 'journey to the West'.

## 94

131 Mount Vernon St.
[Boston]
Feb. 5*th* 1883.

My dear Macmillan.

I return herein, with thanks, the receipt, signed, enclosed in your letter of the 19*th*.[1]

I wrote you only a few days ago, & I am afraid I have little to add to what I may have told you then.[2] I am much interested in your publishing changes & schemes. I should think Morley would give *Macmillan* a considerable impetus, & congratulate you on this prospect – disinterestedly, however, as I presume he will banish frivolous fiction from its regenerate pages.[3] I wish you also all success with your emulation of the *Century* & *Harper*; though I fear it will be a "big job" for Comyns Carr to keep abreast of those breathless rivals.[4] (This fiendish taunt will probably goad you to great exertions.) I will try & think of a name, though it is hard to have to find appellations not only for my stories, but for the magazines in which they appear! "The Vivid" – "The Public" – "Form" – "Style" – "The Day" – "Black & White" – "Art & Life" – "Town & Country" – "The Country" – "Light" – "Visions" – "The Visible" – "Far & Near" – "Far & Wide" – "The Modern" – "The Moment" – "The Period" – "The Bedford" – "The Object" – "The Thing" – "Things" – "Humanity" – "The Fact" – "The Present" – you however see how easily I toss them off![5] Whatever you call the periodical, I shall be very willing to see my name in any list you may issue.[6]

I shall send you a little volume just appearing here: "The Siege of London" & the "Point of View," bound up with the *Pension Beaurepas*, which had never been republished here. When I have a third new story (it won't be long before I do) to substitute for the *P.B.*, I shall probably propose to you to put forth such a volume in England.[7] I think I have told you that I see myself here till the summer.[8] I am quite resigned, as I am enjoying the domestic quiet of my life; though your proposal about the pantomime does make me stifle a sigh. Ever faithfully yours

H. James Jr.

### Notes

1. Although Macmillan's letter of 19 January is not in LB, MA, the receipt obviously refers to the £84 paid to James's tailor (letter 92).
2. See letter 93.
3. John Morley, long an adviser to the firm, had agreed to replace George Grove as editor of *Macmillan's Magazine*. As editor of the English Men of Letters series, he had asked James to contribute a volume on Hawthorne (see letter 21).
4. J. W. Comyns Carr (1849–1916) was to be the first editor of *English Illustrated Magazine*, a new Macmillan enterprise.
5. Some of James's prospective titles for the magazine suggest what an avid namer he could be. The title eventually chosen was the *English Illustrated Magazine* (1883–1913). In 1893 Macmillan sold the periodical to *London Illustrated News*.
6. James contributed an article on Matthew Arnold (January) and two tales – 'The Author of Beltraffio' (June, July) and 'The Path of Duty' (December) – to the journal in 1884, during its first year of publication.
7. Such a prospective collection as James describes was never published by Macmillan, though 'The Siege of London' and 'Madame de Mauves' appeared together in volume 11 of the Collective Edition issued on 13 November 1883. 'The Pension Beaurepas' had been collected in England with 'Washington Square' and 'A Bundle of Letters' in 1881 (*BHJ*, pp. 59, 51–2).
8. James returned to England on 29 August 1883 (Edel, III, 75).

**95**

131 Mt. Vernon St.
[Boston]
March 29*th* [1883]

My dear Macmillan.

Will you please forward the enclosed to Mrs. Green, to whom I have not been able to deny myself the satisfaction of writing a few words? I shall be greatly obliged to you, & owe you a stamp. I don't venture to assume that she is in Kensington Square, & should be very glad to know how she is, poor lady! Green's death has received much extremely appreciative notice here.[1]

I am afraid I haven't anything to tell you about myself, of the least interest. I was never less interesting, & I am afraid less interested, than during these unterminated weeks of Boston & of east wind. Providence owes me some tremendous compensation in the near future, & I depend upon you & your wife to help me to enjoy it when it comes. It must begin at any rate (with your home,) with a dinner in Elm Tree Road.[2] The date of my departure doesn't advance; on the contrary. I shall not leave these shores before midsummer at the nearest, & that is not near when I look out of the window & see a good hearty snowstorm briskly beginning.[3] I go soon for a short time – that is, for April – to New York & Washington.[4] I never cared much for the season, in London; but I should like this year's. Give me a little news of it some day. Many remembrances to your wife. Very faithfully yours

Henry James.

**Notes**

1.  Mrs Alice Stopford Green was the wife of John Richard Green (1837–83), whose histories of the English people (1874, 1877–80) had been published by Macmillan and whose death had occurred 7 March. See letter 96.
2.  As the reference suggests, James now takes for granted his familiar status with the Macmillans.
3.  James left Boston on 22 August and returned to England on 29 August 1883 (Edel, III, 75). James himself writes that he returned on 1 September (*HJL*, III, 4–5). The difference in dates has to do with place. He arrived in Liverpool on 29 August and was back in London 1 September.
4.  James was in New York on April 15, his fortieth birthday, and visited Henry and Clover Adams in Washington shortly thereafter (Edel, II, 72–3). See also letter 96.

**96**

Washington,
Wormley's Hotel
April 19*th* 1883[1]

My dear Macmillan.

Your letter of the 6*th* comes to me here, where, after ten days in New York, I am spending a week. Let me immediately answer your inquiry about my view of the projected new edition of my stories.[2]

I like the idea very much, & only make the condition that the books be as pretty as possible. Can you make them really pretty for 18-pence a volume? I should like them to be *charming*, & beg you to spare no effort to make them so. Your specimen page will enlighten me as to this, & I will after receiving it, lay out the arrangement into volumes as you suggest: though I shall not be sure whether you think it important that the old *grouping* (of the shorter things), be retained or may be departed from: i.e. whether for instance *The Madonna of the F.* might go with *Daisy M.*, &c.[3] I hope fortune will favour the enterprise. I should tell you, à propos of this, that the property of Chatto & Windus in *Confidence* has expired;[4] & that I have parted with the English copyright (prospective) in two books which I am to write as speedily as possible for my American publisher J. R. Osgood. One of these is to be a novel about ½ as long as the *Portrait*; the other a group of three tales, exactly corresponding to the *Siege of London*, &c, which I sent you. I have sold him these things, to do what he pleases with for periodical & serial publication & otherwise, both in England & in this country. I mention this so that you may know in advance that there will ultimately be these several productions as to which, when the time shall come for your wishing to include them in the little "choice" edition, you will have to treat with him – not with me.[5] I have no doubt he will be glad to arrange with you for the appearance of one of the shorter stories in the *Illustrated English.* One of these is to be another international episode, of exactly the length of the *Siege of London*: "Lady Barberina" – an earl's daughter who marries a New Yorker & comes to live in 39*th* St! – of course I shall be at liberty to place the *Siege of L.* & the *Point of View* in your 18 penny edition.[6]

I suddenly remember, by the way, that the short tales above-mentioned (to be supplied to Osgood) (as well as the novel,) have by this time *probably* been disposed of by him in advance to the *Century* – with which my relations are apparently destined to become intimate, as I have been writing three or four essays which are to appear in its pages.[7]

I spent ten delightful days in N.Y., which decidedly is one of the pleasant cities of the world. Washington is also charming at present, with the temperature of a Northern July, & great banks of pink & white blossom all over the place. It reminds me of Rome! The date of my return is I am sorry to say rather more than less uncertain, & there is even a *possibility* of its not taking place till October next.[8] I see however no reason to expect a longer detention than that. I shall then have been away 11 months. Thanks for your few items of London news, all of which I hold "precious." I am very glad to hear something of poor Mrs. Green to whom I lately wrote to your care.[9] Apropos of the ventilation of your affair, with Julian H., I can only say that the invasive impudence of the papers here is something unspeakable & horrible![10] I have suffered much from it myself. Many greetings to your wife & every one who remembers me. Ever faithfully yours

Henry James.

Please, in any more announcements or advertising, (of things of mine), direct the dropping of the *Jr*.[11]

### Notes

1. This letter has previously appeared in *HJL*, ɪɪ, 410–12. The present text differs in several substantive and accidental particulars.
2. Macmillan's letter of 'the 6*th*' is not in LB, MA. The 'projected' edition, the first one of James's writings, had been proposed by Macmillan and was published in fourteen volumes on 13 November 1883 (*BHJ*, pp. 58–9).
3. *The Madonna of the Future and Other Tales* and *Daisy Miller: A Study* had been published separately by Macmillan in 1879. They did not appear in the same volume in the edition.
4. For James's arrangements with Chatto and Windus on the publication of *Confidence*, see letters 59–61.
5. Presumably *The Bostonians* (1886), though the length of its text was almost as long as that of the *Portrait*, and *Tales of Three Cities* (1884), including 'The Impressions of a Cousin', 'Lady Barberina', and 'A New England Winter', all of which fiction Osgood sold to the *Century*, as James subsequently suggests, and none of which appeared in time to be in the Collective Edition of 1883. Osgood's firm failed before he could publish the novel in book form. See letters 122–7, 129, 134–7.
6. None of these stories appeared in the *English Illustrated Magazine*. 'The Siege of London' and 'The Point of View' appeared in separate volumes of the edition (*BHJ*, p. 59).
7. These essays, considerations of Anthony Trollope (July 1883), Alphonse Daudet (August 1883), and George Du Maurier (May 1883), were later collected in *Partial Portraits* (1888).

8.  James returned to England 29 August. See letter 95, note 3.
9.  See letter 95, note 1.
10. For Macmillan's 'affair' with Julian Hawthorne, see the *New York Tribune*, 12 March 1883, p. 5 and 5 April 1883, p. 5. Hawthorne's serial, 'Fortune's Fool', had followed James's 'The Portrait of a Lady' in *Macmillan's Magazine* in December 1881, but had disappeared from the journal without authorial explanation after its tenth instalment in September 1882 and was not resumed until the following July and not concluded until September 1883. This hiatus and some confusion about the reasons for it led to a misunderstanding between Hawthorne and Macmillan that found its way into the press, at least in *part*, according to Hawthorne, because Macmillan's 'friend' George W. Smalley, the *Tribune* correspondent in London, published numerous despatches on it (Hawthorne to Macmillan, 9 March 1883, LB, MA, BL). Smalley, it will be remembered, was also a friend of James's. See letter 1, note 2.
11. After his father's death, James had immediately dropped the 'Junior', even when, as in the case of the appearance of a new impression of his *Hawthorne* in 1887, 'a cancel title-leaf was inserted in remaining copies, eliminating the "Jun$^r$" after the author's name at HJ's specific request' (*BHJ*, p. 46).

# 97

April 25. 1883

My dear James,

I enclose a specimen of the type in which we propose to print the small edition of your stories about which I wrote to you a few days ago.[1]

Our idea is to make volumes of about 250 pages each which can be sold at a shilling. The short stories will therefore require re-arrangement and for this purpose I enclose subjoin a list of them giving the number of pages which each will occupy.

The following will do as they stand

| | |
|---|---|
| Portrait of a Lady | 3 vols. |
| Roderick Hudson | 2 vols. |
| American | 2 vols. |
| Washington Square | 1 vol. |
| Confidence | 1 vol. |

I hope your arrangement with Chatto & Windus will allow of this last being included as without it the set would be incomplete. If I remember right you only ceded the right to publish it to them for a certain time which must now have expired [.][2]

The following short stories must be arranged to make volumes of about 250 pages, or less

| Siege [*sic*] of London | 120 pages |
| Pension Beaurepas | 73 |
| Point of View | 67 |
| Bundle of Letters | 55 |
| Daisy Miller | 78 |
| International Episode | 96 |
| Four Meetings | 40 |
| Madonna of the Future | 57 |
| Longstaff's Marriage | 45 |
| Madame de Mauves | 115 |
| Eugene Pickering | 70 |
| Dairy of a Man of Fifty | 50 |
| Benvolio | 70. |

We propose to issue the books at a shilling a volume in paper and one and sixpence in cloth and to pay you a royalty of 10 per cent on the retail price of all copies sold. If you agree to this and will kindly arrange the short stories as I have indicated, we shall go on at once and publish them all before you get back to England.[3]

This letter is entirely on business[.] I hope to write you a little gossip before long. Believe me

Yours very sincerely,
Frederick Macmillan

Henry James Esq
13 [*sic*] Mount Vernon St:
Boston.

#### Notes

1. See letter 96.
2. The novels were published as listed, with another volume being devoted to *The Europeans*. *Confidence* had been taken by Chatto and Windus for three years in 1879 and was consequently 'free', as James points out in letter 98.
3. James arranged these thirteen stories as volumes 11–14. See letter 98.

### 98

131 Mount Vernon St.
[Boston]
May 8*th*. [1883][1]

Dear Macmillan.

I have arranged the short stories according to your request, to the best of my ingenuity. (The specimen pages you send are charming.)

The tales make 4 vols. of something less than 250 pages each. The division I have made is arrived at after various other attempted combinations, & appears to be the one that satisfies most of the conditions – & the only one which would make the volumes equal. They had better be issued, I should say, in the order I have marked.[2] I should think the little series would be charming & I wish it all success.

I wrote you the other day from Washington – since when, after another week in New York, I find myself back here. My return to London has, alas, apparently quite definitely deferred itself to the last days of the summer. Osgood, who is to publish some things of mine during the next year, tells me he has written to you – but to this correspondence I do not belong.[3] In addition to the three or four new things (mostly short) that he is to bring out, (they *are* all to appear in the *Century*!) he will also put forth *two* volumes of essays (republished,) a volume of short tales (early ones, collected from periodicals,) &, in a small volume, the interminable dramatic Daisy Miller.[4] I don't know what to say to you about the question of your bringing out a *portion* of this multifarious matter in London: e.g. the vols. of essays. If you don't they will probably be cribbed; yet on the other hand I am not very keen about their appearing there. (That is, with the exception of the first vol. of the Essays, which will probably be called *Certain Impressions*, & *contain* articles on Ste. Beuve, A. Daudet, E. Delacroix, Carlyle & Emerson, Anthony Trollope, Du Maurier, Venice, Washington &c. Several of these things are yet to appear, in the *Century*.) The other vol. of essays is to consist of sketches of travel & will possibly be named *Sketches & Studies in local colour*.[5] But I will leave this till it seems more urgent. You are right: *Confidence* is now free.[6] This letter is pure business – I will be sociable another time.

I am hideously homesick. Ever yours
Please make *that* now my name[7]

Henry James

**Notes**

1. Previously printed in *HJL*, ii, 416–17, but the present text differs chiefly in accidentals.
2. See letter 97. James's markings are not available, but one may infer that his 'division' of the short stores was followed. (See *BHJ*, p. 59).
3. See letter 96.
4. James had dramatised *Daisy Miller* in 1882 and the play was appearing in the *Atlantic Monthly* (April–June 1883) at the time of James's letter.

5.  Since Osgood's firm failed in May 1885, he did not manage to publish everything James mentions. *Tales of Three Cities* (1884) included the 'new things' in the *Century*, and *Daisy Miller: A Comedy in Three Acts* appeared in September 1883. Moreover, the only other volume of short tales Osgood brought out at this time – *The Author of Beltraffio, et al.* (1885) – consisted with one exception of tales published in 1884, not 'early ones'. Some of the 'essays' on places in France, Italy, and England were collected first by Macmillan in *Portraits of Places* (1883) and subsequently by Osgood in 1884 (*BHJ*, pp. 60–62). The essays on Daudet, Trollope, and Du Maurier later were included in *Partial Portraits* (1888), long after Osgood had failed.

6.  See letter 97, note 2.

7.  James has drawn a hand with a finger pointing to his name and is thereby indicating again that he is dropping the junior. See also letter 96, note 11.

## 99

Boston
June 11*th* 1883.
131 Mt. Vernon St.

My dear Macmillan.

Your letter of May 30*th* finds me literally just on the point of writing to you.[1] Let me immediately relieve my mind of what was to have been uppermost in this communication – a matter as regards which I have (in general) a tender conscience.

I have given a letter of introduction to you, & it is my bounden duty to forewarn you! I don't think, however, it will hurt you much. The bearer is Lawrence Godkin, the son of our friend of the *Nation*, who goes to London to spend a few weeks, & to whom I have lent my rooms.[2] His Father has been so superhumanly kind to me since I have been in this country that when he asked me for a few notes for Lawrence I could not possibly refuse – though I usually hate to give 'em. Besides, he is a thoroughly nice, discreet young fellow & you will be sure to like him. He is lately from Harvard. Perhaps your wife will ask Mrs. Macmillan of Knapdale to kindly send him a card for her usual garden-party?[3] He would be sure to enjoy that. By the same occasion let me thank her for anything she may do for Miss Lazarus – thank her very cordially. I didn't venture to send Miss L. directly to her, but hoped Mrs. Smalley would work her off a little. She too is a good woman, not likely to be troublesome, I think, & very appreciative of small attentions.[4] I hasten to add that these are my first & only emissaries this season!

I shall be very glad to write you a short story (for the new magazine,) of the length & on the terms you mention. But I am afraid I shall not be able to do it for some little time yet, as it is part of my covenant with Osgood that the things I have engaged to write for him shall be finished before I do anything else. I am, however, getting on pretty steadily with the four works of fiction, of varying lengths, with which I have undertaken to supply him. Three of them are short (& almost written,) & the 4*th* is not long.[5]

Your London gossip is always like water to a thirsty man. I feel as if I could really have danced at Mrs. Lewis's ball. Here no one dances now – the thermometer is in the nineties, & the summer announces itself fiercely. I shall be pretty steadily in Boston, at work, for the next 2 months; till I sail, as I expect to do, in the *Servia* on August 22*d*. I bear the heat very well, & even enjoy it – it is the first summer I have known for years, & is very splendid as such. My sister is in the country, I have a house all to myself, wear no clothes, take 10 big baths a day, & dine on lemonade and ice-cream. Moreover, even under a torrid sun Boston is essentially breezy, i.e. I do very well. It is not absolutely certain that I sail on the 22*d*; I only do so if I can manage to terminate certain affairs & get off. If I don't, I shall wait till October. But I have good hopes of August.[6] I am as yet quite uncertain whether, if I arrive in England on Sept. 1*st*, I shall spend the autumn there or go abroad; but the former is the more probable. I smile at Mrs. Lang's description – from the depths of a homesick soul.[7]

I shall be very glad to see you put forth *one* of the vols. of essays that Osgood counts upon – but the other is a little ambiguous yet – till I see what English subjects are treated of in it. I shall only be willing to publish it there if it seems overwhelmingly *genial*. (It is to be some travel-sketches collected from periodicals of the last several years.[8] Excuse my stupid forgetfulness of the alterations in the *Siege of London*. They had completely passed out of my mind – but they go herewith. Please print the *Point of View* also from the same copy.[9] What do you do in August? Love to Mrs. F.

Ever faithfully yours
Henry James.

### Notes

1.  Macmillan's letter of 30 May is not in LB, MA.

2.  Edwin Lawrence Godkin, founder and editor of *The Nation*, and James had been
    friends since the 1860s, and James had contributed to the journal since 1865.
3.  Mrs Alexander Macmillan, wife of the senior partner of the firm.
4.  James had recently met Emma Lazarus (1849–87), American Jewish poet, and
    written several of his English friends about her. In a letter to her of 9 May [1883],
    he suggests, for example, that she go to one of Mrs Anne Benson Skepper
    Procter's 'afternoons' (*HJL*, ii, 417–18). For Mrs Phoebe Garnaut Smalley, see
    letter 1, note 2.
5.  Presumably some of the works referred to in letter 96, note 5: 'The Impressions
    of a Cousin', 'Lady Barberina', and 'A New England Winter', all of which
    eventually appeared in the *Century*.
6.  James subsequently sailed 'in the *Servia* on August 22*d*' and arrived in England
    29 August.
7.  Apparently Mrs Andrew Lang, wife of the well-known Scottish critic and essay-
    ist whom James had met in 1876. See *HJL*, 11, 86, 92–3.
8.  The 'travel-sketches', indeed, were published first by Macmillan under the title
    *Portraits of Places* on 18 December 1883 (*BHJ*, p. 60). See letter 98, note 5.
9.  James was preparing the texts of these two tales for publication in the Collective
    Edition of 1883.

## 100

Aug: 18. 1883

My dear James,

The printers have sent me a proof of some pages in *Confidence*
with a question which I do not feel competent to answer. Will you
kindly say whether it should be "Mrs. Gordon" or "Mrs. Wright".[1]

I suppose Chatto & Windus quite understand that they have
nothing more to do with this book. I notice that they still advertise it
with their 2/. novels. This ought to be withdrawn & they ought not
to sell anymore [*sic*] copies [.][2]

Yours very sincerely,
Frederick Macmillan

Schloesser has decided against the house so that it is quite at your
disposal.[3]

### Notes

1.  The text of *Confidence* is being set up for volume ten of the Collective Edition.
2.  Since the agreement between James and Chatto and Windus for *Confidence* had
    ended in 1882, Macmillan maintains that the rival firm should stop selling the
    novel.
3.  James was thinking about leaving his flat for a house, and Macmillan here refers
    to a property on Elm Tree Road, St John's Wood, his own neighbourhood. See
    *HJL*, iii, 3, 8, 10, 17 and letter 106 herein. James, it should be remembered, had
    lived in St John's Wood as a child (Edel, iii, 79).

## 101

Sept 6. 1883.

Dear James,

The printer sends us a sheet of "Confidence" in which there are some proper names which he thinks must be wrong.[1] Will you kindly look at it?

Yours ever,
Frederick Macmillan

Henry James Esq

**Note**

1. See letter 100 for other examples of questions concerning proper names in the novel.

## 102

Oct 2. 1883

My dear James,

"Portraits of Places" will make 316 pages.[1] I am telling the printer to go on setting it up & to send you proof.

Yours ever,
Frederick Macmillan

Henry James Esq

**Note**

1. *Portraits of Places* actually contained 376 pages (*BHJ*, p. 60). Macmillan, or his secretary, possibly, inaccurately recorded the number.

## 103

3 Bolton St.
Piccadilly.
Oct. 19*th* [1883]

Dear Mr. Macmillan.

In your brother's absence (if he is absent, as I suppose) will you kindly redress a little injury from which I suffer?[1]

He sent, the latter part of last month, the copy for a little book of mine which you are to bring out, to certain printers in Edinburgh, with the request that they should send me proof with extreme promptitude, in order that I might despatch the sheets of the work to America, where I had agreed that it should immediately appear. I should have sent the copy straight to America, if I had not supposed that the delay of getting proof here would be very short. But it turns out so long that I must beg you to please send the printers word that they must really either begin & send me the sheets or else return me the copy. Their delay has already compelled me to wreck my agreement, as to time, with my Boston publisher, & they show no symptoms as yet of having even begun to set up the book. A week ago your brother wrote to them at my request to hurry them, but they have paid no attention to his remarks. I don't know who they are, or I would write to them myself. Can you not apply the goad – as my necessity is really pressing? I should tell you that the name of the book is "Portraits of Places."[2] *Has* your brother gone to Holland?[3] Yours very truly

Henry James

### Notes

1. This letter is addressed to Maurice Crawford Macmillan (1853–1936), Frederick's younger brother, and a junior partner in the firm.
2. See letter 102. The printers in Edinburgh were R. and R. Clark, and the Boston publisher was James R. Osgood and Company. The book came out in London on 18 December 1883 and in Boston on 29 January 1884 (*BHJ*, pp. 60–62).
3. Frederick Macmillan has gone to Flushing. See letter 104.

## 104

Henry James Esqr
3 Bolton Street
Piccadilly

October 20. 1883

Dear Mr. James

We are very sorry that this delay on the part of the printers has caused you annoyance. We can undertake that you shall receive the whole of the proof by the end of next week at the latest.[1]

My brother went on Thursday evening to Flushing.[2] He will be back by the beginning of the week after next.

Believe me

Yours very truly
Maurice C Macmillan

**Notes**

1.  For James's failure to receive proof, see letter 103, and for a resolution of the problem, see letter 105. James saw 'all . . . proofs' by November 2 (letter 106).
2.  This is in response to James's question in letter 103.

## 105

Nov: 1. 1883.

Dear James,

Osgood has written to say that he will take a duplicate set of our stereotype plates for "Portraits of Places" so that all you have to do is to correct the proofs & let our printer have them.[1]

Are you going to make any alterations in the Tauchnitz "Poets & Novelists" or can we print off at once?[2]

Yours ever,
Frederick Macmillan

Henry James Esq

**Notes**

1.  See letter 103, note 2. James apparently learned that Clark was printing his book.
2.  The Tauchnitz edition of *French Poets and Novelists* was revised by James (see letter 106 and *BHJ*, pp. 36, 384), so according to the date of this letter, *BHJ's* conjectured date of publication – October 1883 – is a bit off the mark (p. 36).

## 106

3 Bolton St. W.
Nov. 2*d* [1883]

Dear Macmillan.

I am glad Osgood takes the plates, & hope you will be able to send them speedily. I have seen all my proofs. The book (though I say it who shouldn't) will be charming! The next time I see you we must settle the question (as to time) of its appearance here. I don't see why it shouldn't come out as soon as it can be got ready, as it must – or had better – anticipate the publication there.[1] The English notices here may help it.

I shall *immediately* send you the (further) revised *French Poets* &c.[2] Please therefore wait a day or two.

Won't you let me come & dine (or "spend the evening") alone some day, & talk about the *House*?[3]

Yours ever<br>Henry James

**Notes**

1.  James is responding to letter 105. *Portraits of Places* appeared in London almost six weeks earlier than it did in Boston (see letter 103, note 2).
2.  This copy of (for) the Tauchnitz edition of *French Poets and Novelists* (see letter 105, note 2) would also serve as text for a new Macmillan edition after the first of the year (*BHJ*, p. 36).
3.  James is still considering the property on Elm Tree Road in St John's Wood referred to in letter 100. He subsequently decided not to move, for 'the place was too far from the centre of things'. See his letter of 11 December 1883 to Elizabeth Boott (*HJL*, III, 17).

## 107

Dec. 27. 1883

Dear James

Fred will not be here till New Year's day so I opened your letter and have given instructions for the books to go out as you wish.[1]

I am<br>Yours very truly<br>George A. Macmillan

Henry James Esq
3 Bolton St.

**Note**

1.  Presumably presentation copies of *Portraits of Places*, published 18 December. George A. Macmillan, the son of Alexander Macmillan, was Frederick's cousin.

**108**

3 Bolton St. W.

Jan. 29*th* [1884][1]

My dear Macmillan.

The last time I saw you in Bedford St, I was interrupted by the arrival of visitors before I had discharged the latter portion of my errand, & last night was of course not an occasion for talking of business. But before I leave town, as I expect to do for some little time on Friday or Saturday, I want to repair my omission.[2]

It is only within a few days past that I have looked over the statement of account you sent me a number of weeks ago, & taken home to myself its melancholy results. I postponed the contemplation of it, as I am apt to do disagreeable things, because I expected the said results would be small, but I now perceive them to be virtually *nil*. The balance owing me is £2.17.6! – for a year's sale of some seven or eight books. The sale is depressingly small; – it appears however to have amounted to some 500 copies for all the books, without counting a quantity of sheets of one of them sent to America. I feel that for the future I must make some arrangement that shall be more fruitful, & such as I made a year ago in America.[3] Even my *old* American arrangement, which still holds with regard to most of my volumes there, yields me an appreciable yearly profit. It is not, however, of this I wish to speak to you now, as there will be time for that before I publish something new. What moves me to-day is the sense of being rather in want of money, owing to having (among other things) expected from the source which has yielded me £2.17.6., a sum less insubstantial, though, as I said just now, not large. It occurs to me to ask you whether the sale of the little books in a box? – or that of the *Portraits of Places* – or the two sales together – may be such as to warrant your sending me a cheque on account. In the natural course, you would not, I suppose, do so for another year; but I shld. be glad if the process might be anticipated.[4] In any case, please debit me with the sum I owe for the printing of my American tale the other day, in the manner most convenient.[5] I had supposed that my share of the profits of my old books would at least cover that. I am trying to leave town on Friday.

Yours very faithfully

Henry James

**Notes**

1. Previously printed in *HJL*, III, 22–3. The present text differs in several accidentals.
2. The firm's headquarters continued to be in Bedford Street until 1897, when the move to new premises on St Martin's Street was made (*LM*, p. 21). The reference to 'last night' is obviously to a social occasion similar to the 'midnight supper' at the Macmillan home on 18 January described in James's letter of 19 January to Grace Norton (*HJL*, III, 21).
3. James is referring to the agreement he had made with James R. Osgood in Boston while he was in America in 1883 (see letter 96). He had, for example, sold for cash certain fiction to Osgood outright, but this 'arrangement' backfired in May 1885 when the Osgood firm failed. See letters 122–7, 129, 134–7, 141–4, among others. By January 1885 James would propose to Macmillan that he receive some 'money down' (an advance) on his books (see letter 114).
4. The 'little books in a box' refers to the Collective Edition of James's work Macmillan had published in pocket-sized volumes the previous November (*BHJ*, pp. 58–9). *Portraits of Places* had appeared on 18 December 1883 (*BHJ*, p.60). For Macmillan's response, see letter 109.
5. James may be referring to the 'pre-publication copyright edition' of 'The Point of View' that Macmillan had brought out, even though it had appeared in July 1882, hardly 'the other day' (*BHJ*, pp. 54–5).

## 109

Jan 29. 1884.

My dear James,

I am not surprised that you are disappointed with the accounts.[1] I was dreadfully disgusted with them myself and had it been possible by any manipulation to make them look more satisfactory I would have done so. This is the first time that the yearly accounts have not included a new novel which has always yielded you something. I am afraid that the old books in the 6d shilling form are not to be counted on.[2]

You will remember that we agreed to pay you a royalty of 10% on the new pocket Edition of your stories and we are quite ready to advance you £100 on account of these royalties, a cheque for which sum I now enclose. If you can see your way when your present engagements are over to write me a story for "Macmillan" or "The English Illustrated" we shall have an opportunity of making more liberal payments.[3]

Believe me
Yours Ever,
Frederick Macmillan

Henry James Esq

**Notes**

1.  See letter 108.
2.  Editions of *The American, The Europeans, Daisy Miller,* and *Roderick Hudson* were issued at this price in 1879–80. See *BHJ*, pp. 33, 38, 40.
3.  In response to this invitation, James sent in 'The Author of Beltraffio', for which he received £80. See letter 111.

## 110

Feb 11. 1884.

My dear James,

I forward a letter from a man who wants to translate your books into French.[1] I have told him that we are referring the matter to you.

Yours ever,
Frederick Macmillan

Henry James Esq

**Note**

1.  James was in Paris at the time, and his response to the request is not in LB, MA, though both *The American* and *Roderick Hudson* appeared in French translations in 1884 (*BHJ*, p. 362). For James's view of another prospective French translator, see letter 145.

## 111

May 14. 1884

My dear James,

I enclose a cheque for £80 for the use of your story "The Author of Beltraffio" in "The English Illustrated. ["] The first part is to appear next month.[1]

Believe me

Yours very truly,
Frederick Macmillan

H James Esq

**Note**

1.  I (June, July), 563–73, 628–39. See letter 109, note 3.

## 112

Aug 25/1884.

My dear James.

I send you a copy of "The Impressions of a Cousin," & we shall be glad to put the new volume in type as soon as you have made your corrections.[1]

Mrs. Macmillan and I came back from Switzerland a fortnight ago, & we sail for America on Saturday. I am happy to say that my wife is a good deal better, & we hope that the sea voyage and a little of her native air may put her quite right.[2] I hope you are quite well. We shall look look [*sic*] forward to seeing you in November at 7 Northwick Terrace which we are already inhabiting.[3]

Believe me

Yours very truly
Frederick Macmillan

Henry James Esq
15 Esplanade [,] Dover

### Notes

1.  *The Century*, xxvii (November, December, 1883), 116–29, 257–75. Reprinted by Macmillan in *Tales of Three Cities* on 18 November 1884 (*BHJ*, p. 68).
2.  For other references to Mrs Macmillan's health, see, for example, letters 113–15, 157, 167.
3.  The Macmillans had moved from Elm Tree Road. See James's response in letter 113.

## 113

15 Esplanade,
Dover
August 26*th* [1884]

Dear Macmillan

I wrote to the "firm" because I supposed you, & every other individual member of it, were absent, but I am glad to have caught you before you sail. (I thought this event had taken place last Saturday.)[1] I fled from the London temperature two or three weeks ago, & came down here for ventilation & privacy. I have found both in due measure, have open tidy little quarters overhanging the French coast (so near it looks) & am working very diligently at a much-delayed novel, which is presently to appear in the *Century*.[2] If I don't languish for some other society than my own, & that of my creation, (which is all I have) I shall stay through September. I am very glad to hear Mrs. Macmillan is better & hope her pious pilgrimage will complete the good work.[3] From the Engadine to the London of the last weeks must have been for you a jump from the pole to the tropics. You have the conviction that America can't feel hot. I make a note of 7 Northwick Terrace, & begin to wish again, I *had* taken Elm Tree Road![4] Many good wishes to your wife & a happy return. My copy goes this evening.[5]

Yours ever
Henry James

### Notes

1. The Macmillans sailed for America Saturday, 30 August. Both Frederick Macmillan and James hoped that the trip home would improve Mrs Macmillan's health. See also letter 112.
2. The reference is to *The Bostonians* (*The Century*, xxix, February 1885, 530–43, to xxxi, February 1886, 591–600).
3. Mrs Macmillan's return home to America.
4. The Macmillans had recently moved. See letter 112. In 1883 James had seriously considered taking a house in Elm Tree Road. See letters 100 and 106.
5. 'Impressions of a Cousin', referred to in letter 112 and soon to appear in *Tales of Three Cities*.

## 114

3 Bolton St. W.
Jan 2*d* 1885

Dear Macmillan.

Osgood is soon to publish for me in Boston a volume consisting of *The Author of Beltraffio*, *The Path of Duty* (from the Eng Illust.) & two other fictions, which appeared last summer in America: entitled respectively *Pandora*, & *Georgina's Reasons*.[1] I want it of course to come out here, & it ought, I suppose, to do so immediately. To the English book I should propose to add (as it is a very good opportunity, for which I have been waiting) two other tales (ancient) published a long time ago in America & never yet reprinted here. One of them *A Passionate Pilgrim*, I have often been asked for, & last winter I completely revised & in a manner rewrote it for Tauchnitz.

It is of course this Tauchnitz form which I should make use of. The other additional tale is called "A Light Man"; it was lately republished in New York by the Scribners. These things would make six stories in all, &, I suppose two volumes, as some of them are of considerable length. Will you publish such a book?[2] I must tell you that I wish to make some other arrangement about it than that which has been going on so long & has yielded me so little profit. What I prefer, for this occasion, is a sum of money down, you in return to have all profits from it for three years. The sum I propose is £150.[3] I have the sheets of the book here & could let you have copy therefore as soon as needful.

I am assuming, you see, that you are back in London, & I hope your journey has been an episode not too dismal – though the return (in particular) cannot have been very much the opposite. I am anxious to hear how you left Mrs. Macmillan.[4]

Yours very faithfully
Henry James

P.S.  I find by the statement of acct. that you sent me some time since that £142 were owing me, mainly on sales of the cheap edition. £100 of this I had in advance, last year, to supplement the £2.17 which fell to me then. There remains to my credit, as I understand it, £42. Will you send me a cheque for them now?[5]

**Notes**

1. All four tales were included in *The Author of Beltraffio*, a collection published by Osgood in February 1885 (*BHJ*, pp. 69–70).
2. Macmillan included all six stories and added eight others to complete the three volumes of *Stories Revived* on 15 May 1885 (*BHJ*, pp. 70–73).
3. James is proposing terms that would provide him an immediate return for his labour, and though Macmillan's letter of 'Monday' (5 January 1885) is not included in LB, MA, he agreed to James's terms in letter 117.
4. Macmillan had taken his wife to St Moritz for her health. See letter 115.
5. Macmillan sent a 'cheque for the balance due' with letter 115.

## 115

Jan. 3 1885

Dear James,

I enclose a cheque for the balance due to you this month. I will write on Monday with regard to the new book. I need not say that we are anxious to be as liberal as possible: there is nothing we like so much as paying large sums to authors, but our ability to do so must depend on the liberality of the British book buyer.[1]

I came back from St. Moritz on Wednesday. My wife is settled comfortably enough, but is inclined to be discontented with her lot, & hates the banishment cordially. If a person happened to like living in a hotel on top of a mountain, the place where she is would please him, but her task is in the direction of living at home.[2]

With best new years [*sic*] wishes

I am,

Yours very sincerely,
Frederick Macmillan

Henry James Esq

**Notes**

1. Macmillan's letter of Monday (5 January) is not included in LB, MA, but he may have suggested that James add enough tales to make a third volume (see letter 116). He accepted James's terms in letter 117.
2. For other references to Mrs Macmillan's health, see letters 112 and 113, for example.

## 116

3 Bolton St. W.
Jan 7*th* [1885]

Dear Macmillan.

I find I can without difficulty supply plenty of copy for 3 vols. Indeed I should like, while I am about it, to include in the three the major rather than the minor list. I enclose them both herein, but what I shall send you will be material for the whole.[1] The things can all be comfortably comprised I think, if the page of the new book contains a little more, without being crowded, than in the case of the shorter list. This will give me a chance to reprint "Poor Richard" (a longish thing,) which I want to do.[2] I find the sheets sent me from America are *un*corrected proof; so I shall have to look over them again, & as the other things need a great deal of revising it will be several days before I send you the whole copy. I will do so next week. In haste, yours ever

H. James.

**Notes**

1.  Macmillan presumably had suggested in a letter of 5 January that James include more tales, especially those that had not appeared previously in England. Neither list is presently in LB, MA, nor is the letter.
2.  'Poor Richard' was included in volume three of *Stories Revived*. For other tales included in the collection, see *BHJ*, pp. 70–73.

## 117

Jan 8. 1885.

Dear James,

We certainly prefer the "Major list" so that the three volumes may not have the appearance of being too much spaced out.[1] For this we shall be happy to give you the price you ask viz: £150 for the use of the stories for 3 years.[2] Believe me

Yours very truly
Frederick Macmillan

Henry James Esq
3 Bolton Street

**Notes**

1.  Though Macmillan may have suggested a three-volume format for *Stories Revived*, he wanted to keep the work from appearing to be 'too much spaced out'. This list is not in LB, MA. See letter 116.
2.  Macmillan here agrees to James's terms proposed in letter 114.

## 118

3 Bolton St. W.
January 28*th* [1885]

Dear Macmillan.

It comes over me that I told you I would send a title for my collection of tales, & that I have delayed longer than I intended.

The best I can think of is: "Stories Revived" (not revised) which is a fair general description of them & of what I have done to them, &

does not seem to me amiss. "Stories Late & Early" is the next best, but not, I think, so good, & all other titles I have been able to think of are wanting in simplicity. If you have a definite objection to "Stories Revived," I fear I must fall back on "The Author of B. & other Tales." In case of the "Revived," I recommend printing on the title-page of each volume (in the French manner,) the contents of the same, as on the reverse of this note.[1] If there were not 3 vols. I should go in for simply enumerating the tales, on the title-page à la française, printing the name of the 1st biggest. I rather like "Stories Revived".

What a gallant little force at Metermuch & what a relief to hear from them![2] I hope you have good tidings from St. Moritz.[3]

Yours ever<br>H. James[4]

**Notes**

1. Macmillan accepted James's title and seriously considered recommendations for the titlepage. See letter 119.
2. Possibly a reference to a group in which Malcolm Kingsley Macmillan (1852–89), Alexander's eldest son and Frederick's first cousin, was involved. For two dangerous incidents in his life, see Graves, pp. 351, 380–81.
3. Mrs Macmillan was temporarily residing in St Moritz. See letter 115.
4. Underneath his signature James has written: '*Stories Revived*. The Author of Beltraffio. Pandora. The Path of Duty. A Day of Days. A Light Man.' These tales compose the first volume of *Stories Revived*.

## 119

Jan 31. 1885

Dear James,

I send you the Title-page set up in five different styles. I rather think No 1. is the best: which do you like?[1]

Yours ever,<br>Frederick Macmillan

H. James Esq

**Note**

1. This example is no longer with the letter in LB, MA, but James accepted a style that included on the titlepage all the names of the stories in capitals.

**120**

Feb 13. 1885.

My dear James,

The letter you speak of as having been written a fortnight ago was either never posted, or, if posted was not delivered. Had it ever reached me I need not say you would have had the money immediately. I am sorry that you should have been inconvenienced by its non-arrival.[1]

I am

Yours very truly,
Frederick Macmillan.

Henry James Esq

**Note**

1.     The reference is apparently to a letter written after 118. Neither it nor the letter to which 120 is in answer is in LB, MA. Apparently James had not received the advance he was to get for *Stories Revived*. A receipt for £150 for this work dated 13 February, the date of Macmillan's letter and signed by James, is in LB, MA.

**121**

April 15. 1885

Dear James,

I shall be very glad if you can conveniently return the proofs of "Stories Revived" for press, as we are anxious to publish it as early in the season as possible.[1]

Believe me

Yours ever,
Frederick Macmillan

Henry James Esq

**Note**

1.     *Stories Revived* appeared 15 May (*BHJ*, p. 71).

**122**

St. Alban's Cliff:
Bournemouth.
May 5*th* [1885][1]

My dear Macmillan.

I am moved to write you a letter of somewhat bewildered inquiry by having culled from the *Times* this a.m. (in the American telegrams) the sweet flower of information that J. R. Osgood & Co, my dear Boston publishers, have failed. The news leaves me at sea in regard to one or two important facts, & it occurs to me that you, having many lights, on such matters, (I have none) may be able to answer two or three of my questions. If you can, I shall be greatly obliged.[2] Osgood owes me about a thousand pounds, eight hundred of which constitute a sum that he was to give me for the *Bostonians* when the completed work was delivered. As the remaining £200 have not (for a long time) been forthcoming (the fact that two letters I had lately written him on the subject were not answered had led me to entertain suspicions that his solvency was not perfect) I see no reason to believe that, in the midst of his catastrophe, the larger amount will be paid me when the smaller is not. As the last instalment of the story (it has developed into a thing double the size I expected when I made my agreement with Osgood) has not yet been sent to America – it is in the hands of the interminable Mouchablon! – I have made no demand for the money; but it is obvious I shan't get it (from Osgood.)[3] He made terms of his own with the *Century* for it, serially, & what I want to know is whether, if the *Century* people haven't paid him that money, I can put forth a claim to it from *them*. If they have paid him, I suppose I must go unrewarded, as the money will have been swallowed up; but if they haven't, would it be a proper line, or mere verdancy, for me to expect they will give it to me, or respectfully to suggest the same? I fear the indebtedness of the *Century* to Osgood (only, & directly) is not altered by his having failed. If you have any idea or impression on the subject I shld take it very kindly of you to let me have it and to let me hear also this: Wouldn't the book become mine, as a book, to do what I please with, on the failure of J. R. O. & Co. to pay me $4000 on receipt of the whole? And can't I also do what I please with my other books (in their hands) for which I shall certainly receive no royalties – judging by all their recent dumbness when appealed to on the subject? I won't bother you with more interrogations (indeed I have no others,) but leave the above to your convenience & discretion.[4]

Bournemouth is very mild, in all senses, especially *not* climatic. In fact in that sense it isn't so particularly, though the quality of the air is of the finest. I have some pleasant rooms on the sea; in the day I work, walk a little, & look after my sister, who is very feeble, but tending to improve; & in the p.m. I go to see Robert Louis Stevenson, who lives here, consumptive & shut up to the house, but singularly delightful.[5] The place itself is meagre & featureless, but the sea is a lovely colour & the Isle of Wight looks pretty on the horizon. I hope Mrs. Macmillan thrives. Ever faithfully yours

Henry James

### Notes

1. Printed in *HJL*, III, 79–80. My text differs in several substantives and accidentals.
2. Under the rubric 'The United States' datelined Philadelphia, 4 May, the *Times* states: 'Messrs. James R. Osgood and Co., publishers, of Boston, have suspended payment' (5 May, p. 5).
3. The 'interminable Mouchablon' was, as James had pointed out in a letter to Osgood on 18 April, 'the only operator of the sort [typist] in this whole big city' (*HJL*, III, 77–8).
4. The *Century* had paid Osgood for the novel, but both James and Macmillan later commented that he received nothing for its serial publication in America, despite the statement in *BHJ* that James's earnings 'for both [English and American] markets, plus serialisation, came to £492' (p. 75). See letters 123–5, 127, 129–30, and 134–6. The novel was not published serially in England.
5. For James's friendship with Stevenson, see Janet Adam Smith (ed.), *Henry James and Robert Louis Stevenson: A Record of Friendship and Criticism* (London: Rupert Hart-Davis, 1948).

## 123

May 6. 1885.

My dear James,

I am very sorry indeed to hear that you are involved in the failure of Osgood's for from what I have heard of him and his affairs I doubt whether his estate can be worth anything to speak of.

Your position as I now understand it is this. You have agreed to sell him the *Bostonians* for £1000 on condition that he pays you the money on delivery of the last instalment. If you send him this final instalment you will be a creditor for £1000 and entitled to whatever composition he may be able to pay. This however may be only 10 or 15 cents on the dollar.

If on the other hand you decline to deliver the final instalment except upon payment of the money, it seems to me that the whole agreement falls to the ground and the book becomes once more your property.[1]

The arrangement with the "Century" folk is a further complication. Osgood has no doubt agreed to hand over the story to them for a certain sum, but as he is, presumably, not in a position to get hold of the story [*sic*] he has been in fact selling what he does not possess. The "Century" people cannot insist upon your giving them the final instalment, for you have entered into no contract with them, and are not affected by any arrangement they may have made with Osgood. The best plan will probably be for you to offer to sell the serial right of the last part to the "Century" for some moderate sum, based upon what they have been in the habit of paying you the last when dealing with you direct. If they have already paid Osgood they will be paying twice over for this last instalment but it will be hard if you are not to get *anything* from the serial publication.

"The Bostonians" being once more your own property you will have no difficulty in getting it published by someone else. We, for instance, should be very glad to publish it, paying you whatever royalty you have been in the habit of receiving from Osgood.[2]

With regard to your old books that are in Osgood's hands you need not be under any apprehension. For whatever he already owes you you will be a creditor & can only get your share, but no more copies can be sold by anyone without giving you the full royalty. I suppose that the estate will be sold and that the stereotype plates will be bought by some other publisher. Whoever buys them will however take over the obligation to pay you a royalty on all the copies he sells. If as is likely to be the case, the plates are sold at auction I shall instruct our agent to try to buy them, that is unless you express any disinclination to have your books sold in America by us.[3]

I will see our solicitor tomorrow and make sure that I am right legally in what I have said above – & I will then write again.[4] In the meantime do not send out the final instalment of copy to Osgood or the Century or anyone.

Believe me

Yours very sincerely,
Frederick Macmillan.

Henry James Esq

Notes

1.  This central point eventually allowed James to recover his property in the book and to recoup some of his loss from his failure to receive anything for its magazine appearance.
2.  Macmillan and Company eventually published *The Bostonians* in 1886 in America and England. See letters 126–7, 133, and *BHJ*, pp. 73–5.
3.  Since only a few chapters of plates had been prepared, James eventually recommended that Macmillan refuse to buy them and to start from scratch on the company's own plates. See letters 134–7.
4.  See letter 124.

## 124

May 7. 1885.

My dear James,

I have seen our solicitor this morning & find that I was right in what I told you as to the legal aspect of your arrangements with Osgood.[1]

(I notice by the way that I misunderstood one point in your letter. The £200 which Osgood owes you has nothing to do with the "Bostonians" but is what he owes you for some previous book. I took it for a payment on account of "The Bostonians", but I understand now that you have as yet received nothing for that book).[2]

The first thing to do is to offer to fulfil your contract with Osgood and to hand over the remainder of the copy on receipt of £800. It is just possible (though improbable) that the Trustee in bankruptcy may think it worth while to take the book at the price agreed upon[;] at any rate you are bound to give him the chance. Should Osgood's Trustee refuse, the book becomes your property. You can then either try to make "The Century" people buy the whole thing from you at Osgood's price for the sake of getting the last chapters, or you can if you like, ask them a smaller price for the *serial* right of what is still unpublished, and keep the right of publication in *book form* in your own hands. Of course it is possible that if you insisted on having the whole £800 from the "Century" they might refuse to give it & stop the publication of the rest of the story in their magazine. If they would be likely to do this, it would probably be wise to ask a smaller sum (so much per page) for the use of the remainder of the story in their magazine & to make other arrangements for the publication in book form.

It is important that the remainder of the manuscript should not be given up to either Osgood or "The Century" except for actual cash down. If you have not anybody in America to act for you, I shall be very glad to instruct our New York Agent, a very intelligent fellow, to do so.[3] The manuscript might be deposited in his hands with strict instructions not to part with it except for cash.

By the way how much of the story is not out – half or a third of what?[4]

Believe me

Yours very sincerely
Frederick Macmillan

Henry James Esq
St. Alban's Cliff
Bournemouth

**Notes**

1. See letter 123.
2. See letter 122.
3. George E. Brett, Macmillan's New York representative, eventually handled the publication of the American edition of the novel. See especially his letters to Frederick Macmillan of 19 March and 18 May 1886 in LB, MA.
4. For the remainder of the copy of the novel not forwarded to the *Century* ('a small fraction'), see James's letter to Osgood of 18 April [1885] in *HJL*, III, 77–8. See also letter 125.

# 125

St. Alban's Cliff
Bournemouth
*May 7th* [1885][1]

Dear Macmillan.

I am much obliged to you for your information in the matter of Osgood's failure – especially for the advice about not sending the last chapters of the *Bostonians*, which is much to the point. I shall keep them back for the present. I am strongly inclined to believe that the Century Co. has by this time paid Osgood the sum he agreed with them for for [sic] the serial use of the novel; he is sure, by the time nearly $9/10$ ths of my copy had been sent, which was the case before his failure came out, to have extracted that money from them. He said something to me when he was in London in the summer (last) that suggested that he should get his cash as soon as they began to publish.[2] Nevertheless, on the *chance* that he may not have been paid, I wrote to Gilder on Tuesday to inquire. The Century people, if they are very chivalrous, may give me something, but I don't see that they are bound to, as I chose to make the bargain (in an evil hour) with him and not with them; but I don't count upon it, & am resigning myself to going unrewarded for the work in its serial character – odious as that idea is.[3] There will be some compensation if I recover the book; & I don't see how I can fail to, not having given it up, literally, nor where else the property can vest in. If this should appear plain, I shall probably offer it to you – that is if you are willing to give me a sum for the copyright.[4] I shall be so out of pocket by the nonpayment of the money due on the magazine use of it, that I shall want for funds, & have to make some such arrangement as that. O's bankruptcy is a most beastly immediate inconvenience to me. My royalties (on five books) for the last year (three new ones,) I don't expect to get at all, & limit my expectation to the books being rescued. I shall be very glad if your people over there will buy them (i.e. the plates,) & you publish them in the U.S.[5] There is a 6*th* ("Tales of Two Cities") of which Osgood owned the copyright (for 5 years,) as well as the plates.[6] I shall be glad to hear what your solicitor says about the effect of Osgood's insolvency on the *Bostonians* as that work stands.

> Yours ever
> Henry James

### Notes

1. Printed in *HJL*, III, 81–2. The present text differs in several substantive and accidental particulars.
2. Osgood had indeed been paid in full by the *Century*. See letter 129.
3. It seems clear that James received no compensation for serial publication. Assuredly, the *Century* had paid Osgood in full for the novel's appearance in the magazine, and though *BHL* implies that James received something for 'serialisation' (p. 75), James himself maintained that he received nothing. See letters 122, note 4, and 127, note 1.
4. For negotiations between James and Macmillan for book publication, see letters 126, 127, 129, 133–7.
5. Macmillan, London, published three of the five books in one form or other: *Daisy Miller: A Comedy* (1883); *The Siege of London* (1883); *A Little Tour in France* (1884); *Tales of Three Cities* (1884); and *The Author of Beltraffio* (1885). See the Collective

Edition (1883) and *Stories Revived* (1885). The New York firm did not acquire any of these titles. See *BHJ*, pp. 59, 68, and 70–73.
6.  James means *Tales of Three Cities*. Macmillan had already brought out an English edition of this title in November 1884 (*BHJ*, p. 68).

## 126

May 13. 1885.

My dear James,

With regard to "The Bostonians" I wish to say that in case Osgood does not carry out his contract & the book becomes yours to deal with again, we shall be happy to publish it both here and in America and to pay you a royalty of 15 per cent of the retail price of all copies sold. We can also advance you the sum of £500 on account of this royalty; this we would pay as soon as the contract with Osgood was definitely abolished.[1]

I am

Yours very truly,
Frederick Macmillan

H. James Esq

**Note**

1.  Though James sought to improve Macmillan's offer – Osgood, after all, had agreed to pay £800 for serial and book rights – he later accepted these terms. See letters 127 and 133. The subsequent sale of the book did not justify such a large advance, and Macmillan accordingly reduced his offer for *Princess Casamassima* by £100. See letter 154, *BHJ*, p. 75, and Anesko, pp. 107, 229.

## 127

May 20 1885.

My dear James,

I return Osgood's letter. You must be careful to remember that you are not his creditor except in respect of what he owes you for royalties on old books. I suppose in a few days you will have some kind of offer from the "Century Company" for the serial right in the remainder of "The Bostonians".[1]

With regard to that book I am afraid we cannot revise the offer I made in my letter of the 13th. We could not offer a large enough addition to the £500 to make it worth your while to part with the copyright entirely, nor should I advise you in your own interest to sell it. It may be that the "Century" people will be induced to pay enough for the serial use of the ms not yet delivered to go some way towards making up the loss you suffer through Osgood's defection, and in any case I have no doubt that should you find yourself short of money we could arrange a further advance on account of general royalties particularly if the American publication of the old books is in our hands.[2] But for "The Bostonians" alone I am afraid we cannot increase our offer.

> Believe me
> Yours very truly
> Frederick Macmillan.

Henry James Esq
St. Alban's Cliff
Bournemouth.

#### Notes

1.  Osgood's letter is not with James's correspondence in LB, MA. James received nothing from the Century Company. See his remark to William James on 9 October 1885: 'I lose every penny – not a stiver shall I have had for the serial, for which [Osgood] received a large sum from the *Century*' (*HJL*, III, 102). See also Macmillan's remark in letter 135 that James had been 'absolutely done out of every penny' that the *Century* had 'paid for the serial publication of 'The Bostonians'.
2.  These books had been mentioned by James in letter 125. See also 125, note 5. All of these were taken over by Houghton Mifflin Company in Boston. See *BHJ*, pp. 56, 57, 64, 67, and 70.

## 128

May 29/1885

Dear James,

Six copies of "Stories Revived" were sent to Bolton Street last week. If you like I can get the parcel back and forward it to Bournemouth.[1]

The copies on the enclosed list all go today.[2] I have taken the liberty of altering the address you give for Mrs. Procter, as it seems to be a mistake – at least I know she is at Albert Hall Mansions for we had a note from her yesterday.[3]

What a delightful change in the weather!

Believe me.

Yours ever,
Frederick Macmillan.

Henry James Esq
St. Alban's Cliff
Bournemouth

### Notes

1.  *Stories Revived* was published 15 May, and author's copies had been sent to James's London address.
2.  The list is obviously a duplicate of one sent by James for presentation copies and is no longer enclosed with the letter. For several names on the list, see the references to Mrs Procter below and to Mrs Lewis and Mrs Howard in letter 130.
3.  Anne Benson Skepper Procter, the widow of Barry Cornwell (Bryan Waller Procter) and an old friend of James's, was also a friend of Macmillan's. See letter 80, note 1.

## 129

St. Alban's Cliff
Bournemouth
June 2*d* [1885]

Dear Macmillan

Will you please send for the parcel of the 6 copies of my book that were sent to Bolton St. & cause the following disposition of them to be made? (I enclose it on another sheet.)[1]

I have heard from my lawyer in Boston[2] & from the *Century* about the Bostonians, but inconclusively, that is, Osgood's assignees appear inclined to maintain his offer & take the book giving the money down, – *if I insist*. But I don't insist & have telegraphed on the subject. I expect an answer tonight, & if the agreement *is* cancelled shall probably accept your offer. I shall therefore write to you again in a day or two. Osgood was paid by the *Century* months ago – & money was lent him therewith![3]

I hope you have in town something like these soft airs. Summer is here & Bournemouth has become charming. I am probably in for another month of it. I hope the balminess is a help to your wife.[4]

Yours ever

Henry James

Notes

1.  See letter 128. Though the list is no longer available, see letters 128 and 130 for names probably on it.
2.  James's lawyer was Joseph Bangs Warner, the family attorney.
3.  A clear indication that James could hardly expect any compensation from the magazine.
4.  Another of James's periodic references to Mrs Macmillan's health.


**130**

St. Alban's Cliff
June 5*th* [1885]

Dear Macmillan.

It is all right about Mrs Lewis's copy – I am sorry to have deprived her of *your* gift; but, however, haven't really done so. Besides, the essential is her having the book.[1] I wonder if you can ascertain for me whether I *did* ( I can't for the life of me remember) direct a copy to be sent to:    Hon. Mrs George Howard[2]
                    1 Palace Green
                    Kensington, W.
& if I didn't, kindly cause that one that didn't go to Mrs. Lewis to be sent to her? I meant to give her name, & wrote to her I should send her the book; but am very vague in mind about it. Perhaps your sender has some note or record or has even kept my list: the 2*d* one. Mrs. H's name was not in *the first*.

I still get no telegram from Boston.[3] There is evidently some hitch; & I am must [*sic*] wait – cursing – for more letters. Ever yours

H. James


Notes

1.  The reference is presumably to a presentation copy of *Stories Revived* for Elizabeth Lewis, the wife of George Henry Lewis, a well-known London solicitor who later was knighted and thence awarded a baronetcy, and an old friend of James.
2.  Rosalind Frances Stanley Howard was another frequent recipient of James's presentation copies during this period. Her husband was George James Howard, MP (1843–1911), who subsequently became the ninth Earl of Carlisle (1889–1911). See letter 132 for Macmillan's response.
3.  James impatiently waits for news from his lawyer regarding his situation vis-à-vis the bankruptcy of James R. Osgood and Company.

**131**

St. Alban's Cliff
Bournemouth
June 8*th* [1885]

Dear Sirs
Will you kindly direct that an author's copy of *Stories Revived* be forwarded to the address I subjoin, & oblige yours very truly

Henry James

A copy of *Stories Revived* (from the author) to:
Mrs. Sands[1]
25 George St.
Hanover Square W
[Macmillan & Co.]

Note

1. Mary Hartpence Sands (1853–96), American wife of Mahlon Sands and friend of James from 1883 until her death. Her husband's sister Katherine had in 1884 married E. L. Godkin, founder of the *Nation* and a staunch friend of James's. See Robert L. Gale, *A Henry James Encyclopedia* (New York: Greenwood Press, 1989), pp. 586–87.

**132**

June 10 1885.

Dear James,
I have been away for a couple of days (on the Mowbray Morrisian trip to Stratford) & find your note lying on my table. I write to say that a copy of Stories Revived was sent to Mrs. Howard on the 6*th* inst.[1]

Yours ever,
Frederick Macmillan

H James Esq

Note

1. Mowbray Morris (1847–1911) had recently become editor of *Macmillan's Magazine* and on occasion invited friends to the Shakespearean plays in Stratford. James himself was once a guest. He had inquired about Mrs Howard's copy in letter 130.

**133**

Aug 5 1885.

Dear James,

We have this day paid in to your account at Brown Shipley & Co. £500 as arranged. If you will kindly sign & return the enclosed form of receipt it will serve as an agreement.[1]

I am

Yours very truly,
Frederick Macmillan

Henry James Esq
15 Esplanade
Dover

**Note**

1.   The agreement is for the copyright of *The Bostonians* in book form for which James received £500. See letter 126. A receipt for this amount signed by James on 6 August is in LB, MA.

**134**

15 Esplanade
Dover
August 25*th* [1885]

Dear Macmillan

I have received from my lawyer in Boston the enclosed form of cancellation of my agreement with Osgood, but before signing it I want you to look at the clause, marked *Second*, bottom of last page but one, which at the request of Ticknor & Co. has been included in it, providing for the purchase of the plates (so far as they exist) of the "Bostonians."[1] Osgood was stereotyping the book as the successive parts came out, & sending proof to me; but when he stopped payment, & other operations, but 2 or 3 chapters had been done. I don't *exactly*, that is, know how much had been done, but a quantity at any rate, for which the said $150 is asked. Since my lawyer has acceded to Ticknor's request, & the plates would otherwise be sacrificed, I hope you will be disposed to buy them – they can be continued & will serve for the American edition of the book.[2] The last page of proof I received is the enclosed. The actual stereotype may continue beyond it. The book, with that page, will be a fattish one – ought to sell for $2.00. If you agree to buy the plates it would be perhaps better to tell your agent in N.Y. to communicate the fact to Ticknor & Co. The plates were being made by John Wilson & Son, University Press, Cambridge, Mass., who naturally, I suppose, in this case, will go on with them, with you. Please return Warner's letter as well & believe me ever yours

Henry James

### Notes

1. Joseph Bangs Warner. See letter 129, note 2.
2. See letters 135–7 for the decision not to buy the plates.

## 135

Aug 26. 1885

My dear James,

I think your lawyer has been unnecessarily tender with Ticknor & Co: Considering that you have been absolutely done out of every penny that the Century paid for the serial publication of "The Bostonians" it seems hardly your place to relieve Ticknor of their useless stereotype plates.

However Mr. Warner has agreed to the clause and I will therefore take over such plates as are finished at the rate of not over $1. per page. I must put in this proviso to protect myself against imposition.[1]

I will write to our agent in New York & put him into communication with Wilson & Son & Ticknor.[2]

Believe me<br>Yours ever,<br>Frederick Macmillan

Henry James Esq

### Notes

1. See letter 134. It is worthy of note that Macmillan was willing to go against his better judgement and buy the plates in order to publish the novel expeditiously. In the end, however, he did not buy them.
2. George E. Brett served as the firm's agent in America at this time. He died in June 1890 and was succeeded by his son, George P. Brett, who became president in

1896 when the Macmillan Company of New York, an American corporation, was
established (Morgan, pp. 83, 163).

## 136

15 Esplanade [Dover]
Aug. 27*th* [1885]

Dear Macmillan.

Further consideration, as I telegraphed you this a.m., makes me
much prefer that you should have nothing to do with Ticknor's
plates; so, if, as is probable, you have taken as yet no step in the
matter, please give yourself no trouble about it. I agree with you
that Warner made a very injudicious concession, & I shall write to
him in this sense & shall myself have as little to do with the plates
as possible. It will be much better for you to have fresh ones made
for the book & not have to conform to the few first pages established
by Ticknor.[1] The page I should like is that (if it contains enough
words) of "Mr. Isaacs," &c.[2]

In haste, yours ever

Henry James

### Notes

1. See letters 134–5, 137 for discussion of the 'plates'. Joseph B. Warner is James's
   lawyer.
2. F. Marion Crawford's *Mr Isaacs* had been published by Macmillan in 1882.
   Macmillan's favourable response follows in letter 137.

## 137

Aug 29 1885.

Dear James,

I had not taken any steps about the stereotype plates of "The
Bostonians" when I got your telegram & I shall be, as you will have

gathered from my note, glad to be relieved of the necessity of taking them.[1]

We will certainly give you the same type as "Mr. Isaacs" if it is possible. I am waiting to receive proofs of the latter chapters before deciding. I wrote to Gilder to ask for them.[2]

I am
Yours ever,
Frederick Macmillan.

H. James Esq

**Notes**

1. See letters 134–6 regarding the 'stereotype plates'.
2. 'The Bostonians' was still appearing in the *Century* and would not be concluded until February 1886. For Richard Watson Gilder, see letter 31, note 2.

## 138

Sept 9 1885.

My dear James,

We are about to bring out a cheaper edition of "Stories Revived" in 2 6/. volumes. In order that the volumes may be sold separately would you allow us to drop the title "Stories Revived" & to call the first volume "The Author of Beltraffio & other stories" and the second volume "The Passionate Pilgrim & other stories"? I should propose to leave the name of all the tales on the title page.[1]

Believe me
Yours very truly,
Frederick Macmillan.

Henry James Esq

**Note**

1. The two-volume edition appeared the following November under the old title, but the volumes were labeled 'First Series' and 'Second Series', the only changes being 'some rearrangement of the order of the tales' (*BHJ*, p. 73). See also letters 139–40.

**139**

15 Esplanade
Dover
Sept. 10*th* [1885]

Dear Macmillan.

I have no objection at all to your dividing the "Stories" & naming each of the 2 volumes separately; but would it not be possible, while calling one of them "Beltraffio," to keep for the other the title of "Stories Revived?" I like that so much better than "A P. P. &c". In this case the preface (of the 3 vols.) might be prefixed to this 2*d* volume; it suits it better than the "Beltraffio" lot, which are mostly newer stories.[1] I should be glad if you saw no reason against this.

I am still at this place, where I have been ever since August 1*st*; but tomorrow my retirement ceases, as I cross to Paris, where I shall remain a month, or even two.[2] I was in town last week for a day or two, very hurriedly, & saw Mr. Morris, who told me you had taken a house for the winter at Brighton. I hope it will be pleasant & profitable, as it ought to be, for your wife; but I hope also that you don't go there very early, & that I may have a glimpse of you when I return to town. I was very pleased to see Morris in possession of an editorship, & have promised him some contributions.[3] I don't know anything about anyone, & haven't heard a social echo. I learn from a note I got yesterday from Sargent that I am supposed to be "elaborately hiding" – on the highway between London & Paris.[4] Ever faithfully

Henry James

**Notes**

1. The two-volume edition appeared in November as 'First Series' and 'Second Series' (*BHJ*, p. 73). See also letter 138, note 1.
2. James remained in Paris until 1 November (*HJL*, III, 103).
3. For Mowbray Morris, see letter 132, note 1.
4. John Singer Sargent (1856–1925), a young American expatriate painter, had met James in the winter of 1884, a few months before he achieved a *succès de scandale* with 'Madame X' at the Paris Salon (Edel, III, 108–9).

**140**

Sept 11. 1885.

My dear James,

As you have a fancy for the title "Stories Revived" I think we will retain it and distinguish the volumes as "First Series" and "Second Series" which will allow of their being sold separately.[1]

Many thanks for the photograph which is very good & which I am very glad to have. We go to Brighton on October 1*st* – three weeks hence – but I hope our being there will not prevent our seeing you this winter, as we shall have a spare bedroom very much at your service.[2] I send this to Bolton St. as I suppose you have given up your rooms at Dover.[3]

Believe me
Yours ever,
Frederick Macmillan.

H James Esq

**Notes**

1. See letters 138–9.
2. The social amenities continue even when the Macmillans are away from home.
3. James had spent August and early September in Dover and left for Paris about the time of Macmillan's letter (*HJL*, III, 97, 100, 102).

## 141

Sept 14 1885

My dear James,

You will remember that I spoke to you sometime ago about the arrangement which Osgood made with us in reference to "Tales of Three Cities" & "The Bostonians" & told you that he had sold us the absolute English copyright. I was rather surprised when you said that he had only bought from you the right of publication for five years, & when Ticknor & Co. applied for the payment we agreed to make for "Tales of Two Cities" [*sic*] I asked for an explanation. I have received the enclosed answer from them this morning, from which it would appear that there has been some mistake, & that they really did buy outright the copyright in England. Will you kindly refer to the original agreement if you can get at it & let me know whether Ticknor & Co. are right.[1]

Believe me
Yours Ever,
Frederick Macmillan.

Henry James Esq
3 Bolton St.

## 142

29 Rue Cambon
Paris
Sept. 15*th* [1885][1]

Dear Macmillan.

I haven't here my copy of my contract with Osgood, & I am afraid that I cannot get it for you very well, as I only know that it is somewhere among my papers in Bolton St. These are stuffed away in various drawers and trunks, & though if I were there I could put my hand on the document promptly, I am afraid I cannot tell any one else how to do it.[2] Meanwhile in regard to the matter in question my statement to you was an allusion to the fact that – according to my very definite recollection, unless I am very strangely mistaken – my cession to Osgood of the property of the two books was qualified by a clause giving me a right to recover control of them at the end of five years, on certain terms. I have not looked at the contract for a long time – since I signed it – but I cannot imagine what put this into my head unless there is a paragraph to this effect in the document. My recollection is *vivid* of Osgood making this point in the last talk I had with him before I left America, & it is almost equally so of the contract, which was sent to me in London afterwards, having – as I had every reason to expect – a repetition of it. As Ticknor makes no mention of this – with the paper before his eyes – I can only conclude that I am the victim of some strange *mis*recollection, or that the clause in question refers only to the U.S.[3] Certainly, when I spoke of the matter to you and you told me that Osgood had agreed to give you the *Bostonians* out & out, forever, I said to myself – "What in the world thus becomes of that right reserved to me, of reacquiring the book at the end of five years?" The arrangement with you appeared to me made over the bind of that clause, & this made me say to you that Osgood had not the right to dispose of the book *indefinitely*. The explanation of these words of mine is either in a complete mistake of memory about the whole matter, or else what is much more probable, (though with the paper out of my sight I can't be sure of it,) is in the fact that there *is* in the agreement a provision giving me an interest in the books at the end of five years, but that such provision applies only to the U.S. If there is none at all, all I can say is that I have been the dupe of a singular trick of memory. Of course the paragraph quoted by Mr. Ticknor is, in fact, incompatible with my qualification of the property in the book that was to have been made over to you. I think you had better send him this letter as it explains my allegation – though what explains it, having been erroneous, is, I fear, only my surprise to-day, at the state of mind in which I made, at the time of the agreement, so clean a sweep of all my rights for so small a sum.[4] I shall look at the contract as soon as I return to London, for my own satisfaction, as I shall be still more surprised if it doesn't reveal the grounds of my mistake.

Ever, faithfully yours
Henry James

**Notes**

1.  The original of this letter is in the Library of Congress, but I am printing from a photocopy of it at Harvard.
2.  The contract in question deals with *The Bostonians* and *Tales of Three Cities*. See letters 143–4.
3.  Benjamin Ticknor of Ticknor and Company, successor to James R. Osgood & Co.
4.  James, indeed, had leased the domestic rights to the two books to Osgood & Company for five years and sold the firm the foreign rights altogether. The memorandum of agreement between James and Osgood is printed in Anesko, between pages 83–4.

# 143

3 Bolton St. W
Nov. 4*th* 1885

Dear Macmillan

Here is the agreement with Osgood, by which you will see I was, as I said I should probably prove to be yesterday, only ½ right. It contains the clause I remembered (the 4*th*,) but it applies only to the U.S. – & is preceded by another giving up the book fully for other countries. As to this my memory was by no means clear, as it easily isn't about many things; & I recalled only the 5 year limitation – without the prior concession.[1]

I am very sorry I had to miss your dinner. On leaving you I had to go to the city, where I got more seedy – so that I had to come home & go to bed. I am better today.

> Ever yours
> Henry James

**Note**

1.    See letter 142 for discussion of the contract.

## 144

Nov. 4 1885

Dear James,
     There is no doubt that Osgood – or rather Ticknor [–] is right & that we must pay him the money.[1] I will do so at once.

> Believe me
> Yours Ever,
> Frederick Macmillan

Henry James Esq

**Note**

1.    See letters 142 and 143. Macmillan, in effect, is negotiating a second time for *The Bostonians* – first with Osgood and now with Ticknor and James.

## 145

3 Bolton St.
Piccadilly
Nov. 20*th* [1885]

Dear Macmillan.
     I omitted yesterday one of the principal things I wanted to ask you – if you would please have the books I name on the enclosed leaf sent to their address. I in a moment of weakness consented to let a Frenchman's wife to [sic] translate 2 or 3 of my tales; & now she

wants some of my other things, as her translation is to be prefaced by an introductory essay, & there are some she hasn't read – hang her! The whole thing is a bore to me as I want neither her translation nor her essay, but I consented, to oblige my brother, whose friends she & her husband are, & believing that they wouldn't find a publisher. But they have found one, & he demands the introductory essay.[1] A demain. Yours ever

Henry James

**Note**

1. The 'enclosed leaf' is not included in LB, MA. Apparently James is sending copies of *Daisy Miller: A Study. An International Episode. Four Meetings* (2 vols, 1879) to Mme F. Pillon, for these tales appeared in her translation in Paris in 1886 (*BHJ*, p. 362). Mme Pillon was the wife of François Pillon, a French philosopher and friend of William James, who by translating some of James's essays into French helped him become known in France. See Gay Wilson Allen, *William James: A Biography* (New York: Viking Press, 1967), pp. 202–3, 252–3.

# 146

Nov 27 1885.

Dear James,

Our man in New York has provided the enclosed proofs of "The Bostonians" which he got from the Century people. They do not seem to go to the end of the book but I think they go further than the corrected sheets you sent me the other day. I am not sure about this because the latter are in the printers' hands.[1]

Believe me
Yours Ever,
Frederick Macmillan

H James Esq

**Note**

1. Macmillan is supervising the publication of *The Bostonians* in book form and is printing the text from James's revisions of instalments in the *Century*. The novel did not complete its run in the magazine until the following February. The Macmillan agent in New York was George E. Brett.

**147**

3 Bolton St. W.
December 4*th* [1885]

Dear Macmillan.

I yesterday, in the most solemn & irrevocable manner, took a lease (for 21 years!) of a "residential flat" (in De Vere Gardens, Kensington;) & the proprietor, as appears to be usual in such cases, asked me for a "reference." I took the liberty of giving him your name; so that if he should apply to you perhaps you will testify to my general respectability & solvency; which latter quality depends, after all, very much on you.[1] It is probable that the thing is only a form & that he will let you alone; but I send you this line in order that, if he *does* write to you, you may know what it's all about. The flat is in rather an unfinished state, & with all that has to be done to it, in the way of furnishing &c., I shall not get into it for three or four months. But it shines before me as a promised land. I hope there is prosperity at Brighton.[2] Ever faithfully

Henry James

**Notes**

1.  In such financial matters, James usually turned to good friends of substantial reputation and connections, as, for example, when he asked his friend Edmund Gosse for a recommendation for a flat in Chelsea in 1912 and for support for his application for British citizenship in 1915. See *SLHJEG*, pp. 271, 307–8. He moved into his new quarters on 6 March 1886. See *HJL*, III, 114.
2.  The Macmillans were temporarily living in Brighton. See letter 140.


**148**

3 Bolton St. W.
January 25*th* [1886]

Dear Macmillan

I enclose a list for author's copies of the "Bostonians" in the U.S., if you will be so good as to forward it to New York.[1]

With regard to such copies of the book as I may wish to have sent out *here*, would it not be possible to keep back some of the 1 vol. lot (say a couple of dozen,) that you are sending to America, that I may use them here for presentation, instead of the 3 vols?[2] I don't care to give away more than $\frac{1}{2}$ a dozen of the latter. Very likely you will have a part of the 1 vol edition ready here (for subsequent British use) at the same [time] that the 3 volumes appear? Ever yours

Henry James

### Notes

1. The list includes the following names: Mrs E. L. Godkin, Charles A. Dana, Edgar Fawcett, Mrs [Catherine] Walsh, Mrs [John Jay] Chapman, Edmund Tweedy, Mrs Caroline Tilton, Miss [Katherine Prescott] Wormeley, Mrs John LaFarge, William James, Miss Grace Norton, Mrs E. W. Gurney, T. S. Perry, Mrs J. L. Gardner, Mrs [Henry Cabot] Lodge, T. B. Aldrich, Francis Parkman, and W. D. Howells. Addresses on the list have not been included in this note.
2. Though *BHL* dates the three-volume edition as 16 February 1886 and the one-volume edition as May 1886, James knows that a portion of the one-volume printing is intended for export to America, an issue that appeared in March. See *BHJ*, pp. 73–5. Actually both issues were ready at the same time, but Macmillan did not wish to allow them to compete with each other in the beginning. See letter 149.

## 149

Feb 10 1886

Dear James,

We hope to publish "The Bostonians" next week & we shall be glad to receive the list of people to whom you wish presentation copies to go. I should prefer to send the 3 volume Edition to anybody who is in England as it will be confusing to have copies of the cheap edn about before it is on sale.[1] We do not charge you for the copies you give away so it will make no difference.[2]

I sent out the list of American presentation copies to our New York agent.

Believe me
Yours very truly
Frederick Macmillan

H James Esq

### Notes

1. The one-volume 'cheap edn' would certainly hurt the sale of the three-volume work, and it was not due to appear until May.
2. From the beginning of their business association, Macmillan had not limited James to six author's copies and had provided gratis numerous presentation copies, though James from time to time, had, in turn, written to ask that extra copies be charged to his account.

## 150

March 22 1886

Dear James,

We are out of your book for a few days but the three copies shall go about the middle of the week.

We printed 500 to begin with, but are now exhausted & we are at press with another 100.[1] There has not yet been time to hear anything about the reception of "The Bostonians" in America.[2]

Yours ever,
Frederick Macmillan.

H James Esq
13 De Vere Gardens West[3]

### Notes

1.  Macmillan apparently did not print more than one hundred copies of the three-volume edition because the one-volume edition was available in adequate numbers and soon to appear. See letter 148, note 2.
2.  On 9 March James had written his brother William in America that the novel 'appears to be having a goodish success here' (*HJL*, III, 116).
3.  James had moved to De Vere Gardens on 6 March. See letters 147, note 1 and 151, note 1.

## 151

13, De Vere Mansions West, W.[1]
*Friday noon* [June 18? 1886][2]

My dear Macmillan

Will you read the enclosed & forward them to Mowbray M., whose no. in Holywell St. I have forgotten. They constitute an appeal from Arthur Collins, whom you met here one day, on behalf of an article describing the Gordon Boys' Memorial Home. He is earnestly wrapped up in it, & as it is an enterprise worthy of high promotion – as I suppose – I hope Morris will be able to print his paper.[3] Will you stick this also into the envelope for him? Yours ever in haste –

Henry James

### Notes

1.  James had leased a flat at this address in December 1885 (see letter 147), but he did not move there 'definitively' until 6 March 1886 (*HJL*, III, 114). He describes the flat and location – 'three minutes of Kensington Gardens . . . just out of the Kensington Road' – in a letter to Grace Norton of 16 July [1886] (*HJL*, III, 124).

2.  The date is based upon the day given by James and Macmillan's answer in letter 152. Letters were frequently written, received, and answered the same day by both writers.
3.  For Arthur Collins's article, 'The Gordon Boys' Home', see *Macmillan's Magazine*, LIV (August 1886), 296–300. Lieutenant-Colonel Collins was Princess Louise's equerry. For Mowbray Morris, see also letter 152.

## 152

June 18 1886

Dear James,

I have sent your letter to Mowbray Morris, but I know that he has already agreed to take Col: Collins's paper. It cant be in the July no as that has already gone to press but it will appear in August.[1]

> Yours ever,
> Frederick Macmillan

Henry James Esq

**Note**

1.  For James's effort to promote Lieutenant-Colonel Collins's 'paper' with Mowbray Morris, editor of *Macmillan's Magazine*, see letter 151 and note 3.

## 153

13, De Vere Mansions West, W.
June 24*th* 1886

My dear Macmillan.

I send you herewith a considerable part of the revised copy for the *Princess*: that is the 1*st* volume & about half the second. I will let you have the remainder as soon as possible. I think you will find that the same page & type as the *Bostonians* will be the right thing.[1]

Nothing has passed between us in relation to the terms on which this book shall be published – & I don't know what your own ideas may be. I should like the same arrangement as we made for the *Bostonians*.[2] Please let me hear from you about this & believe me yours ever

> Henry James

**Notes**

1.    Macmillan brought out *The Princess Casamassima* 22 October 1886. In June the novel was still appearing in the *Atlantic Monthly*, and instalments ran until October. James was apparently revising from the *Atlantic* text. He is, of course, referring to the 'same page & type' of *The Bostonians* in book form.
2.    James received £500 for the copyright of *The Bostonians* and 15% of the retail price of each copy sold. See letters 126–7, 133, and the memorandum of agreement itself in Anesko, between pages 83–4. For Macmillan's reply, see 154.

## 154

June 24 1886

My dear James,

   I have received your letter and the instalment of revised copy of "The Princess" which shall be put into type at once. We shall be happy to publish it on the same terms as the "Bostonians" – viz: a royalty of 15 percent on the retail price of all copies sold here and in America. We should like however to make the preliminary payment on account rather less, say £400 instead of £500.[1] I hope this will be satisfactory.

Believe me,
Yours ever,
Frederick Macmillan

Henry James Esq
13 De Vere Mansions West W

**Note**

1.    Since the firm had not managed to recover its investment in *The Bostonians*, Macmillan reduced the advance from £500 to £400 and retained the 15% royalty. James's reply is not included in LB, MA. but he signed a receipt for the first instalment on these terms (£150) on 26 June (LB, MA). See letter 156.

## 155

June 15. 1886

Dear James,

   I have much pleasure in sending you a cheque for £150 on account of "The Princess Cassimassima" [*sic*].[1]

Yours ever,
F.M.

H. James Esq

**Note**

1.  This is a down payment on the advance of £400 mentioned in letter 154. James's receipt dated 26 June is in LB, MA. See also letter 156.

## 156

34, De Vere Gardens, W.[1]
September 20*th* 1886

My dear Macmillan

I sent the last page of the final proof [of] the *Princess* back to the printers last week, & I suppose, & hope, that the rest of the business of bringing the book out will go on rapidly. It will make pp. 595 – the one volume edition. That is a good many – but I don't think it will make an awkward book if paper *not thick* is used. I have before me a 1 vol. novel ("East Angels," by Miss C. F. Woolson, Sampson & Low) of just that length & it is very handy, the paper being thin – not of course too thin.[2] I don't know what your idea will have been as regards the time of paying me the remainder of the £400 on acct. of royalties for which we covenanted & of which I had £150 when the book began to be printed. But as my part of the business seems over I won't conceal from you that it would be rather a convenience to me to receive it now.[3]

I heard the other day (from Smalley) that you were going, or had just gone, to Brighton – & called in Bedford St. to get news of you & of your wife. But you were not there, which confirmed these tidings. If you are spending any time at B. I would come down for a Sunday – except the next. I hope Mrs. Macmillan isn't banished thither.[4] I have been much away. Ever yours

Henry James

**Notes**

1.  James has not moved. He lived in an apartment building – De Vere Mansions – at 34 De Vere Gardens. From this date, he usually gives the latter as his address.
2.  *The Princess Casamassima* appeared in three volumes on 22 October 1886. Concurrently, a one-volume edition for American and domestic markets was printed, though the American issue was published on 2 November and the English issue in August 1887 (*BHJ*, pp. 75–6). James is referring to the English issue of *East Angels* (1886) by his old friend Constance Fenimore Woolson (1840–94).
3.  These terms are partially described in letters 154–5; Macmillan promptly sent the cheque for £250 in letter 157.
4.  George W. Smalley was a mutual friend (see letter 1, note 2). The Macmillans from time to time spent part of the fall and winter in Brighton or Bournemouth for Mrs Macmillan's health and invited James to come down for a weekend. See letter 140, for example, but see also letters 157 and 159.

**157**

Sept 21. 1886

My dear James,

I was sorry to miss you on Thursday. I was not out of town but had stayed at home because I was not very well. I have much pleasure in sending a cheque for the £250 which is now due to you on account of the "Princess." We shall have her out very soon now & will take care that she is not too fat.[1]

We are not at Brighton and I hope shall not have to go now. My wife is only pretty well but the doctor says she may safely stay in London until Christmas if the weather remains fairly decent.[2]

> Believe me to be
> Yours ever,
> Frederick Macmillan

H James Esq

**Notes**

1.   See letter 156. The one-volume edition of *The Princess Casamassima* contained 596 pages. James's receipt for the cheque is dated 22 September and is included in LB, MA.
2.   Within a month the Macmillans were 'ordered out of town' to Bournemouth (letter 159).

**158**

Oct 14 1886

Dear James,

I send you by post a copy of the American edition of "The Princess Casamassima". Its fellows are already on their way to New York and the English edition in 3 volumes will be ready next week.[1]

Please send me the names of any persons to whom you would like presentation copies sent.

> I am
> Yours ever,
> Frederick Macmillan

Henry James Esq

**Note**

1.   Compare letter 156, note 2, and *BHJ*, pp. 75–6. The one-volume American edition

apparently was printed, at least, before the three-volume English edition was published.

## 159

34, De Vere Gardens, W.
October 22*d* [1886]

My dear Macmillan

I have just sent the list to Bedford St.[1]

I am very sorry indeed to hear that you are ordered out of town – & wish greatly I might follow you to Bournemouth. My hope of being able to do so is not of the keenest – there being so many things I want to do (in the way of writing) before I go abroad; & I can only write in my regular quarters – not on a perch of 2 or 3 days. I have taken a vow not to leave town till I go abroad – & yet have made a couple of engagements for short absences in November. I am under a promise to go & see Stevenson before Dec. 1*st*, & if he were at home I wd. make my visit now – so as to have the resource of your company as well – but he is in London, where he has been very ill (he is getting better.) If you shld. stay anytime [*sic*] however, I would come down for a couple of days – especially if he were back & I should be able to redeem my pledge to him. I hope your wife will immediately find herself better – & will find sun & a blue sea; both of which are usually to be had at Bournemouth. Please to give her my very good wishes.

I hope the Princess will have a career – & almost think it probable – though I am cured of presumption.

I see you expect to be away 2 weeks. In this case I shall *try* & come down at the last, & will certainly do so if R.L.S. is back. He goes back as soon as he can.[2] Ever yours

Henry James

**Notes**

1. The list refers to those chosen to receive presentation copies of *The Princess Casamassima* as requested in letter 158. It is not included with the James letters in LB, MA. The novel was published on the day of James's letter (*BHJ*, p. 76).
2. Instead of a stay in Brighton (see letters 156 and 157), the Macmillans had gone to Bournemouth for Mrs Macmillan's health. Since, apparently, Stevenson did not return to Bournemouth before the Macmillans left, James presumably did not visit his friends at this time. See *SLHJEG*, p. 41.

## 160

Dec 10. 1886

Dear James,

A copy of the "Princess" has gone to Miss Broughton. I hope it will do her good & improve the style of her next book.[1]

I am glad to hear that Sunshine & warmth is to be met with in the South. We start in ten days time and are looking forward to it eagerly. I am afraid there is no chance of our getting as far as Florence.[2]

Believe me

Yours ever,
Frederick Macmillan

Henry James Esq

### Notes

1.  Rhoda Broughton (1840–1920), English novelist and friend of James, may have been on the list referred to in letter 159.
2.  James had gone to Italy on 3 December and had reached Florence on 8 December (*HJL*, ɪɪɪ, 151), from which place he had apparently written Macmillan. His letter is not in LB, MA.

## 161

34 De Vere Gardens
October 19*th* [1887][1]

Dear Macmillan.

I have during the last few years written certain little articles of a critical nature which I should like to collect into a *small* volume, if for such a volume I can get some money. There are enough to make a little book – or even more than enough; & though I shall probably write some others, I think it better to work these off first. I enclose a list of the papers in question – the sequence in which they stand not being definitive. I have also prefixed to them a title which is only provisional – in order to put something. Will you publish such a volume – in England & America – & what will you give me for it? My idēa is that it should be a book smaller & more unassuming in aspect, as it were, than *French Poets & Novelists* in the 1*st* edition (of F.P. & N.), but as pretty as possible.[2] Believe me yours ever

Henry James

**Notes**

1.  The year of this letter is fixed by a note in another hand on the letter dated 21 October 1887 and by Macmillan's reply in 162. James had returned 21 July from a stay of almost eight months 'on the continent' (*HJL*, III, 195).
2.  James suggested a title of 'Half-Length Portraits' and proposed including the following essays: 'Emerson, Carlyle and Emerson, R. L. Stevenson, George Eliot, Ivan Turgénieff, Anthony Trollope, Alfonse Daudet, Emile Zola (apropos of *Nana*), Sainte Beuve, Matthew Arnold, Ernest Renan, The Art of Fiction, Du Maurier, J. S. Sargent, E. A. Abbey, Miss Woolson, Coquelin, Salvini.' In a note scrawled across one side of the page, someone at the firm cautions: 'I am not sure they would *all* go in.' For discussion of terms, length, and other matters of what eventually became *Partial Portraits*, see letters 162–4, 167, 169–71.

# 162

Oct 20 1887

Dear James,

I write to say that we shall be very pleased to publish your proposed volume of "Half length Portraits" and to give you a royalty of 15 per cent on all copies that we sell either in England or the United States.[1]

I should propose to make the volume uniform in size & general appearance with Frederic Harrisons [*sic*] "Choice of Books" which I dare say you know.[2] If you will kindly send me the copy I will have it cast off & let you know how many of the papers can be included in a volume of moderate size.[3]

> I am
> Yours ever,
> Frederick Macmillan

Henry James Esq

**Notes**

1.  These terms as regards royalty are the same James had received for *The Bostonians* and *The Princess*. It is worth noting that Macmillan offers no advance. James accepts these terms in letter 163.
2.  Harrison's *The Choice of Books and Other Literary Pieces* had been published by Macmillan & Co. in 1886.
3.  For Macmillan's suggestions concerning 'the papers', see letter 169.

**163**

34 De Vere Gardens W.
Oct. 21*st* [1887]

Dear Macmillan.

I accept your terms of 15 per cent royalty on each copy sold, for the volume of Critical Sketches – would that do, by the way, for a title?[1]

I am afraid, & I was afraid at the time I wrote, that the compatibility between a *small* volume & the inclusion of *all* the papers whose names I gave you will not be complete. Two or three of them are rather long. Yet the volume had better be small – & the form of "The Choice of Books" would be good for it.[2] I will get together the things as soon as possible – there will be a little delay. The Emerson doesn't appear till the December *Macmillan* & the R. L. Stevenson – which is one of the longest – till the November *Century*. But I will make an assortment & let you measure it.[3]

Yours ever:
Henry James

**Notes**

1.  The title eventually became *Partial Portraits*. See letters 169–71.
2.  James agreed with Macmillan about his suggestion in letter 162 as to the form of the book.
3.  'The Life of Emerson', *Macmillan's Magazine*, LVII (December, 1887), 86–98, but 'Robert Louis Stevenson' was delayed: *The Century*, XXXV (April, 1888), 868–79. Both articles appeared in *Partial Portraits* (1888), a collection of eleven essays. The 'assortment' James refers to is not included with his letters in the LB, MA.

**164**

Nov 14 1887

My dear James,

It would be a pity to omit the paper on Stevenson from your "Half Length Portraits" so I suppose the publication of the book must be postponed until it has appeared in the magazine. However as you say the printing can go on and everything can be prepared for publication immediately after the appearance of the March "Century".[1] I take it for granted that you have reserved the right of separate publication.

I like the title "Half Length Portraits" & should be inclined to stick to it.[2]

Believe me
Yours ever
Frederick Macmillan.

H. James Esq

**Notes**

1. The Stevenson essay actually appeared in the April *Century* (see letter 163, note 3).
2. This projected title was eventually dropped when it was discovered that someone else had used it. See letter 169.

## 165

34 De Vere Gardens W.
November 30*th* 1887

My dear Macmillan.

I had a couple of days ago a talk with Morris – which he perhaps will by this time have mentioned to you, on the subject of my giving him a tale, in three parts, for *Macmillan*.[1] We talked considerably about the magazine & I professed myself ready to contribute to it to that extent or even further. But I told him I would communicate with you directly on the great money-question. I have been reflecting on this & with the following result. He mentioned that you had paid, or were to pay some novelist (I think Mrs. Ritchie) £2.10.0 (two pounds ten shillings,) a page for some past or future serial.[2] This same rate would content me on condition of your assent to my attaching to the matter the following modification. More than a year ago the editor of Harper's Weekly (not *Monthly*) wrote to me to ask if I wouldn't give him the use from week to week of anything that I might be publishing from month to month in an English periodical & inasmuch as the said *Weekly* has absolutely no circulation here (I think it is never even seen) & would accordingly not in any degree compete with or injure my English appearance – I returned him an indefinite answer, as I was not then "running" in an English periodical & had not a present prospect of so doing. But to-day the case comes up & it occurs to me that my problem will be satisfactorily solved if I may give Harper's

Weekly my *Macmillan* sheets from month to month – on the rigid understanding of course that they are not to appear till *after* they have come forth in the magazine. This can be assured by my not sending them till a day which would render prior publication over there impossible. The Harper's plan would be I think to publish a Macmillan instalment either in a monthly or fortnightly form: that is a monthly quantity (of the English issue) is too short for them to cut it into quarters. As £2.10.0 a page is considerably less than I get for my productions from the American magazines, I suppose I could look to the Harpers payment (though their idea is *not* to pay me the full American price – as I gather) to equalize the thing. If this arrangement suits you I shall be glad to give Morris the story – & if it works well in practice I daresay we shall be able to go on with it in other cases. I *think* that I myself can look to the Harpers to do their part. My view is of course to give the Harpers the simple *use* in their journal of the sheets (the understanding being definitely for the *Weekly* only – on behalf of which only their proposal was made,) leaving you the *book* into which the tale, or tales, would ultimately be resolved, in America as well as in England.[3] I don't know that there is more to say of this, save that in regard to this particular story of which I have talked with Morris & which is to consist of three monthly instalments of *about* 18 pages, it wd. be a comfort to me to receive the full amount, for the three months, on delivery of the complete MS. The value of this you will naturally estimate when it *is* delivered.

Believe me yours ever

Henry James

Frederick Macmillan esq.

### Notes

1. This is the first reference to 'The Reverberator', a short novel that appeared in *six* instalments in *Macmillan's Magazine*: LVII (February 1888), 263–75 to LVIII (July 1888), 161–75.
2. Mowbray Morris, as editor of *Macmillan's*, would normally handle decisions concerning the acceptance of and payment for contributions. It is worth noting that James wishes to deal directly with Macmillan on 'the great money-question', in part, at least, because he usually dealt with him and, in part, because he wanted to work out the concurrent publication of the same work in *Harper's Weekly*. Mrs Ritchie was Anne Isabella Thackeray Ritchie (1837–1919), the daughter of Thackeray and a well-known writer of fiction herself. The serial referred to may have been 'Mrs Dymond', *Macmillan's*, LI (March 1885), 321–35 to LIII (December 1885), 141–52.

3.   *Harper's Weekly* did not reprint *The Reverberator*, but Macmillan published the
      book in England and America.

## 166

Nov 30. 1887

My dear James,
     We shall be very glad to print your story in "Macmillan" on the
terms suggested by yourself viz a payment of £2/10/. per page, and
an understanding that you are to be at liberty to send early sheets to
New York for simultaneous publication in "Harper's Weekly."
     We shall be very pleased to pay for the whole story as soon as the
ms. is in our hands & we can accurate[ly] estimate its extent.[1]

> Believe me
> Yours very truly,
> Frederick Macmillan

Henry James Esq

### Note

1.   Macmillan agreed to James's proposal regarding his 'story' for *Macmillan's* that
      subsequently becomes *The Reverberator*. The terms as described in this letter are
      written in another hand on the last page of James's letter (number 165).

## 167

Jan 12 1888

My dear James,
     I have written to our man in New York telling him to get the title
of "The Reverberator" entered at Washington according to the re-
quirements of the law.[1]
     Enclosed I send a cheque for the February & March instalments as
requested.[2]
     By the way what about "Half Length Portraits"[?] Is that to be
ready for publication this spring?[3]

My wife is down at St. Leonards & I come up to town for three days each week. We have had plenty of sunshine & the place seems to suit her very well. I think she will stay there until the end of February. I hope you are well & flourishing.

> Believe me
> Yours Ever
> Frederick Macmillan

Henry James Esq
34 De Vere Gardens

**Notes**

1.  This is the first mention of the title of the work under discussion in letters 165–6.
2.  At the rate of £2.10 per page for twenty-four pages, this cheque would have approximated £60 ($300 at the rate of $5.00 per pound).
3.  'Half-Length Portraits' became *Partial Portraits* and appeared the following May.


## 168

> 34 De Vere Gardens W.
> January 26*th* [1888][1]

Dear Macmillan.

It will give me great pleasure to dine with you on Wednesday 1*st*, at the Devonshire Club at eight o'clock.

> Yours ever
> Henry James

**Note**

1.  Dated by James's reference to the dinner engagement on Wednesday, 1 February. Such social exchanges continued until James's final illness in December 1915.


## 169

> Feb 7 1888

Dear James,

We find that your volume of reprinted essays will be about 50 pages too long as it stands. The printers calculate that it would run to 558 pp: whereas 500 is as much as we ought to give, & we should not be sorry to limit the volume to 450. I think that you said you could cut it down if necessary; will you please let me know which papers can be omitted?[1]

I find that there is already in existence a book called "Half Length Portraits" by one Gibson Craig – so we must think of some other title.[2]

Yours Ever<br>Frederick Macmillan

H. James Esq

### Notes

1. James's response is not in LB, MA, but a comparison of his proposed list in letter 161 with the contents of the first edition reveals that nine essays were dropped and one on Maupassant and another on Eliot were added.
2. Gibson Craig, *Half-Length Portraits* (London: Sampson Low, 1876).

## 170

34 De Vere Gardens W.<br>March 21st [1888][1]

Dear Macmillan.

I am just sending back the last proofs of my volume to Clark.[2] Therefore don't you think the enclosed title-page would perhaps do? I have thought of 20 things (Portraits Reduced, Figures Reduced, Faces and Figures, Smaller than Life, Essays in Portraiture, Likenesses, Appreciations &c. &c. – somehow they all sound – don't they? – like advertisements or *signs*:) & this seems, on the whole, the least objectionable.[3] It preserves the idea of the portrait, which is necessary, & conveys in a graceful & not obtrusive double meaning, both that the picture is *not* down to the feet, as it were, & that the appreciation is favourable – which in every case it happens to be. If however you should take a wild fancy to "Smaller than Life," I would give place to it. I think this improbable. If the title satisfies you will you please cause the note to Edinburgh to be posted? The sooner the book comes out the better, for I have an ardent wish that at as early a subsequent period as possible certain accumulated tales, which are panting to see the light in volumes, should be collected together. There will be by that time eight or nine of them – some of them rather long – & they will all have come out in periodicals by the time the last *Reverberator* (July 1*st*,) is published in *Macmillan*. Therefore one might be getting them ready. Yours ever

Henry James

P.S.    I have left out 6 or 7 of the original papers – & still the volume makes *408* pages![4]

### Notes

1.    Previously printed in *HJL*, III, 226–7 and *HJ:SL*, 221. The present text differs in various accidentals.
2.    The firm of R. & R. Clark in Edinburgh was printing the book.
3.    Though the title page is no longer with the letter in LB, MA, the context of the letter and Macmillan's response in number 171 make it clear that James is proposing the title by which the book was published: *Partial Portraits*.
4.    James actually left out nine of the proposed essays: Carlyle and Emerson, Emile Zola, Sainte Beuve, Matthew Arnold, Ernest Renan, J. S. Sargent, E. A. Abbey, Coquelin, and Salvini. All of these essays were subsequently reprinted, though those on Carlyle and Emerson, Arnold, Renan, and Salvini were collected posthumously. The text of the book contained 408 pages and four pages of advertisement (*BHJ*, pp. 76–7).

### 171

March 21 1888

Dear James,

I do not think that any of the alternative titles suggested in your letter are improvements on the one you have chosen & I am therefore sending your copy for Title page etc on to Clark to be set up in type.[1] We shall publish as soon as possible – immediately after Easter.

Believe me
Yours Ever
Frederick Macmillan

I suppose people will say that a portrait ought to be *im*partial!
Henry James Esq

Note
1.    The title, as Macmillan implies below, is *Partial Portraits*. The book was published 8 May 1888 (*BHJ, p. 77*).

**172**

April 3 1888

My dear James,

We have just begun the publication of a new series of Two Shilling Editions of novels bound in paper boards in a style which we think is as showy as the ordinary "yellowback" but not as vulgar. Are you inclined to allow us to bring out two of your novels in this style with the idea, if the experiment proved successful, of publishing the others in the same way? We have the stereotype plates hitherto used for the 6/. Editions from which the books could be printed, and as you know from our accounts the sale of the old books is unfortunately so small that no harm can be done by bringing them out in a cheaper form. It may be that the effect apart from any profit that the cheap editions brought in, might be good by making your work more widely known & so educating readers for your future books. I send a copy of one of the new 2/. editions by this post so that you may see the kind of appearance I am proposing for you.[1]

> Believe me
> Yours very truly,
> Frederick Macmillan.

Henry James Esq

**Note**

1. *The Princess Casamassima*, apparently, was the copy of the new two-shilling edition Macmillan sent. See letter 173. The other novel published in this format at this time was presumably *Roderick Hudson* (*BHJ*, p. 31). See letter 173, note 1.

**173**

April 5 1888

Dear James,

I am much obliged for your letter. We will at once print & publish a 2/. Edition of "The Princess" & if that turns out to be successful we can follow it up with the other books.[1]

It is a long time since I have seen anything of you. Can you come and dine quietly with us at Northwick Terrace (7.30 o'clock) on

Monday next – & indeed any other day you like to name (except tomorrow)?

Believe me
Yours ever,
Frederick Macmillan

Henry James Esq.

**Note**

1. James's letter is not included in LB, MA. At least two other novels appeared in the two-shilling 'yellowback' format: *Roderick Hudson* and *Washington Square* (*BHJ*, 31, 52).

## 174

April 7 1888

My dear James,

The printers tell me that they are waiting for the return by you of the proofs of "Partial Portraits" which were sent out to you in revise.[1] Can you kindly send them marked for "press"?

Yours ever,
Frederick Macmillan

Henry James Esq

**Note**

1. James apparently returned the proofs promptly, for the book was published 8 May (*BHJ*, p. 77).

## 175

April 16 1888

My dear James,

I have much pleasure in sending you a cheque for the final instalment of "The Reverberator" [.][1]

Am I right in thinking that you said you would leave the publication of this book in our hands for England & America on the same terms as the last book – a royalty of 15 per cent?[2] If so I will see to the printing at once. Will you wish to make any further corrections?

Yours ever,
Frederick Macmillan

Henry James Esq

#### Notes

1. Since the final instalment of the novel appeared in the July issue of *Macmillan's Magazine*, Macmillan may be in error. He may have remembered that the serial was originally to appear in three instalments. The cheque presumably was for £30. See letter 167, note 2.
2. The 15% royalty had served as the basis for terms on James's books since *The Bostonians*. Though James's direct response to this proposal is not in LB, MA, he accepted the royalty, but asked for an 'advance' on it. See letter 177. In letter 178 Macmillan proposed £125 down on *Partial Portraits* and *The Reverberator*.

## 176

May 9 1888

Dear James,

We sent you a couple of copies of "Partial Portraits" which was published yesterday.[1] If you will let me have a list of persons to whom you wish presentation copies to be sent it shall be attended to.[2]

Yours very truly,
Frederick Macmillan

Henry James Esq

#### Notes

1. *Partial Portraits* appeared 8 May 1888 in an edition of 2000 copies, 'divided between domestic and American issues' (*BHJ*, p. 77).
2. The list is not in LB, MA.

## 177

34 De Vere Gardens W.
May 24*th* 1888

Dear Macmillan.

I have been wishing to write to you for three or four days past, but have waited, on the supposition that I should be hearing from you in relation to what I wrote to you ten days ago on the subject of McClure: so that then having occasion to write again I should make one job of it. But now it occurs to me that possibly (as I *don't* hear from you) my letter about McClure (of the 15*th* or 16*th*,) failed through some error or accident to reach you. The purpose of it was to ask you to offer him *The Patagonia* – a tale of mine, of about 18 or 20 thousand words, now in the possession of Comyns Carr – for his American use, on those terms of which you spoke to me the night I dined with you last. Did you ever receive it – or is McClure simply delaying to answer?[1]

I have various tales (this is the other matter) which are ready, if not to appear, at least to prepare to appear as books – especially if it is a practical question with you to get something more done in America (in my case) before the copyright matter comes into effect – if it be destined to do so.[2] I send you herewith the substance of one of these small collections (complete;) it goes in another cover – ready for the printers. In spite of *P. Portraits* & the *Reverberator* being already in the field I should like to see "The Aspern Papers &c" take a forward step.[3] It makes a book a little (not, I believe, much) larger than the *Reverberator* – & I think a better one. I have other things coming on behind it – a possible volume, "A London Life," composed of a longish tale of that name & two or three others ("The Liar," "The Patagonia," before mentioned, & another.)[4] These two books correspond in dimensions & both correspond, *about*, with the *Reverberator*: that is, are the stuff of two volumes. I am doing a good deal of work now, which I wish to put forward in its order – & I don't wish these little publications, therefore, to accumulate. But, to speak only of "The Aspern Papers" to-day, will you take them in hand & will you let me know the idea you may have about them? I must tell you that an essential part of the idea, for me, is to have some money. I said nothing to you about it in regard to the *Reverberator*, but my aspirations in regard to these two volumes as well (& to the volume in America,) will not have been fulfilled unless I receive something "down" – a certain sum in advance, of course I mean, on that 15 per cent royalty which I should otherwise have a long time to wait for.[5] I shall be glad to know your views on this subject & on that of a sum down, on the same system for "The Aspern Papers," if you take them in hand. I may mention further, since I have wound my courage up to the point of talking about money, that it would fall in wonderfully with my convenience to be paid for the story about to appear in the Eng. Illus. (as I understand Carr, in July & August,) now. I am used to this with my American magazines.[6] I have rec'd. proof of the 1st instalment, which makes just 11 & ¹/₂ pages. The 2d is longer – I suppose there need be no great delay in its being set up. Excuse me if I am importunate on the subject of the McClure letter – or any other. Ever yours

Henry James

### Notes

1. Though this letter is not in LB, MA, Macmillan presumably received it, for, as he indicates in letter 178, he had written S. S. McClure (1857–1949), the American publisher, on 16 May. Comyns Carr was editor of the *English Illustrated Magazine*, where 'The Patagonia' appeared in the issues for August and September 1888.
2. As it happened, the US Congress did not pass legislation on copyright until 1891.
3. *The Aspern Papers, Louisa Pallant, The Modern Warning*, despite Macmillan's word of caution in letter 178 about the book's close proximity in appearance to *The Reverberator* (June 1888), was published in late September 1888 (*BHJ*, pp. 78–80). But see letter 185, note 1, for a later date.
4. The unnamed tale was 'Mrs Temperly' (originally 'Cousin Maria'). *A London Life* (including the three other tales mentioned) appeared in April 1889 (*BHJ*, p. 82). In letter 190 Macmillan specifies 30 April as the date of publication.
5. James had received nothing 'down' on his books since *The Princess Casamassima*, though in letter 178 Macmillan offers £125 in 'anticipation of royalties' on *Partial Portraits* and *The Reverberator*. Eventually – see letter 183 – Macmillan proposes an advance of £200 for *The Aspern Papers* and two other books: *A London Life* and *The Lesson of the Master*.
6. James received £75 for the two-instalment appearance of 'The Patagonia' in the *English Illustrated Magazine*. See letter 178. Such a sum would be based on a figure of £3 per page on twenty-five pages, an advance from the £2.10 James had been receiving. Moreover, this payment was made further in advance of publication than the firm had been in the habit of paying.

## 178

May 25 1888

My dear James,

I wrote to McClure on the 16th inst but have not yet had any reply to my letter. I find on inquiry at the American Exchange (which is his address) that he is on the continent but he has his letters forwarded and I will write again today to stir him up. Of course it is possible that he is not a serious person at all. I have had no dealings with him, and people of his kind, even when they come from the United States, are sometimes inclined to make large promises which it is difficult to get them to perform.[1]

We shall be very pleased to publish "The Aspern Papers" and I have already sent the copy to our printers, but I think it would not be giving "The Reverberator" a fair chance to bring it out just yet. Our experience leads us to think that if two novels of the same writer are published within a short time of one another the sale of the first is damaged. The "circulating library" life of a book is not very long but while it lasts it should be treated tenderly. We will get on with the printing of "The Aspern Papers" and have it ready to issue as soon as the "Reverberator" stops selling.[2]

Carr tells me that "The Patagonia" is to appear in "The English Illustrated" for August and September, but we shall be glad to pay for it now as you suggest, & I propose therefore to send you £200 – £75 on account of the EIM and the remainder in anticipation of royalties on "Partial Portraits" & "The Reverberator [.]"[3]

I am glad to be able to report that the Two-shilling edition of "The Princess" seems likely to be a success. Smith & Sons have ordered 700 copies for their bookstalls.[4]

> Believe me
> Yours very truly,
> Frederick Macmillan

Henry James Esq

### Notes

1.  S. S. McClure's rather flamboyant approach to publishing obviously did not appeal to Macmillan (see also letter 179). Though the American publisher had approached James about the purchase of some of his fiction, he apparently never published 'The Patagonia'. See *HJL*, III, 241n.
2.  Though Macmillan is naturally reluctant to publish *The Aspern Papers* too soon in relation to *The Reverberator*, he nevertheless accepts the new work, but offers no advance until letter 183.
3.  The sum for 'The Patagonia' is actually an improvement on the rate of payment for James's fiction in Macmillan magazines (see letter 177, note 6). The figure for the two books, however, is a smaller advance than James had received for his long novels (£500 for *The Bostonians* and £400 for *The Princess Casamassima*).
4.  Smith's order was larger than usual and contributed to the printing of 3,000 copies of a one-volume edition shortly after the appearance of the first edition (*BHJ*, p. 76). The sale of the novel led eventually to the publication of three other titles in two-shilling editions. See, for example, letter 179.

**179**

May 29 1888

Dear James,

As the booksellers seem to have taken kindly to the two shilling edition of "The Princess", I think it would be a good plan to bring out two or three of your other books in the same form. What do you say to "Daisy Miller" [,] "The Madonna" and "Washington Square"?[1]

I think that McClure's only connection with the American Exchange is that his letters are addressed there – but for all that I dare say he is a *farceur*.[2]

> Believe me
> Yours ever,
> Frederick Macmillan

Henry James Esq

**Notes**

1. Each of these three titles appeared in a two-shilling edition. See *BHJ*, pp. 40, 43, 52.
2. Macmillan's opinion of McClure is consistent with what he had said earlier. See letter 178.

**180**

June 11. 1888

Dear James,

I am glad you like the appearance of "The Reverberator": the sale has begun fairly well – Mudie having subscribed for 150 copies.[1] The presentation copies are going out today.

No: I was not at the international supper-party, nor is it the kind of entertainment that would have given me much satisfaction. I can imagine the kind of speeches they would make.[2]

> Believe me
> Yours ever,
> Frederick Macmillan.

Henry James Esq

**Notes**

1.   This well-known circulating library had, for example, purchased 100 advance copies of *Washington Square*. See letter 77. The novel had appeared on 5 June (*BHJ*, p. 78).
2.   Though Macmillan and James advocated international copyright, both eschewed 'supper-parties' when possible. James's view of this kind of affair is expressed in a letter written later in the month– 29 June – to Edmund Gosse in which he reports his 'absolute & immitigable aversion to public dinners' (*SLHJEG*, pp. 57–9).

# 181

June 13 1888

Dear James,
    We are sending a copy of "The Reverberator" to Mr. Reinhart.[1]
                                    Yours Ever
                                    Frederick Macmillan
H James Esq

**Note**

1.   Charles S. Reinhart (1844–96), the American illustrator, had illustrated 'Cousin Maria' (later 'Mrs Temperly') in *Harper's Weekly*, XXXI (6–20 August 1887), 557–8, 577–8, 593–4. See also letters 182 and 187.

# 182

34 De Vere Gardens W.
July 5*th* 1888[1]

My dear Macmillan –
    Will you please ask your people in America to have the enclosed title-page copyrighted for me? It is the title of a tale in two parts about to appear in the *Universal Review* here (July 15*th* & August 15*th*) which will of course be sure to reach the U.S. & be exposed to reproduction there.[2]
    And will you also direct that a copy of *The Reverberator* be sent to:
        Leslie Stephen esq.
        Talland House
        St. Ives,
        Cornwall?[3]

Making these little requests of you brings to the head a purpose I have entertained for several days past – & into which I will plunge without more delay. It is connected – I suppose I ought to be ashamed to confess it – with a certain need of money & a desire to learn if I may successfully *faire valoir*, as the French say, to the end of obtaining some from you, [for] various as yet unpublished but as I think eminently publishable productions. The case with me is that (stated as simply as possible) I have on the one hand a need for a considerable sum & on the other the sense that the material of three books of about the size of the *Reverberator* is about to burst (in so far as it has not already burst) from the periodical press. I think I have mentioned these things more or less definitely to you already, but I will enumerate them again for correctness' sake. Let me premise that each of the said books would make two volumes of rather fuller contents than the *Reverberator* – there is in each case, in other words, rather more copy.

*First*, there is the "Aspern Papers," which I sent you some time ago & which you sent on (I think you told me,) to the printers. It consists of three tales.[4]

*Second*. There is: A London Life (terminated in *Scribner* about August 20*th*) The Liar: (out of the *Century*.)[5]

*Third*. There is:  The Lesson of the Master
                      The Patagonia
                      Mrs. Temperley.[6]

The 1*st* of these three last things appears in the July & Aug. *Universal Review*; the 2*d* in the corresponding nos. (or rather the August & September nos.) of the *English Illustrated*. The 3*d* came out a year ago in Harper's [*sic*] *Weekly*, with big pictures by Reinhart. Having them there I want to do something with them (in a pecuniary sense) & the question is What can I do? Are you able, to answer this question, without inconvenience, in any accommodating sense? Of course I know that you don't wish to publish three books (or five, counting the 2 lately published) all in a heap: but nevertheless I can't forbear to sound you. Would there be any money owing me on the sale (already) of the two-shilling volumes lately put forth, & of which a parcel of copies – they are very pretty – came to me yesterday? Or on anything else? I am settling down to write a longish novel (it begins in the *Atlantic* in January next & runs a year,) so that for the next few months I shall be engaged on work without immediate returns – a strain I am sorry to say that I am not, just now, rich enough easily to stand.[7] I may be asking something so unusual that it is impossible – but without asking I can't know. If it is consistent with your powers to make me such an advance as will ease off the said strain, I shall greatly appreciate the service to Yours ever

Henry James

**Notes**

1.  This letter is printed in *HJL*, III, 237–8. The present text differs chiefly in accidentals.
2.  'The Lesson of the Master', *Universal Review*, I (16 July and 15 August 1888), 342–65, 494–523.
3.  James had known Stephen since 1868, and as editor of the *Cornhill* (1871–82), Stephen had published 'Daisy Miller', 'An International Episode', and 'Washington Square'. *The Reverberator* had been published 5 June (*BHJ*, p. 78).
4.  'Louisa Pallant' and 'The Modern Warning' were published the following September with 'The Aspern Papers' (*BHJ*, p. 80). But see also letter 185, note 1.
5.  'A London Life' appeared in *Scribner's Magazine*, III (June 1888), 671–88, IV (July–September), 64–82, 238–49, 319–30 and 'The Liar' in the *Century*, XXXVI (May–June 1888), 123–35, 213–23.
6.  'The Patagonia' and 'Mrs Temperly' (James subsequently dropped the final 'e') were added to 'A London Life' and 'The Liar' when the collection was published in April 1889 (see letter 187 and *BHJ*, pp. 82–3). 'The Lesson of the Master' was not collected until 1892.
7.  The 'longish novel' is *The Tragic Muse*. For Macmillan's reply, see letter 183.


## 183

July 6 1888

My dear James,

I will have the title of "The Lesson of the Master" registered at Washington – & a copy of *The Reverberator* goes to Leslie Stephen by today's post.[1]

I am sorry that the sale of your books does not enable us to be as liberal in our advances as we should like to be but of course in matters of this kind we have to look facts in the face. If it will be of any assistance to you I shall be glad to send you a cheque for £200 on account of royalties to come from the three books you mention viz 1) The Aspern Papers 2) A London Life 3) The Lesson of the Master.[2] The books to be published at intervals of 4 months from October 1st or thereabout.

Believe me<br>Yours ever<br>Frederick Macmillan

Henry James Esq

**Notes**

1.  See letter 182.
2.  *The Aspern Papers* was published in October 1888, *A London Life* in April 1889, and The *Lesson of the Master* in February 1892. The delay in the publication of the third volume was due, in part, to the publication and poor reception of *The Tragic Muse*, James's decision in 1890 to leave the novel for the drama, and his failure to publish enough short fiction until 1891 to make a volume. He touches on the matter of 'short lengths' in a letter to Robert Louis Stevenson of 31 July [1888] (*HJL* III, 240). James signed a receipt for this advance on 11 July (LB, MA).

## 184

July 10 1888

My dear James,

I enclose a cheque for £200 as agreed.[1]

My wife and I start tomorrow morning for a driving tour to Cheshire by way of Bucks, Warwickshire, Worcestershire & Shropshire. If we get on all right we ought to arrive at our destination on Saturday week. Of course in a thing of this kind it is quite possible that our horses may break down & that we shall have to finish the journey by train but if no accident happens it ought to be a pleasant experience. We expect to be back at the end of the month & then we go for Weybridge where we have taken a house for six weeks. I hope that if you are in town then you will come down and stay with us.[2] Believe me

Yours ever
Frederick Macmillan

Henry James Esq

**Notes**

1.  The 15% royalty James had received on the retail sales of his books since *The Bostonians* was also a part of the contract. James's receipt of 11 July for £200 is in LB, MA.
2.  James may well have taken advantage of Macmillan's usual hospitality, for he was 'in town' until the following October.

## 185

Oct 10 1888

Dear James,

I have your list of persons to whom presentation copies of "The

Aspern Papers" are to go and will attend to it. The book is to be published next Tuesday. I will let you have certainly one & most likely two copies by tomorrow evening.[1]

Yours ever,

Frederick Macmillan

Henry James Esq

### Note

1.    Since James was leaving immediately for Switzerland, Macmillan was trying to provide copies of the soon-to-be published *Aspern Papers*. James's letter and list are not in LB, MA. The date of publication – 16 October – is different from that given in *BHJ*: 'Published September 1888. . . . First advertised, as ready "Immediately", in the *Athenaeum*, 29 September 1888' (p. 80).

## 186

Geneva, Switzerland.

Oct. 13*th* [1888]

Dear Macmillan

I meant to thank you before leaving London for the two copies, timely in their arrival, of the Aspern Papers – & to thank your wife, by the same occasion, for a very delectable looking little sealed pot (of which I didn't dare to penetrate the mystery the last thing before embarking at Dover,) which she was so kind as to send me.[1] Please express to her my appreciation of the graceful gift – it is something to look forward to on my return – to hurry back for. The book is charmingly pretty – & if the public would only show some practical agreement in this estimate there would be no wormwood mingled with my honey. Apropos of honey this place looks as lovely to me as ever – & the "little change" as they say in London, is already doing me good. I am at the Hotel de l'Ecu but *may* leave it tomorrow for another – so that if you should have occasion to write to me 34 De Vere Gardens is. . . .[2]

### Notes

1.    See letter 185. James had gone to Switzerland for a working holiday – he was writing 'The Tragic Muse' – and to visit Constance Fenimore Woolson, an old American friend and fellow novelist. See Edel, III, 250–51 and *HJL*, III, 246–7. Mrs Macmillan's continued attentions should also be noted.

2.   Though James appears to be concluding the letter, there is no more text and no
     signature in LB, MA.

**187**

34 De Vere Gardens W.

January 22*d* [1889]

Dear Macmillan.

Three minutes after I had left you this afternoon I remembered
that I *had* made a strange blunder, through crass forgetfulness, and
had not included with my sheet of copy for the "London Life" a
certain tale of *Cousin Maria* (I shall change its name) which appeared
in three nos of Harper's *Weekly* [*sic*] 18 mos. ago (with ugly big
drawings by Reinhart) & which I mentioned to you in my list, last
summer, of the tales of which these volumes should be composed.[1]
Here I find it in a drawer, all ready to go – & having failed to go (with
the *Life* & *The Liar*, the other day) apparently because I was in such
a blundering hurry to get over my delay. I send it now with *The
Patagonia* – & they ought *both* to be included, as my very mistaken
estimate of the amount of material that you already have will probably leave ample room for both. The "Life" was not, as I accidentally
said to you a couple of hours ago, 3, but 4, instalments of *Scribner*; &
the "Liar" was 2 of the *Century*: making in all 6 magazine instalments. *The Reverberator* had been 6 short instalments of *Macmillan*, &,
as my *Century* parts were longer than any of *those*, I said to myself
that this would represent the right sort of thing; with the *Cousin
Maria* added: viz, a couple of volumes containing sensibly more stuff
than the *Reverberator* but not so long as the *Aspern Papers*.[2] Of course
it was stupidly oblivious of me (but I am always playing myself such
tricks) to drop out the *Cousin Maria* – which for the moment, I not
only forgot that I had named to you, but forgot that I had written! I
have only [one] copy of it, & had to move heaven & earth to get my
request for *that* attended to; therefore I send the big sheets (of the
paper) just as they are; not being able to *arrange* them, by the aid of
a duplicate. There is apparently (if the report you had today is
confirmed,) some strange shrinkage of the *Scribner* pages in transfer-
ence to a bookpage; for the said Scribner page contains 75 words
more than a *Macmillan* one. The *Century* page contains 350 more – &
the union of 6 instalments of such pages was my foundation for

expecting a considerable excess of printed matter on that of the 2 vol. *Reverberator*.

> Ever yours
> Henry James

### Notes

1.  'Cousin Maria' became 'Mrs. Temperly' in *A London Life* (1889). For James's list of tales, see letter 182.
2.  *A London Life* included three tales in addition to the titlepiece: 'The Patagonia', 'The Liar', and 'Mrs. Temperly'. *The Aspern Papers* contained 'Louisa Pallant' and 'The Modern Warning'.

## 188

Jan 23 1889

Dear James,

The copy for "The Patagonia" and Mrs. Temperly (Cousin Maria) has reached me. I will make the printers go over their calculations of quantity once more.[1]

> Yours very truly
> Frederick Macmillan

H James Esq

### Note

1.  James's miscalculation (see letter 187) leads to another measurement of the copy. He has obviously changed the title of 'Cousin Maria' to 'Mrs. Temperly'. At this stage of production the new title is spelled Temperly and Temperley interchangeably.

## 189

April 25 1889

Dear James,

The presentation copies of "A London Life" *from the author* shall be sent out on Monday next when the book will be published.[1]

> Yours ever,
> Frederick Macmillan

H James Esq

**Note**

1. The publication date would appear to be 29 April 1889. According to *BHJ*, the book was 'published April 1889. . . . The publisher reports publication date as March 1889. The earliest advertisement noted, reading available "Immediately", is in the *Athenaeum*, 6 April' (p. 82). But see letter 190 for a correction.

## 190

May 4 1889

Dear James,

We are sending a copy of "A London Life" to Mrs. Richie [*sic*] and another to you. The book, as I told you, was published on Tuesday and has started fairly well – that is to say we have sold 280 copies.[1]

Yours ever
Frederick Macmillan

H James Esq

**Note**

1. The publication date was Tuesday, 30 April, not 29 April as indicated in letter 189 and note 1. Mrs Ritchie was Anne Isabella Thackeray Ritchie, daughter of Thackeray and an old friend of James.

## 191

May 9 1889

Dear James,

We are sending copies of "A London Life" to Lady Rosebery, F. Myers, & Miss V. Paget. You are welcome to as many copies as you find it convenient to give away.[1]

Yours ever,
Frederick Macmillan

H James Esq

**Note**

1. Lady Rosebery, the former Hannah de Rothschild and wife of the Earl of Rosebery, recent foreign minister; Frederick Myers, graduate of Trinity College, Cam-

bridge and a founder of the Society for Psychical Research; and Violet Paget, British novelist and woman of letters. Macmillan's generous policy regarding presentation copies still obtains. James's list is not in LB, MA.

## 192

May 20 1889

My dear James,

The 2 volume edition of "A London Life" (500 copies) is all but exhausted but I have just been able to scrape together a couple of copies which are going to the persons named in your letter.[1] We intend to bring out a second & cheaper edition in one volume next week.[2]

We were sorry not to have you on Saturday. As you must of [sic] conjectured we took the liberty of asking you to fill up a place left open by the defection of a man at the last moment.

Yours ever,
Frederick Macmillan

H James Esq

### Notes

1.  Since James's letter is not included in LB, MA, the names of the persons are not available. Having been published 30 April, the edition, consequently, was 'exhausted' in three weeks.
2.  *BHJ* states that the one-volume edition of 2,000 copies was included under 'Books of the Week' in the *Pall Mall Budget*, 23 May (p. 83).

## 193

34, De Vere Gardens. W.
June 16*th* [1889]

Dear Macmillan.

Will you kindly say to the French lady, for me, that, with many thanks, my preference is that the *Portrait* &c shld. *not* be translated into French & that I have expressed to you my wish that my assent to any such undertaking be respectfully withheld?

I am tired of giving this assent to similar proposals (they are all quite in the air & highly irresponsible) from which no results have *ever* proceeded. This lady is careful not to give you the name of her "editeur", & one knows nothing whatever about her qualifications. The refusal will come with a better grace from you than from me & I return you *Mme* Gabillard's letter – for the address – & the stamp – if you can get it off![1] Till Thursday. Yours ever

Henry James

**Note**

1.  James was quite successful in keeping the *Portrait* from being translated into French, for the first translation did not appear until 1933 (*BHJ*, p. 363).

## 194

June 26th 1889

Dear James,

Mr. Fisher Unwin of Paternoster Square writes to say that he is going to publish a volume to be called "Love Scenes from Modern Literature" and he wishes to have permission to include in his book the extracts from your writings of which I enclose copies. Will you let me know whether you would like him to have leave. So far as we are concerned we do not care whether it is given or refused but would like to do just what you wish.[1]

Yours ever
Frederick Macmillan

Henry James Esq

**Note**

1.  The enclosed 'extracts' of James's writings are not included in LB, MA, nor is James's response in the James Papers in the MA. The title mentioned by Macmillan is listed neither in the LC *Union Catalogue* nor in *The General Catalogue of Printed Books in the British Museum Library* (now called the BL).

## 195

Hotel de Hollande,
r. de la Paix
November 13*th* 1889.

Dear Macmillan.

Will you please take some near occasion to send your people in New York, with the request that they will copyright it in my name in the U.S., the enclosed title-page of a tale in three parts which is immediately to begin to appear in the *New Review*? The editor of that periodical has had it in his hands for the last six months but has been keeping it back till he was ready to go into fiction. He is apparently to do so with a vengeance in his Dec. or Jan. no, as my story, or the 1*st* instalment of it, bids fair to take up a large part of his magazine.[1] This is why I have not been able, before this, to place it in your hands as a contribution to the *third* series of collected short tales about which we covenanted so many months ago & which I have suffered to wait (gathering that you were not reluctant) so much beyond its literal time. When this thing has run its course of three months I shall clap it into the book.[2]

I am spending this November in Paris, now sufficiently quiet & comfortable, the exhibition being dead & buried.[3] I had the last week of it – it was worth a week. I return to London Dec. 1*st*. I suppose this will find you at Brighton, where I hope you are breathing health.[4]

Ever yours
Henry James

### Notes

1. 'The Solution', *New Review*, I (December 1889), 666–90; II (January–February 1890), 76–90, 161–71.
2. 'The Solution' was included in the collection entitled *The Lesson of the Master* (1892). For the discussion of the three series of tales James mentions, see letter 182.
3. The Paris Exhibition of 1889 celebrated the centennial of the French Revolution.
4. The Macmillans actually planned to go to Brighton 30 November. See letter 196.

## 196

Nov 15 1889

Dear James,

I have forwarded the title page of "The Solution" to our man in

New York telling him to register the title at Washington. Will you please ask the Editor of the New Review to have 2 copies of each number of his periodical containing your story posted as early as possible to Macmillan & Co. 112, Fourth Avenue New York in order that they may be deposited at Washington in accordance with the Statute.[1]

I am glad to hear that you are having a pleasant month in Paris. I am afraid we shall just miss one another when you come back, as we hope to go to Brighton on Nov. 30th.[2]

> Believe me
> Yours ever,
> Frederick Macmillan

Henry James Esq

### Notes

1. Macmillan is helping James protect the American copyright of the tale. See letter 195.
2. James proposed to return to London on 1 December. See letter 195.

## 197

March 22 1890

My dear James,

Mess [rs.] Houghton & Co. of Boston have written to say that they will publish your "Tragic Muse" at the end of April & suggest that our edition should appear simultaneously. You have not yet said anything to us about this book, but I presume (& hope) that you intend to have it published in England.[1]

Is it the case that you are engaged on a translation of a new Tartarin book by Daudet?[2]

> Yours ever,
> Frederick Macmillan

Henry James Esq
34 De Vere Gardens. S.W.

### Notes

1. *The Tragic Muse* actually was published by Houghton, 7 June 1890 (*BHJ*, p. 84). Macmillan's query about an English edition led James to seek new terms from the firm. See letters 198–204.

2.    James translated Alphonse Daudet's *Port Tarascon: The Last Adventures of the Illustrious Tartarin* for *Harper's New Monthly Magazine*, LXXXI (June–November 1890), 3–25 to 937–55. The book was published by Harper & Brothers in New York on 30 October 1890 (*BHJ*, 210, 337). For James's comment on this work, see letter 199.

# 198

34, De Vere Gardens, W.

March 24*th* 1890[1]

Dear Macmillan

The very long novel ("The Tragic Muse") which, ever since Jan. 1889, I have been contributing to the *Atlantic Monthly* is to terminate there in May. When it was a question of arranging for it there two years ago, I found it indispensable to meet Houghton & Mifflin's condition that *they* should publish the book in the U.S. The terms they offered me for the serial were so much better on this condition that I couldn't afford not to agree to them, even though they constituted an implication that such tales as I shall hereafter publish in the *Atlantic* shall also come, as books, to its proprietors. The *Atlantic*, on this basis, is more hospitable & remunerative to me than any other periodical appears anxious to be on any other. I thought it injudicious to appeal to you, as an alternative, for other conditions; but I have all along taken for granted, not fallaciously, I trust, that in England you will still be glad to issue the book. I have just got the revised copy all ready to sent you if you will have it. Will you let me know your ideas about it?[2] I must frankly add that the book is, I fear, almost formidably long – it is to make (probably) 2 volumes even in the U.S. At the same time I think it only fair to add that it is, in my opinion – & I believe in those of such "admirers" as Providence has vouchsafed me – the best of my productions. (This, I suppose, however, will strike you as what "we all" say.)[3] It is altogether, in subject, a matter of English life. Ever yours

Henry James

P.S.    I am [not] unaware or oblivious that I am actually in your debt to the extent of whatever fraction of £200 on acct. (which you paid me July 9*th* 1888), is represented by the third of the books then covenanted for here & in the U.S. – the *Aspern Papers* & *A London Life* being the 2 others. I will engage that this last member of the batch (about 5 short tales) shall appear in the autumn – if that will suit you.[4] – H.J.

### Notes

1. Previously printed in part in *LM*, pp. 170–71. The present text differs in several substantives and accidentals and contains a postscript not included in *LM*.
2. Since Macmillan had been publishing James's books in both England and America since *The Bostonians* in 1885, James explains more fully his arrangements with his American publisher than he might have done otherwise. He is also, to be sure, letting Macmillan know that he has received better terms from Houghton, Mifflin, though he still assumes Macmillan will issue the book in England, if an agreement can be reached.
3. In the US the novel was published in two volumes (882 pages) by Houghton, Mifflin and Company on 7 June 1890 (*BHJ*, p. 84). Macmillan published the novel in three volumes on 7 July (*BHJ* proposes June publication – p. 86 – but letter 208 clearly states this day as that of first appearance).
4. *The Lesson of the Master* included six tales, but it did not appear until February 1892 (*BHJ*, p. 88). Since James had been paid for this book in July 1888, he decidedly had the better of the deal. This postscript, by the way, is mistakenly included with the text of letter 203 in *HJL*, iii, 275–6.


## 199

34, De Vere Gardens, W.
March 24*th* 1890[1]

Dear Macmillan

I find your note of today on coming in – having posted you a letter on the subject of it three hours ago.[2]

I will send you the revised copy therein alluded to, by hand tomorrow a.m. – you can then estimate its length. It is complete save for 17 pp. (*Atlantic* pages,) which I haven't yet had the sheets of from Boston, but am daily expecting. I shld. considerably doubt whether the book will come [out] in Boston so *early* as the end of April; that is, the date of their receipt of revised copy over there wld. make this a hurry greater than I shld. suppose H. M. & Co. likely to take. I imagine some time in May more probable. You will judge how long the matter represented by the *332* "Atlantic" pages will take yourselves to produce as a book.[3]

Oh yes, I translated three months ago an unpublished *Tartarin* novel of Daudet's [,] the last, killing the hero off, for the Harpers, who are to produce it as a 6 months serial, (& then as a book,) in their magazine in advance of its issue in France. It begins in the U.S., I think in June – & appears in France only for Xmas. I was bribed with gold – more gold than the translator (as I suppose,) is accustomed to receive.[4] The book is charming.

Yours ever<br>Henry James

**Notes**

1.  Printed in *HJL*, III, 274. The present text differs in several accidentals.
2.  Macmillan's letter of 24 March is not included in LB, MA. Its content may be partially inferred from James's letter.
3.  The *Atlantic* pages refer to the text of *The Tragic Muse* as it appeared in that magazine. Houghton, Mifflin & Company, Boston, did not publish the novel until June. See letter 198, note 3.
4.  For James's translation of Daudet's *Port Tarascon*, see letter 197, note 2. He received $1,700 from Harper for the translation. See Anesko, p. 191.

## 200

March 25th 1890

My dear James,

We shall be very glad to publish "The Tragic Muse" as a 3 vol. novel in England if you will agree to be paid by results, and will accept *two thirds* of whatever profits there may be. In view of the fact that we only have one market, we feel that this is the best offer we can make, & in the event of the book being successful, it will not be a bad one for you.[1]

I am<br>Yours ever,<br>Frederick Macmillan

Henry James Esq
34 De Vere Gardens. W.

**Note**

1.  Though Macmillan is well aware that James will want something 'down', he assuredly remembers that the firm had lost money on large advances on *The Bostonians* and *The Princess Casamassima*. He also knows that the firm has only the English market to depend upon. Whatever his rationale, the effect of this offer to share profits was to revert to an arrangement as to terms similar to that he had proposed to James in the beginning of their business relationship. For James's counter offer, see letter 201.

## 201

34, De Vere Gardens, W.
March 26*th* 1890[1]

My dear Macmillan

I am afraid I can't meet you on the ground of your offer in regard to the publication of "The Tragic Muse" in this country – two thirds profits in the future. That future is practically remote & I am much concerned with the present. What I desire is to obtain a sum of money "down" – & I am loth to perish without a struggle – that is without trying to obtain one. I gather that the terms you mention are an ultimatum excluding, for yourselves, the idea of anything down – which is why I make this declaration of my alternative. But I should be sorry to pursue that alternative without hearing from you again – though I don't flatter myself that I hold the knife at your throat.[2]

Yours ever
Henry James

**Notes**

1. Printed previously in *HJL*, III, 274–5. The present text differs in several accidentals.
2. James is adamant about wanting something 'down', though he realises Macmillan may not change his offer; nevertheless, he presents him a chance to modify his proposal.

## 202

March 26 1890[1]

My dear James,

My reason for putting my proposal for the publication of "The Tragic Muse" in the form contained in my last letter was not any objection on our part to pay promptly, but a desire to guard against loss. I am sorry to say that this caution arises from the fact that the commercial result of the last few books we have published for you has been anything but satisfactory. At the same time we like to be your publishers and are anxious to fall in with your wishes about terms as far as we can prudently do so.

I propose therefore that in order to meet your views as to immediate payment, we should pay you "down" a sum equal to two-thirds of the estimated profits of an edition of 500 copies. I cannot say off hand how much this would come to but it would not be less than £70.[2]

> Believe me
> Yours very truly,
> Frederick Macmillan

Henry James Esq
34 De Vere Gardens S.W.

**Notes**

1. Printed, in part only, in *LM*, p. 171.
2. The advance of £70 is a figure roughly equivalent to the advances Macmillan had paid on the last collections of James's tales: *The Aspern Papers* (1888) and *A London Life* (1889).

## 203

> 34, De Vere Gardens, W.
> March 28*th* 1890[1]

My dear Macmillan.

I thank you for your note & the offer of £70.0.0 Don't, however, think my pretensions monstrous if I say that, in spite of what you tell me of the poor success of my recent books, I still do desire to get a larger sum, & have determined to take what steps I can in this direction. These steps I know will carry me away from you, but it comes over me that that is after all better, even with a due & grateful recognition of the readiness you express to go on with me, unprofitable as I am. I say it is "better" because I had far rather that in these circumstances you should *not* go on with me. I would rather not be published at all than be published & not pay – other people at least. The latter alternative makes me uncomfortable & the former makes me, of the two, feel least like a failure; the failure that, at this time of day, it is too humiliating to consent to be without trying, at least, as they say in America, to "know more about it." Unless I can put the matter on a more remunerative footing all round I shall give up my English "market" – heaven save the market! & confine myself to my American. But I must experiment a bit first – & to experiment is of course to say farewell to you. Farewell then, my dear Macmillan, with great regret – but with the sustaining cheer of all the links in chain that remain still unbroken.[2]

Yours ever<br>
Henry James

### Notes

1. Previously printed in *LM*, pp. 171–2 (in part) and in *HJL*, III, 275–6. The present text differs from *HJL* in accidentals and in *not* including a postscript that according to LB, MA, belongs to letter 198.
2. Despite his farewell note, James did not give up on Macmillan. After all, the firm had most of James's revised copy of the novel and presumably was ready to print proofs for the book. James now turned to Alexander Pollack Watt (1834–1914), a literary agent he had hired in 1888 mainly to deal with the English periodical market, and Watt, realising that the firm was practically committed to the book, negotiated better terms with Macmillan: £250 for the exclusive rights to the novel in England and the dominions for five years and two months, or until 30 June 1895. See James's letters to Watt of 2 April and 9 April (NYPLB) and Macmillan's letter to Watt of 2 April, only five days after James's farewell letter (LB, MA). See also letter 205; receipt for £250 signed by James on 9 May 1890; *LM*, p. 172; and Anesko, p. 130.

## 204

April 29 [1890]

My dear James,

I have received the concluding chapters of "The Tragic Muse" & have forwarded them to the printers. Proofs of the first 96 pages (about a fifth of the whole) go to you today & the remainder will follow quickly.[1]

I am<br>
Yours ever,<br>
Frederick Macmillan

Henry James Esq

### Note

1. Preparations for the publication of the book proceeded rapidly, and the novel was in type early in May (see letter 205).

**205**

May 6 [1890]

My dear James,

"The Tragic Muse" will be all in type by the end of this week. I shall be obliged if you will let us have it back for press as soon as possible. I have sent your Mr. Watt a cheque for the £250.[1]

Yours ever,
Frederick Macmillan

H James Esq
34 De Vere Gardens

**Note**

1. See Macmillan's letter to Watt of this date (LB, MA). Though the work was in the type early in May, it was not published until 7 July, in part at least because of the slowness of the printers (letter 207). For A. P. Watt, see letter 203, note 2; Anesko, pp. 129–30; and *SLHJEG*, p. 51. The cheque for £250 is for English and colonial rights to the novel until 30 June 1895.

**206**

Villino Rubio,
1, Via Palestro.
Florence.
May 29*th* 1890

My dear Macmillan.

I assume that *The Tragic Muse* is now on the point of bursting on (I trust) [a] not altogether indifferent world; & I send you herewith the names of a few persons to whom I shall be glad to have a few copies sent. The list is not long – my lists grow shorter with every book.[1] I am rejoicing in Italy in hot weather & in a simplified life. This truly amiable country has never seemed to me more faithful to its character. I am afraid I am not the least little bit homesick for London – but I expect suddenly to become so about August 1*st*. Kindly instruct that no "notice" of any kind be sent me,[2] & believe me, with salutations in St. John's Wood, yours ever

Henry James

P.S.   I go on Saturday for a fortnight to:
Palazzo Barbaro
Canal Grande
Venice[3]

Notes
1.  The list is not included with James's letter in LB, MA.
2.  James had gradually decided not to read any reviews of his books. For James's decision to divorce himself from the 'circulation and "popularity"' of his books, see also his letter of 23 July 1890 to William James (*HJL*, III, 300).
3.  James often visited his old friends Daniel and Ariana Curtis, American expatriates, at the Barbaro.

## 207

June 17 [1890]

My dear James,

   I have put off acknowledging your letter of the 29*th* May from day to day in the hope that I might be able to say when answering it that "The Tragic Muse" was ready. The printers have been very slow about it and we have not got the book yet but they promise it next week and we shall then publish without further delay. As soon as it is ready we will send presentation copies to the people whose names you give [.][1] I am glad to hear that you are enjoying Italy. We shall look for you early in August & hope that you will come & see us at Weybridge where we shall be then. I am,

Yours ever,
Frederick Macmillan

Henry James Esq

Note

1.  Nevertheless, the book was not published until 7 July, at which time the presentation copies were sent out. See letter 208. James's list of those to receive presentation copies is not in LB, MA.

## 208

July 6 [1890]

My dear James,

   I am afraid you will think we have been a very long time in getting "The Tragic Muse" into her 3 volumes. She is however now ready & will be published tomorrow.[1] Your presentation copies will all be sent out at once.

I presume that you are still in Florence.[2] We go down to Weybridge in ten days from now & shall hope to have the pleasure of seeing you there before we sail for America which event is to occur on Sept 13th.

With kind regards, I am

Yours very truly,<br>Frederick Macmillan

Henry James Esq
Villino Rubio
1 Via Palestro
Florence.

### Notes

1.  *BHJ* incorrectly states that the three-volume English edition was 'published June 1890' (p. 86).
2.  James remained in Italy until mid-August (see letter 209 and note 2).

## 209

Paradisino,<br>Vallombrosa,<br>Pontassieve:<br>Toscana: Italy.<br>July 20th 1890

My dear Macmillan.

My eyes were gratified by the copy of the *Muse* which you sent me to Florence & which made me at last believe in the reality of a great literary event.[1] I feel so far away from all realities (of the practical, professional & commercial order,) in this romantic eyrie, that my hopes & calculations had indeed sunk to a most amiable languor. But may no such detrimental spirit overtake the circulation of the book.

I am lingering on here till the Season – yours – is over, when (some time before the middle of August, certainly,) I hope to be reinstalled in my high-perched London nest.[2] Meanwhile I am more than 3000 feet in the air, & in the most exquisitely beautiful spot I have ever seen in my life: mountains & woods – wonderful views – deep, romantic shade – all hanging in the cool blue Italian air. Below it's furiously hot, but here it's almost too fresh. I am startled by your

American journey – but shall catch you before it begins.[3] Friendliest remembrance meanwhile to your two ladies – & to Mrs. Lewis if she is at hand.

Ever yours<br>
Henry James

### Notes

1. James had considered *The Tragic Muse* as being near publication since May. See letter 206.
2. James returned the 'middle of August' (*HJL*, iii, 303).
3. The Macmillans planned to sail on 13 September. See letter 208.

## 210

Paris,<br>
Hotel Westminster<br>
Rue de la Paix<br>
March 4<i>th</i> '91

My dear Macmillan.

I give this line to my friend W*m* Morton Fullerton, who has asked me to put him in direct relation with you – which I am delighted to do – especially if it turns out that it shall have been a service to both of you. You will know of Mr. Fullerton as holding a highly responsible position in the office of the *Times* – & as the author of the charming article on Cairo in this month's *English Illustrated* – as well as of other things.[1] He will explain to you better than I can do an idea that he has in relation to the paper on Cairo – as the nucleus of a little immediate book – with a Cairene public which, as he has mentioned it to me, strikes me as highly practical & promising.[2] But these are details – I leave you together – & am, dear Macmillan, ever yours

Henry James

### Notes

1. James had known Fullerton (1865–1952), a young American who subsequently represented *The Times* in Paris, for about a year. Fullerton's article on Cairo appeared in the *English Illustrated Magazine*, viii (March 1891), 435–45. For James's continued interest in Fullerton, see letters 287–8.
2. Macmillan also published Fullerton's *In Cairo* in 1891.

## 211

21$^{st}$ Nov 1891

My dear James

I write to acknowledge the receipt of the "copy" for your new volume of stories "The Lesson of the Master etc." As I told you the other day we shall print this in America.[1]

I presume that as it is all from printed matter you will not require to see proofs.[2]

I am
Yours very truly
Frederick Macmillan

Henry James Esq
34 De Vere Gardens W.

### Notes

1.  *The Lesson of the Master* was printed in America and published in New York in February 1892. Sheets from this edition were issued later in the month in London as the first English edition (*BHJ*, pp. 88–9).
2.  For James's response to the query concerning 'proofs', see letter 212.

## 212

34, De Vere Gardens, W.
November 22*d* [1891]

My dear Macmillan

I always greatly deplore not seeing proof – & would almost rather wait, in this case, the extra time that the seeing of it demands than forego it altogether. At any rate, if the book is to be set up in America, which I didn't realise (though I think you mentioned it,) at the moment I sent you the copy. Would you kindly let me have the copy back a couple of days, that I may give it another look to make sure – absolutely – that no errors have been left uncorrected? I shall feel easier – & I will restore it to you as instantly as possible.[1]
Yours ever

Henry James

### Note

1.  Macmillan returned the copy and James read it again. See letters 213 and 214.

## 213

23<sup>rd</sup> Nov 1891

My dear James,

    In compliance with your request I return the copy for the "Lesson of the Master etc," to receive your final corrections.[1]

I am

Yours ever

Frederick Macmillan

Henry James Esqr
34 De Vere Gardens W.

**Note**

1.   Since this collection of tales was to be published in New York and James would not be reading proof (the English edition consisted of sheets of the American issue), he wished to give 'the copy' a final check. See letter 212.

## 214

Dec 1 1891

My dear James,

    The revised "copy" for your new volume of stories will go to New York this week and I shall impress on our people there the importance of having it accurately printed.[1]

I am

Yours ever,

Frederick Macmillan

H James Esq

**Note**

1.   James was nervous about not reading proof of *The Lesson of the Master* (1892). See letter 212.

**215**

> Reform Club,
> Pall Mall. S.W.
> Feb. 29*th* 1892

My dear Macmillan

I ought already to have thanked you for the ½ dozen copies of my book; to which I wish as much success as anything of mine may have. I wish the type had been bigger & the book fatter – but it will do very well. Will you please have the few copies I give addresses for (on an enclosed sheet,) in the U.S. as well as here sent out?[1]

> Yours ever
> Henry James

P.S. Will you kindly order 4 more copies to be sent to *me*?

**Note**

1.  The English edition of *The Lesson of the Master* appeared in late February (*BHJ*, p. 89). Neither James's list nor Macmillan's reply, though Macmillan was unfailingly generous with presentation copies, is included in LB, MA.

**216**

> 34, De Vere Gardens, W.
> April 7*th* 1892

My dear Macmillan.

I committed to Mowbray Morris some time since a tale in 3 parts entitled "Lord Beauprey," of which the 1*st* part appeared in the last *Macmillan*. It would be a comfort to me if you would kindly cause a cheque for the same to be sent me. The 1*st* part is of ten pages; the second will be of eleven; the third will be of twelve – 33 pages in all.[1]

> Yours ever
> Henry James

**Note**

1.  'Lord Beauprey' (later 'Lord Beaupré') appeared in *Macmillan's* LXV (April 1892), 465–74; LXVI (May–June 1892), 64–74, 133–44. Macmillan sent a cheque by return mail. See letter 217. If James was still being paid at the rate of £2.10 per page as stated in letter 167, note 2, he would have received around £80 for this tale.

**217**

April 7 1892

My dear James,

I have much pleasure in sending you a cheque for the story now appearing in "Macmillan's Magazine" [.][1]

I am
Yours very truly
Frederick Macmillan

H James Esq

**Note**

1. This cheque is for 'Lord Beauprey'. See letter 216 and note 1.

**218**

34, De Vere Gardens. W.
September 26*th* 1892

My dear Macmillan.

I have in my hands the material for a volume of short tales – more than enough in fact for one book, which, in the case of short tales, ought to consist, I think, of one volume. I am collecting such of them as will go best together – under the title, probably of the 1*st* of the stories – "The Real Thing." Should you be disposed to publish it, both in England & the United States, on the basis of a "sum down" – on account of royalties? I should like the "sum down" to be, I confess, the most of one that I can arrange for. Will you please let me know what view you would take of it? The stories would make a book of about a 100,000 words – or I could keep it down to eighty thousand if that is preferred – as I must keep some of the things over for another book – they are too numerous for one. The last volume of mine that you published was I think in too small a type; it would be advisable this time to put less on a page.[1]

I hope the country home – & its inmates – is blooming.[2]

Yours ever
Henry James

**Notes**

1.  Macmillan proposed terms in letter 219 that James accepted in letter 220. *The Real Thing and Other Tales* was handled in the same way as the *Lesson of the Master* and was published in New York in March 1893 and in London from American sheets also in March 1893. It included only five tales, one fewer than the earlier collection, and it was sized 7 $^{3}/_{8}$ × 5 inches in comparison with 7 $^{7}/_{16}$ × 5 inches for the 1892 book. See *BHL*, pp. 88–90.
2.  Possibly a reference to a Macmillan home in Weybridge. See letter 208.

# 219

Sept 29 1892

My dear James,

We are willing to give a royalty of 15 per cent on the sale in England & America of your proposed new volume, and to advance £50 on account of royalties. We can further pay you £25 for permission to include the book in our Colonial Library – a sort of Australasian Tauchnitz & we can give another £25 if you will let us deal with 'The Lesson of the Master' in the same way. This would altogether mean a cheque for £100 the very utmost that we can prudently afford.[1]

Mrs. Macmillan and I are coming back to town this day week & I hope we shall see you at Northwick Terrace soon after that day.[2] With kindest regards

I am
Yours ever
Frederick Macmillan

Henry James Esqr

**Notes**

1.  See letters 218, 220 and 221 for other references to these negotiations on *The Real Thing and Other Tales*. During this period, of course, James was concentrating on the drama.
2.  Northwick Terrace is the current Macmillan home 'in town'. James accepts the invitation in letter 220.

**220**

34, De Vere Gardens. W.
October 3*d* 1892

My dear Macmillan.

Please consider that I accept (in reply to your letter of Sept. 29*th*,) the terms you enumerate in relation to my projected volume of tales – viz, the "cheque for £100" – "down" – representing £50 on account of royalties in England [and] in the United States; £25 for the inclusion in the Colonial Library; & £25 for the same application of "The Lesson of the Master." A condition, however, that I am much moved to make is that it be possible for me to see proofs of the book, which will be set up from a considerably revised & corrected copy (of the original magazine sheets,) a circumstance that is apt to engender mistakes. "The Lesson of the Master" was printed in the U.S. – could not "The Real Thing" be printed here? Even if not, I should still like to see proofs. I will send you the copy in the course of this month – it requires a last hand which a press of something else prevents my instantly giving it.[1]

I am very glad to hear of your nearness to town – & shall very soon turn up in Northwick Terrace.[2] Believe me yours ever

Henry James

**Notes**

1. James signed receipts, now in LB, MA, for these sums on 31 December 1892 and 1 January 1893. These terms are written across the top of this letter in another hand and are also stated in letters 219. Macmillan agrees to let him see proof in letter 221.
2. A response to the invitation in letter 219.

**221**

Oct 6 1892

My dear James,

I am afraid that "The Real Thing" will have to be printed in America as the provisions of the Copyright Act demand it; but there is no reason why you should not see proofs, & if you will send me the corrected copy as soon as you have it ready, I will forward it to our people in New York with instructions to send you proofs. I will take care that they use a better type than last time.[1]

Believe me
Yours ever,
Frederick Macmillan

H. James Esq

**Note**

1.  The responses regarding type and proof are to requests made in letters 218 and 220, respectively. The United States Congress had passed legislation on international copyright in 1891.

## 222

Oct 19. 1892

My dear James,

Your letter was forwarded to Crawford who is at Sorrento for the moment, but I heard from him yesterday to the effect that he was going to sail for New York from Genoa on Nov 3rd [.] After that, his address will be care of Blair & Co, 85 Wall Street, New York.[1]

Believe me
Yours ever,
Frederick Macmillan

H James Esq

**Note**

1.  James had known Francis Marion Crawford (1854–1909) for many years, though he did not admire his work. See, for example, his unfavourable remarks to W. D. Howells and R. L. Stevenson on it in *HJL*, iii, 27, 407.

## 223

Oct 25th 1892

My dear James,

I am forwarding the copy for "The Real Thing" to New York with instructions that proofs are to be sent to you and that the type is to be an improvement on that employed for "The Lesson of The Master".[1]

> I am
> Yours very truly
> Frederick Macmillan

Henry James Esq
34 De Vere Gardens W.

**Note**

1. Macmillan is following through on his promises in letter 221.

## 224

Dec 31 1892

My dear James,

As you are going abroad it may be convenient to you to receive before you start a cheque for the small balance due to you in January.[1] With best wishes for the New Year,

> I am, my dear James [,]
> Yours ever,
> Frederick Macmillan

Henry James Esq

**Note**

1. Presumably royalties due on *The Lesson of the Master*, published the previous February.

## 225

Feb 1*st* 1893.

My dear James,

I understand from New York that all the proofs of "The Real Thing" are in your hands. If you will correct and send them in to us, I shall be happy to forward them.[1]

> I am
> Ever yours
> Frederick Macmillan

Henry James Esq
34 De Vere Gardens W.

**Note**

1.   For James's 'wonder-stricken' response – he had returned the last proofs 'about
     a fortnight ago' – see letter 226.

## 226

34, De Vere Gardens. W.
Feb. 1st 1893.

My dear Macmillan

I am wonder-stricken by your news from New York about the
proofs of "The Real Thing" – & asking myself for what you can
possibly take me. What can have *happened* to the proofs?[1] Every one
of them I instantly corrected and sent back to the Printers, J. S.
Cushing & Co, 192 Summer St. Boston, Mass, whose address was
stamped conspicuously on each 1st leaf. The last (the end,) I sent off
about a fortnight ago; all the preceding ones punctually as they
came. The only thing I have here is a bit of revise stamped with a
request that it should *not* be returned. These things were scrupulously & safely done up, stamped & posted – often by my own hand.
I didn't *think* of retransmitting them through Bedford St: the way I
proceeded seemed more direct & expeditious. Surely there must be
some explanation of the mystery – but I am alarmed & distressed. I
understand that the last sheets shouldn't have come back when your
N.Y. correspondent wrote; but the preceding ones – ?[2] Please instruct
him, at any rate, that every *word* of proof that has come to me has
been corrected & returned.

Yours ever
Henry James

**Notes**

1.   See letter 225. Apparently the proofs reached America safely. See letters 228 and
     229.
2.   On occasion, James sent correspondence to the New York branch through the
     Company's Bedford Street office. The 'N.Y. correspondent' was now George P.
     Brett, the son of George E. Brett who had died in 1890.

**227**

Feb 2*nd* 1893

My dear James,

I am afraid I upset you unnecessarily about the proofs of "The Real Thing". They could not have reached America at the time my agent there wrote, but I have no doubt that they are in his hands by this time.[1]

Believe me
Ever yours
Frederick Macmillan

Henry James Esqr
34 De Vere Gardens W.

**Note**

1. Since James refers to '(the revise of) the whole book' in letter 229, the corrected proofs apparently arrived safely in New York. The 'agent' is George P. Brett. See letter 226, note 2.

**228**

Feb 15*th* 1893

My dear James

We have received this morning a revise of the last pages of "The Real Thing" from our American printers, and are forwarding them to you. If you will kindly correct and return them to us we will send them out to Boston.[1]

I am
Yours ever,
Frederick Macmillan

Henry James Esqr
34 De Vere Gardens W.

**Note**

1. Macmillan was still seeking to get James to return proof to the London office so that it could be forwarded to America. Though the book was published in New York, it was printed in Boston by Norwood Press (*BHJ*, p. 89).

## 229

34, De Vere Gardens. W.
February 17*th* 1893

My dear Macmillan

Of all the revise that I have received (of "The Real Thing,") there has been nothing except *one* error, in a page sent the other day, to correct. That makes only one in (the revise of) the whole book. I send it to you herewith, as you offer to transmit; & I add to it two other pages on which there is a word, apiece, that since opportunity offers, I should like altered. To these I add five or six other pages on which the proofreaders have made inopportune queries – to show that their queries are wrong. But in sending me the beginning of the revise they accompanied it with a remark to the effect that all that was remarked "T" (or perhaps it is meant for "F") was *not* to be returned to them. I therefore haven't returned it & have taken for granted that they haven't waited for it. (*All* the revise has been so marked.) Will you at any rate please cause them to be instructed that they may now print – on repairing the error on p. 233, which I enclose & altering, if it is not too late, the two other words. If it is late they don't particularly matter. The thing is all right.[1] Yours ever

Henry James

**Note**

1.  *The Real Thing and Other Tales* appeared in New York in March and in London later in the same month (*BHJ*, pp. 90–91).

## 230

Feb. 21 1896[1]

My dear James,

I understand from my neighbour Heinemann that he is going to publish a novel of yours & that you have left it to him to arrange for its publication in America. I write to ask whether you will allow him to offer it to us. Mr Brett our American partner who is in England just now is very anxious to publish for you & undertake to give at least as good terms as anybody else [.][2]

Believe me
Yours very truly,
Frederick Macmillan

Henry James Esq
34 De Vere Gardens

**Note**

1.  The three-year hiatus in the correspondence may be explained, in part, by James's efforts to seek elsewhere for better terms for his work and by his concentration on the drama during this period. Consequently, from 1893 to 1900 Harper and Brothers published seven titles in New York; Osgood, McIlvaine & Co., four in London (his old friend and debtor, James R. Osgood, had established an English firm and momentarily offered him higher royalties); Herbert S. Stone & Co., two in Chicago and New York; Houghton Mifflin and Company, one in Boston; Duckworth & Co. and Methuen & Co., one each in London; and William Heinemann, another old friend, seven in London. This letter renewed James's relationship with the firm, resulting in this period in the issue of four books in New York.
2.  James's novel, *The Awkward Age*, was being handled by Harper in America (see letter 231), but he and George P. Brett agreed that the firm should bring out the American issue of *The Other House* and a collection of tales entitled *Embarrassments*. For negotiations on terms for these volumes, see letters 231 ff.

## 231

34, De Vere Gardens. W.
February 24*th* 1896.

My dear Macmillan

Thanks for your inquiry of the 21*st*. I am afraid you mistook Heinemann's meaning – or that he misremembered the circumstance, or was unaware of it – in regard to the question of the novel in the U.S. *That* particular novel – one with regard to which I have for some time had an agreement with him on the basis of it coming out *straight* – as a book, without being serialised – *is* arranged for in America: the Harpers are to publish it.[1] But I have since had an understanding with him (within the last few days) about two other books, short novels (65,000 to 80,000 words,) which are to be serialised first – during a period ending next October. I should be very glad if you will take charge of one of these in the U.S. The one you take had, I judge, better be the one appearing in an American periodical – beginning in the April *Atlantic* & entitled "The Old Things." I will write to [you] more on the subject – a short time hence, in time for you to make all arrangements.[2] Believe me yours ever

Henry James

**Notes**

1.  The novel was *The Awkward Age*, a book whose publication was delayed until April 1899 and that was, despite James's present understanding, eventually serialised in *Harper's Weekly*, XLII (1 October 1898), 966–7 to XLIII (7 January 1899), 13–18.

2.    The two 'short novels' were 'The Old Things' (later called *The Spoils of Poynton*) and 'The Other House', but since the *Atlantic* was publishing the former, Houghton, Mifflin brought it out in book form in America in 1897. Macmillan, consequently, published 'The Other House' in New York in October 1896, after its serialisation in the *Illustrated London News*, CIX (4 July 1896), 9–11 to CIX (26 September 1896), 395–98.

## 232

34, De Vere Gardens, W.<br>April 14th 1896.[1]

Dear Mr. Brett.

The *Illustrated London News* is to publish from July 4*th* next to the end of September a shortish novel of mine – 65000 words in 13 weekly instalments of 5000 words each. As a volume, the book will be published in the autumn, here, by Heinemann.[2] I shall be glad to arrange with you to publish it in the United States; & what I am now particularly writing to you about is to ask if you can, as a preliminary to that, do anything in the way of placing there the *American serial rights*. These I have retained & should like not to sacrifice. They would be only valuable of course to a weekly periodical. I have offered them to Harper & Bros. who, however, tell me that the offer comes too late for their two or three organs – at the right dates. They offered them to the *Evening Post* (weekly edition) & have just cabled me that the Post cannot use them. Does any other possibility present itself to you? If it should, I am willing – perfectly – to leave the matter to your discretion. As regards terms it occurs to me that – if I am late in the field for July–September, I had better leave you a certain margin. The *Illustrated L.N.* gives me £300 for the English serial rights. The American ought, in good conditions, not to be worth less – I surmise. But if I am at a definite disadvantage in not giving longer notice, that should perhaps be considered. I don't think I ought to accept less, at any rate, than £250.[3] I shall send this to Messrs. Macmillan to forward to you;[4] & am yours very truly

Henry James

**Notes**

1.    The present text is based upon a photocopy of the manuscript at NYPL.
2.    'The Other House' appeared in the *Illustrated London News*, CIX (4 July to 26 September 1896), 9–12 to 395–8. William Heinemann published the book in London on 1 October 1896 and Macmillan in New York later in the month (*BHJ*, pp. 106–7).

3.   Brett could not find an American periodical for the novel. See letter 235 and *BHJ*, p. 107.
4.   James, on occasion, sent letters and messages to the New York branch through the London office.

## 233

Apr 15*th* 1896

My dear James,

   I am forwarding your letter to Mr. Brett by today's post and hope that he may be able to place your story with an American paper.[1]

I am
Yours ever,
Frederick Macmillan

Henry James Esq
34 De Vere Gardens W.

**Note**

1.   See letter 232. The reference is to 'The Other House', which Brett subsequently failed to 'place' with an American periodical.

## 234

20th April 1896.

My dear James,

   Mr. Heinemann tells me that the volume of short stories which he is to publish here & which our people are to publish in America is now ready for press, and he reminds me that no actual agreement has been made between you and ourselves as to the American publication. I write therefore to suggest that we should give you a royalty of 15 per cent on the retail price of all copies sold, and to make a payment of Fifty Pounds (£50) on publication in anticipation of the said royalty. If this will be satisfactory I will have an agreement sent to you for signature.[1]

Believe me
Yours ever
Frederick Macmillan

Henry James Esqr
34 De Vere Gardens. W.

**Note**

1.   James accepted these terms for *Embarrassments*, and the collection appeared under the imprint of Heinemann in London and of Macmillan in New York. See letter 235, note 2.

## 235

34, De Vere Gardens, W.<br>
May 30<i>th</i> 1896.<sup>1</sup></div>

Dear Mr. Brett.

I promised Heinemann yesterday that I would write you a word expressive of the urgency of our desire that there should be as little delay as possible in the publication of *Embarrassments* in the U.S. The book is all ready here, & only waiting, to appear, for that event. Will you kindly see that it takes place at your earliest convenience? The things I am publishing later – in the year, make all the interval I can get advisable.<sup>2</sup>

'I take for granted from hearing nothing more from you that you have been unable to do anything at all with the American rights of my serial – the thing ("The Other House") appearing here (beginning in July) in the *Illust: London News*. I am much obliged to you for trying – but I had, in truth, very slender hopes, & must make the best of the failure. I am sending you as soon as I can get them from the office of the paper the sheets (galleys) of the first instalment – to copyright in the U.S. They will go to you next week.<sup>3</sup> Believe me yours very truly

Henry James

**Notes**

1.   The present text is based upon a photocopy of the manuscript at NYPL.
2.   *Embarrassments* appeared in London on 12 June and in New York later in the month (*BHJ*, pp. 103–5).
3.   Brett was not able to sell the serial to an American journal, but he copyrighted it and published it in book form. See letters 232, note 2, and 236. The galleys of the 'first instalment' refer to the novel as it appeared in the *Illustrated London News*.

## 236

July 15. 1896.

My dear James,

Mr. Brett writes to say that he hears from you that the serial publication of "The Other House" which he has been copyrighting for you, comes to an end in September, but he does not seem clear as to whether he is to publish it. I presume therefore that no terms have been arranged between you & him. Is this so? & if so can I make terms with you on Mr. Brett's behalf & what do you ask? Would the arrangement which was made for "Embarrassments" do?[1]

I hope you are enjoying your Sussex retreat. We have been panting in town until now, but go to Temple Dinsley tomorrow.[2] In the autumn (October) my wife intends to carry out a project for a visit to her mother land to see her mother & sister. We all think it very enterprising of her.

Believe me
Yours ever,
Frederick Macmillan

Henry James Esq

### Notes

1. See letters 231–2, 235, 237–41 for negotiations on *The Other House*.
2. James had rented a house on Point Hill, Playden, near Rye, earlier in the summer. See letter 237. The Macmillans had acquired a country retreat at Temple Dinsley.

## 237

Point Hill
Playden. Rye.
July 16*th* 1896.

Mr dear Macmillan.

I just have your letter of inquiry about the publication in the U.S. of *The Other House*. I applied to Mr. Brett about the copyright over there fully, of course, on the ground of desiring that you shld. issue the book in America & I shall be very glad that you shall do so. But I am not clear at this moment as to what I shld. say to you about terms – beyond the fact that I shld. wish them to be the same as those on which the book is published in London. It is here to be published by Heinemann – the details of my arrangement with whom I have forgotten: only remembering that it is not the same as for "Embarrassments". I was to have for that volume 15 per cent. & £50 on acct. My sum *on account*, from him, for the *Other House* is to be larger – I *think* £150, but I am not certain, & I have nothing, in this cottage, to refer to; so I will write & ask him; & then let you know. "Embarrass-ments" appears to have been out some time in New York – but does the sum "down" for that work proceed from Fifth Avenue or from Bedford St?[1]

I am an absentee for the autumn – having just rivetted another stake into the grass by taking – from the end of this month, when I have to give up this happy perch, the Vicarage at *Rye* for the rest of the summer. I hope Temple Dinsley is not far off for you & am yours ever.[2]

Henry James

**Notes**

1. For agreement on terms for *The Other House*, see letters 239–41. Macmillan encloses a cheque for the sum 'down' on *Embarrassments* in letter 238.
2. James moved to the Vicarage on 1 August and stayed until the end of September. See James's letters to Gosse of 8, 25 July and 28 August 1896 in *SLHJEG*, pp. 144, 145, 147. Macmillan had mentioned Temple Dinsley in Letter 236.

## 238

July 20 1896

My dear James,

I am obliged to you for your note and shall expect to hear from you in a day or two as to the terms for "The Other House." In the meantime I am enclosing a cheque for fifty pounds (£50) on account of the American royalty on "Embarrassments" as arranged.[1]

I am,<br>Yours very truly<br>Frederick Macmillan

Henry James Esq
Point Hill
Playden
Rye

**Note**

1. See letter 237. Since the advance for *Embarrassments*, according to the terms agreed upon by author and publisher, was to be paid 'on publication' (letter 234), it is possible that the volume appeared later than June, the general date given in *BHJ* (p. 105).

**239**

> Point Hill,
> Playden, Sussex.
> July 21st 1896.

My dear Macmillan.

Many thanks for your cheque, this morning received, for £50 in payment of advance on royalties on *Embarrassments*. I hear from Heinemann as to the terms on which *The Other House* is to be published in this country by them; viz: a royalty of 15 per cent. & an advance thereon, on publication, of £150. If this suits you for the American issue,[1] please let me know & oblige yours ever

> Henry James

Frederick Macmillan, Esq.

**Note**

1. For Brett's modification of these terms as reported by Macmillan and for James's acceptance of the proposal, see letters 240–41.

**240**

> 23 July 1896

My dear James,

In receipt of your last letter I telegraphed to Mr. Brett and have this morning received a reply from him to say that he will be glad to publish "The Other House" on a 15% royalty but that one hundred pounds (£100) is the utmost he is prepared to advance on account of such royalty. Perhaps you will consider the matter and let me know whether you are willing to accept these terms.[1]

> I am
> Yours ever
> Frederick Macmillan

Henry James Esq
Point Hill
Playden
Sussex.

**Note**

1.   Though James accepted the terms, such modifications by Brett in this instance
     and others eventually led James to deal with him infrequently after 1900. More-
     over, Brett occasionally failed to pay promptly (see letters 244 and 245), in part,
     possibly, because of a failure of co-ordination between Brett and the London
     office. At any rate, James held Brett responsible. See his letter of 22 February 1900
     to James B. Pinker, his literary agent, where he notes that the *Soft Side* 'will
     terminate, in all probability, my relations with [Brett] (for the future) . . . ' (Yale).

## 241

Point Hill
Playden [,] Sussex.
July 24*th* 1896.

My dear Macmillan

I have your letter of yesterday about the terms, in New York, for
*The Other House.* Let us say 15 per cent., then, and *One Hundred
Pounds* on account.[1] I assent to those conditions & am yours ever.

Henry James

Fredk. Macmillan Esq.

**Note**

1.   See letters 239–40.

## 242

34, De Vere Gardens. W.
September 17*th* : 1896[1]

Messrs. Macmillan & Co., [New York]
Dear Sirs.

I am much obliged to you for your remittances of cuttings from
the American newspapers on the subject of *Embarrassments* – but
reproach myself with not having originally mentioned to you that I
would not trouble you to send me any reviews – as I have for a long
time made a point of making – with my books – this request.[2] Kindly,
when *The Other House* is published, neglect, as far as I am concerned,
the reviews. I mean, please *don't* forward them. I am assuming that

Mr. Heinemann will have notified you of the date of issue in London.[3] Be so good as to send a copy of the book to the few addresses I enclose on a separate sheet[4] & oblige yours very truly

Henry James

### Notes

1. The present text is based upon a photocopy of the original in NYPL.
2. James maintained such views about cuttings of reviews throughout much of his career. See, for example, letter 318.
3. The book came out in London on 1 October 1896 (*BHJ*, p. 106).
4. The list is not included with the letter in NYPL.

## 243

Nov 25 1896

My dear James,

The enclosed came in an envelope from our New York house without a word of comment. I presume that it is intended to be forwarded to you.[1]

I am
Yours ever,
Frederick Macmillan

H James Esq

### Note

1. The enclosure is no longer included with the letter in LB, MA.

## 244

34, De Vere Gardens. W.
Jan: 24*th* 1897.

My dear Macmillan.

Has there not been some long oblivion in regard to the matter (the £100, for *The Other House*, "down," on publication,) mentioned in your letter to me of 23*d* July last, which, for greater clearness, I enclose? I replied to it, immediately, that I accepted the arrangement on the basis of the said 15% & the £100 in advance on royalties – & you then either rejoined by a confirmatory word (which, in that case, I seem to have mislaid,) or simply accepted my letter as settling the matter.[1] But the sum in question has never arrived; & I *forget* now whether I did get a further line from you & lost it or simply regarded the agreement as complete. I supposed it was, at any rate, when the book was published & my letter to that effect is probably among your records. Hasn't there therefore been a neglect, since early in October, of sending me the cheque?[2] Believe me yours ever

Henry James

### Notes

1. See letters 240 (23 July 1896) and 241 (24 July 1896).
2. *The Other House* appeared in New York about 17 October (*BHJ*, p. 107). Macmillan apologised and sent a cheque the next day (letter 245).


## 245

Jan 25 1897

My dear James,

I must apologise for not having sent you the money due by our New York house on the publication of your last novel. I enclose a cheque herewith and remain[1]

Yours very sincerely
Frederick Macmillan

Henry James Esq
34 De Vere Gardens, W.

### Notes

1. The cheque is for £100, the advance on *The Other House*. See letter 244.


## 246

(Dictated)                                   34, De Vere Gardens, W.
1st March, 1897.[1]

Dear Mr. Brett,

I am glad to learn, by your letter of the 19th, that there is a prospect of seeing you in London this month; when I shall be better able to give you an idea of how the case stands with me in respect to the possibilities you mention. Please let me know when you do arrive; in expectation of which – as it is near at hand – I won't attempt now to say more than that my "plans of publication" are always, in their very essence, the most contingent and precarious things in the world and wholly dependent on my surmounting that element of delay and difficulty which, I fear, is the only constant one in my work.[2] I have, I may add, a couple of old pledges out – still to be redeemed – over the top of which I don't as yet pretend distinctly to see.[3] I expect to go abroad about April 10th – which means, however, that I shall be in London the whole of the time that you are. I am glad to hear news not wholly disastrous of "The Other House."[4] It just occurs to me that this may, after all, not quite catch you; but I launch it without further delay, and am,

Yours very truly,<br>
Henry James

### Notes

1. TLS. The present text is based upon a photocopy of the manuscript at NYPL.
2. Brett's letter of 19 February is not available, but it is clear that he seeks more of James's work to publish; and one may infer that the two discussed James's fiction not then committed (see letter 248). James's comments on the contingency and precariousness of his 'plans of publication' suggest a basis for the hiring of a literary agent a year later.
3. The 'old pledges' presumably refer to *What Maisie Knew* and *The Awkward Age*. See also letter 248, note 2.
4. Brett had printed 2150 copies of the novel – a larger initial run than usual – but the sale led to no further printings in America. See *BHJ*, pp. 106–7.

## 247

Mar 23 1897

My dear James,

I have promised Mr Brett who is in England just now to enquire whether you had any novel in contemplation that you would be willing to put in [his] hands for the United States. I think you will find him able to make you at least as good an offer as any other American publisher.[1]

I am, Yours very truly [,]<br>
Frederick Macmillan

Henry James Esq
34 De Vere Gardens W.

**Note**

1.  It should be noted that Brett, though perfectly capable himself of approaching James and of making terms with him (letter 246), still seeks aid from Macmillan when James seems diffident, one supposes, because of the twenty-year friend-ship between publisher and author, even though James had not published with the London house since 1893.

## 248

Dictated.                                    34, De Vere Gardens. W.
                                             24th March, 1897.[1]

My dear Macmillan,

   I wrote Mr. Brett last month a note, in answer to one of his own, which I am afraid he will have left New York before receiving. Will you please say to him that I then told him that arrangements already exist for the next two books – as regards the u.s. [*sic*] – that I am more or less on my way to publish; one of these arrangements, already a couple of years old, and the other forming a part of that of the serial publication of a short novel now running. Therefore I am afraid I can't yet speak definitely of anything beyond – especially as the more important of the two books just mentioned (the old arrange-ment with the Harpers, – for a novel *not* to be serialised) looms too large for me to see, for some time to come, over the head of it.[2] But I should like to talk with Mr. Brett – as I told him in my letter; and will immediately communicate with him to this effect – so that he will perhaps be able to come to see me.[3]

   Believe me yours ever,

                                             Henry James

**Notes**

1.  TLS. In the summer of 1896 James had fallen behind with the instalments of 'The Other House', had injured his hand and arm in trying to meet deadlines, and after the turn of the year frequently dictated his letters to a typist. See *HJL*, IV, 41–8, 50–6.
2.  For James's 'note' to Brett, see letter 246. The 'next two books' are apparently *What Masie Knew* and *The Awkward Age* (the novel for Harper), though the latter did not appear in America until 12 May 1899 (*BHJ*, p. 116).
3.  Though James's next title with the New York branch, *The Two Magics*, did not appear until October 1898, it is likely that he met with Brett at this time and discussed plans for future books with him.

**249**

34, De Vere Gardens, W.
22nd December, 1897.[1]

Dear Mr. Brett.

I should have thanked you before this – and my only excuse for my delay is "pressure" – for the very pretty little copyrighting volume, which duly and safely reached me. This small fiction will form, in due course, part of a volume (though *not* be the first thing in it) which I shall be glad to see you publish when the rest of the material, I mean four or five other short tales, shall have accumulated. They will probably do so rather rapidly.[2]

Meanwhile the other matter I wrote you about has taken more definite shape. The tale I then alluded to, and which is too long to participate in such a collection as I just mentioned, appears serially in *Collier's Weekly* from some time about the beginning of the year and will be run, in shortish instalments, for about ten weeks. This is the publication – "The Turn of the Screw" – that I more particularly alluded to. My idea has been that I should like, for the book form, to make it only half a volume, accompanying it with another story of the same length and of a rather distinctly different type. It is possible, however, that that course may be something of a waste of opportunity – with things long enough each to stand on its own feet. This reflection I have made in the light of the *Collier* people appearing to think the little work in question – for *their* purposes at any rate – much of a hit. At all events I had probably better let the question I here refer to stand over till the story has run something of its course: then I shall be able – from the impression it makes on me printed – more effectually to pronounce one way or the other; that is for a couple of longish things together or of shortish things apart. The *T. of the S.* is, as I think I mentioned, of about 40,000 words; which wouldn't, I suppose, be inadequate for a little volume if the other omens were propitious.[3] I hope the early part of the year is again bringing you over, and am yours very truly,

Henry James

George P. Brett, Esq.

**Notes**

1. TLS. The present text is based upon a photocopy of the original at NYPL.
2. The 'pretty little copyrighting volume' is *John Delavoy*, a tale Brett had brought out for James in a pre-publication copyright edition in November (*BHJ*, p. 111). The volume of tales alluded to eventually became *The Soft Side* (1990).

3.   'The Turn of the Screw' appeared in *Collier's Weekly*, xx (27 January 1898) to xxi
     (16 April 1898) and was published as part of *The Two Magics* the following
     October by Heinemann in London and Macmillan in New York (*BHJ*, pp.
     113–14).

## 250
(Copy)                                                             Jan. 4, 1898[1]
Dear Mr. James:-

I am glad the little volume prepared for copyright purposes reached
you safely and that you are pleased with its general appearance. I am
holding the type standing in the expectation that we may be able to
arrange with you for the publication of the volume containing it as
you very kindly suggest may be possible.[2]

I am very much interested in what you say in regard to the story
entitled "The Turn of the Screw" and I hope that you will send me
promptly the proofs which you kindly promise. I could then give
you, I feel sure, a much better judgement as to the possibility of the
publication by itself. At first sight, I must say, that I am rather
against the inclusion of two stories of about equal length in a single
volume, but my opinion would only be worth something if formed
on reading the story itself to which I am looking forward with a
good deal of interest.[3]

I hope to do myself the pleasure of calling on you in the early part
of March next.[4]

Yours very truly,
George P. Brett

Henry James, Esq.

### Notes

1.   Typed letter ('copy') for George P. Brett's signature, unsigned, NYPL. The present
     text is based upon a photocopy of this typescript.
2.   See letter 249. 'John Delavoy' eventually was collected in *The Soft Side* (1990).
3.   Despite Brett's initial disinclination, 'The Turn of the Screw' joined 'Covering
     End' in *Two Magics* in October 1898.
4.   Brett frequently came to London on business in February or March. See letters
     230 and 247, for example. Brett and James may well have met during Brett's visit
     to England and discussed plans for publishing 'The Turn of the Screw' and the
     volume of tales subsequently called *The Soft Side*.

**251**

Lamb House, Rye.
20th September, 1898[1]

Dear Mr. Brett,

I have suffered myself to be prevented by complications, for too many days past, from letting you know with what dismay and regret I some short time since heard from Mr. Heinemann that a delay in your issue of *The Two Magics* was unavoidable by reason of your not having, all this time, received copy for the same. The non-despatch of copy to you still stupefies me in so far as it may have been a result of some monstrous oblivion of my own: or rather not so much oblivion as absolute taking for granted that as a matter of course you had long since been provided. It was my earnest intention that you should be and I fully supposed I had made, to this effect, a definite request of Mr. Heinemann. On the other hand I have no document to prove it, and am obliged to fall back more or less on my constitutional superficiality, as I fear I must call it, in matters of rigid business. In short I never dreamed but that the English sheets of the book were long ago in your hands, and I am very sorry you are having to do the thing in anything of a hurry. If you had only been so good as to send me a word of reproach, my eyes would have been opened to the omission, and I would, on the spot, with my own hand, have hustled you off the material.[2] Please now, as the case stands, take your comfort with the matter – a little novel of mine having lately come out. I shall be very sure, on any future occasion, myself to transmit you copy, and I am, with renewed regrets, yours very truly,

Henry James

**Notes**

1. TLS. The present text is based upon a photocopy of the original in NYPL.
2. The fact that Brett failed to receive corrected proof for the American edition of *Two Magics* puzzled both James and Sydney S. Pawling, of Wm. Heinemann, Publisher. Apparently Brett should have received James's corrected copy for *Collier's* from the magazine, but, for some unexplained reason, neither received it nor reported not getting it. The result was a delay of slightly over a month. Heinemann had originally wanted to publish on 30 August, but waited until 5 October (letter to Brett, 9 August 1898, NYPL; *BHJ*, p. 113) so that Brett could copyright his issue on 30 September. See Pawling's letters to Brett of 3, 6, and 24 September (NYPL) for discussion and resolution of this matter.

**252**

> Le Plantier
> Costebelle [,] Hyéres [*sic*].
> March 29*th* 1899[1]

Dear Mr. Brett.

Your letter reaches me here after delays caused by my having for a week past been in movement & practically without an address. I am spending a few days with some friends in the South of France on my way to put in a month or two in Italy.[2] I am very sorry to miss your visit to England by reason of these things (it's the 1*st* time for 5 years that I have quitted those shores,) & also that of Mr. Lewis Gates, whom I should have been very glad to see. I am practically living in the country, for the most part, at present – where *Lamb House, Rye* is an address that always finds & quickly (if I be absent) follows, me;[3] &, were I not at this distance I should have proposed to you both, to come down there for 24 hours. There are one or two matters I shld. have liked to talk to you about & I am particularly sorry to lose the opportunity to ask you to have patience with me in regard to the vol. of short tales for which (the contents of which,) I made some time ago a beginning. I have now more material & I shall before very long have enough, but it accumulates only piece by piece. I shall let you know as soon as the *book* properly results.[4] I hope you are enjoying your London weeks & that they are doing you all sorts of good. Believe me yours very truly

> Henry James

**Notes**

1. The present text is based upon a photocopy of the manuscript at NYPL.
2. James was visiting his old friends, Paul and Minnie Bourget, on the way to Italy (*HJL*, IV, 100–2).
3. James had leased Lamb House in 1897 and moved there the following year.
4. Brett, on his annual business trip to England, had proposed a meeting with James to discuss his work and plans, particularly his progress on the volume of tales they had been discussing for two years, a collection eventually published in 1900 as *The Soft Side*. Lewis E. Gates (1860–1924), a member of the faculty at Harvard to whom Frank Norris had just dedicated *McTeague* (1899) and the author of a Macmillan book entitled *Three Studies in Literature* (1899), had been suggested by Brett as another guest.

**253**

Lamb House, Rye.
August 15*th* 1899.[1]

Dear Sirs.

I am much obliged to you for your account of the sales of *The Two Magics* & for your cheque for £28.18.1 just received.[2] Believe me yours very truly

Henry James

The Macmillan Company, [New York]

P.S. Please note the present as my most regular & constant address.[3]

**Notes**

1. The present text is based upon a photocopy of the manuscript at NYPL.
2. Though James B. Pinker had been James's literary agent for over a year, the New York firm still sent James sales accounts and cheques for some of his work. Negotiations for *Two Magics*, however, had begun before Pinker was hired.
3. James had moved to Lamb House in 1898.

**254**

W.B.                                                                        Nov. 3rd. 1899.[1]
Henry James Esq.
Rye, Sussex.

My dear James,

We are very anxious if possible to obtain the publication of Professor William James's Gifford Lectures both in England and in the United States. We had some correspondence with him about it more than a year ago but as at that time the lectures were unwritten he was unwilling to consider any proposals. I should like to attack him again on the subject, unless, as I fear may be the case from what you said when you were last in town, he is too ill either to deliver the lectures or to attend to other business. Will you kindly let me know how this may be, and if you think I might write to him, in which case will you kindly give me his address?[2]

I am, Yours sincerely,
Frederick Macmillan

Notes

1.  TLS. The typist's initials cannot be identified.
2.  Despite Macmillan's efforts, William James's Gifford Lectures, University of Edinburgh, 1901–2, were eventually published by Longmans, Green & Co. in both London and New York as *The Varieties of Religious Experience* (1902).

## 255

Lamb House, Rye.
January 23d 1900[1]

Dear Mr. Brett.

I have accidentally delayed to write to you till, I imagine you will have heard, already, from Mr. J. B. Pinker, who now is looking after my "literary business" for me, to my own great saving of time & worry.[2] I asked him, very lately, to communicate with you on the subject of the volume of Tales which I a year or two ago mentioned to you that I should eventually have at your disposition, & one of the intended component features of which – a story called *John Delavoy* – you may remember, that you copyrighted for me in the U.S. at the time it appeared in "Cosmopolis."[3] The material for this volume has, for good reasons, never properly accumulated till now – but now I have got it together, & Methuen is to publish it here. I enclose a contents-list of it. It will make *about* 80,000 words. There are some ten stories, & I think it best simply to call the book by the name of the first – "The Great Good Place."[4] I shall be very glad if you can arrange for a simultaneous issue of it in N.Y. with Mr. Pinker. It is important it should come out this spring. I should propose to make "John Delavoy" the last tale but one – or quite the last, if the book shld. have to be shortened by the omission of one (in which case I should omit *The Third Person*.) There is perhaps rather too much than too little material – as the table of contents I send you stands. I hope you are coming as usual this spring – though, alas, I am not, this year, in town. I am not, probably, however, to be, as I was last April, abroad – only down here. I hope I may have the pleasure of seeing you, & am yours most truly

Henry James

George P. Brett, Esq.

Notes

1.  The present text is based upon a photocopy of the manuscript at NYPL.
2.  Pinker had written Brett on 5 January that James's 'new book of short stories' was 'ready' and proposed terms for the American book rights: 'a royalty of 15 per cent. on the first 2000; 20 per cent. after, with £150 on account' (NYPL). For further discussion of terms see letters 256–8.
3.  See letter 249, note 2. 'John Delavoy' also appeared in *Cosmopolis*, IX (January–February 1898), 1–21, 317–32.
4.  The list contains the following tales: 'The Great Good Place', 'Europe', 'Paste', 'The Real Right Thing', 'The Great Condition', 'The Abasement of the Northmores', 'The Tree of Knowledge', 'The Given Case', 'John Delavoy', and 'The Third Person'. Two more stories were later added: 'Maud-Evelyn' and 'Miss Gunton of Poughkeepsie'.

## 256

Lamb House, Rye.
February 26*th* 1900[1]

Dear Mr. Brett.

In answer to your letter of February 6*th* touching the question of a vol. of Tales of mine ("The Great Good Place" &c,) I beg to say that Mr. Pinker is writing to you by this post, at my request, to meet you in the matter by arranging with you for the book on the same terms as those on which you published *The Two Magics* &c. Kindly therefore consider that as settled.[2] It was my wish that it should have been so settled from the first – but I accidentally failed to make this entirely clear to him, & he proposed the same terms for which the book has been disposed of in London. He now however writes to you in the sense of the present,[3] & I am, with regret for delay thus caused, yours very truly

Henry James

Mr. George P. Brett.

Notes

1.  The present text is based upon a photocopy of the manuscript at NYPL.
2.  Brett's letter of 6 February is not available, but the volume mentioned eventually became *The Soft Side* (1900). The terms suggested are not those mentioned in Pinker's letter of 5 January (see letter 255, note 2), but a modification of them (see note 3, below). Part of the confusion and misunderstanding was based upon the difference between terms for a novel and for a book of tales. Brett's changes led James to write Pinker on 22 February that this volume 'will terminate, in all

probability, my relations with him (for the future) . . . ' (Yale). James did not completely 'terminate' business with Brett, but his future books with Macmillan were published in London.

3.    The collection was published in London by Methuen. The terms of publication are described in Pinker's letter to Brett of 26 February (NYPL): 'that you [Brett] agree to pay him [James] the sum of Fifty pounds (£50) in advance & on account of a royalty of 15% on the first 1,000 copies of the book sold, & 20% on all copies over and above that number, – that is to say on the same terms as for his previous volume "The Two Magics".'

## 257

The Reform Club
March 23, 1900.[1]

Dear Mr. Brett.

I return you the agreement for "The Great Good Place" &c, (or whatever it may be finally determined to call the vol. of Tales,) duly signed – keeping the other of the two you sent me.[2] Mr. Pinker will let you know about the designed time of publication here – I haven't yet receive any proof from Methuen & Co. – who desire, I think, to keep back the book till this cruel war is over.[3]

Believe me yours very truly

Henry James

### Notes

1.    The present text is based upon a photocopy of the manuscript in NYPL.
2.    For terms of the agreement, see letter 256, note 3.
3.    The collection was eventually titled *The Soft Side* and was published by Methuen in London on 30 August 1900 and by Macmillan in New York late in September (*BHJ*, pp. 116–18). The 'cruel war', the Boer War, was over in 1902.

## 258

Lamb House, Rye.
March 29*th* 1900.[1]

Dear Mr. Brett.

I received only to-day here your letter of the 24*th* – having left town before it arrived at its address, & I am afraid you will on your side have left London before this reaches you. I am much obliged to you for the cheque for £50, payable down, by our agreement, in advance on royalties for the volume of "The Great Good Place." I send the contract that I have signed back to you, as you request – & think it better to address these things only to St. Martin's St. to be forwarded.[2] I am sorry to have inconvenienced you by delay.

Believe me yours very truly

Henry James

George P. Brett, esq.

### Notes

1.  The present text is based upon a photocopy of the manuscript at NYPL.
2.  The terms for 'The Great Good Place' (*The Soft Side*) are described in Pinker's letter to Brett referred to in letter 256, note 3. Brett had been in London on his annual business trip and sent James the advance there on the collection of tales.

## 259

Lamb House, Rye.
June 28*th* 1900.[1]

Dear Sirs.

I beg to say in answer to your letter of June 18*th* in relation to *The Soft Side* that a complete set of sheets will probably have been posted to-day to you direct from London. If they *haven't* gone to-day, they will unfailingly go by the next post, & I will then write you more fully. I send this off only in time to catch the mail; & I enclose a list of contents, complete. The London volume will make but a few pages less than *400*.

Believe me yours very truly

Henry James

The Macmillan Company
New York.
P.S.   I find I haven't a copy of of [*sic*] the set-up contents; but I write the list on another sheet.[2]

### Notes

1.  The present text is based upon a photocopy of the manuscript at NYPL.
2.  This list is included with the letter and contains all twelve stories in the volume in both English and American editions, though James inadvertently reversed the order of 'The Third Person' and 'Maud-Evelyn'. See *BHL*, pp. 116–18. See also letter 255, note 4.

## 260

> Lamb House, Rye.
> July 6*th* 1900.[1]

The Macmillan Company, [New York]
Dear Sirs.

    I learn from London that a full set of *corrected* proofs of "The Soft Side" will have been sent you this week – as well as uncorrected set a week ago. Please, naturally, have the *second*, only, set up. The book was not – according to intentions unchanged till within a very short time – to have been published till the autumn, & as this appeared to allow a margin I was waiting impatiently only to *receive* the correct Revise, complete, to send it to you for copy. It is has [*sic*] now become desirable it should be issued here before *August* is over, & I am greatly hoping you will be able to manage this, for simultaneity, in New York. My agent, Mr. J. B. Pinker, who will have despatched you the sheets, will have written you also about this. Permit me to add that it will be a great convenience to me to be able to count on it in New York for the particular date he may have mentioned to you[2] – & that I am yours very truly

> Henry James

**Notes**

1.    The present text is based upon a photocopy of the manuscript at NYPL.
2.    The book was published in London on 30 August and copyrighted in the United States on 23 August, though published in New York in September (*BHJ*, pp.117, 118). Pinker had written the New York office on 29 June that Methuen was proposing 28 August for publication in London. He had mailed the sheets in two batches on 1 July and 4 July (NYPL).

## 261

E.M.                                  October 9*th* 1900.[1]
Henry James, Esq.,
Lamb House,
Rye.
Dear Sir,

    We regret to say that we have no stock left of Roderick Hudson in crown 8vo., or of Princess Casamassima in the crown 8vo form.[2]

> We are, Yours faithfully,
> Macmillan & Co. Ltd.[3]

**Notes**

1. TLS. The typist's initials cannot be identified.
2. Macmillan had published a one-volume edition of *Roderick Hudson* of 1,500 copies in crown 8vo. in May 1880 (*BHJ*, p. 31) and in October 1886 had brought out a similar edition of *The Princess Casamassima* in 3,000 copies (*BHJ*, p. 76).
3. Though the company's name is handwritten, there is no initial or signature at the close.

## 262

Lamb House, Rye.
October 16*th* 1900.[1]

[The Macmillan Company, New York]
Dear Sirs.

Will you be so good as to send out another copy of *The Soft Side* for me? – one to *Miss Evelyn Smalley, 125 West 73d St., New York*,[2] & much oblige yours very truly

Henry James

**Notes**

1. The present text is based upon a photocopy of the manuscript at NYPL.
2. Evelyn Garnaut Smalley was the daughter of George W. and Phoebe Garnaut Smalley, old American friends of James's in London. Years later Miss Smalley selected and arranged *The Henry James Year Book* (1911). See *BHJ*, pp. 146–7.

## 263

Lamb House, Rye.
August 16*th* 1901.[1]

The Macmillan Company. [New York]
Dear Sirs.

Returning home from an absence I find your letter of July – with a cheque & a statement of sales, royalties &c, for which I enclose, with my thanks, signed receipt.[2] Believe me yours very truly

Henry James

**Notes**

1.    The present text is based upon a photocopy of the manuscript at NYPL.
2.    The receipt is no longer with the letter.

## 264

W.B.                                                          June 4th. 1902.[1]
Henry James Esq.
Lamb House,
Rye.
My dear James,

Do you happen to know the London address of Mr. James Ford Rhodes?[2] He is, I think, a friend of yours. He called here the other day, left a card with no address upon it, and I do not know where to get at him.

> I am,
> Yours very sincerely,
> Frederick Macmillan

**Notes**

1.    TLS. The typist's initials cannot be identified.
2.    James Ford Rhodes (1848–1927) was the author of a *History of the United States from the Compromise of 1850* (seven volumes, 1893–1906).

## 265

Reform Club,
Pall Mall, S.W.
Feb: 24*th* 1903[1]

Dear Mr. Brett.

In answer to your letter of the 9*th*, which I have but just somewhat belatedly received, I shall be very glad to send you a short story for the series you designate; but my agent Mr. Pinker will immediately endeavour to learn from you by cable if you can possibly, in this case, give a slight extension to the term "short." To learn that is, if *30,000* words wd. suit you equally with *20,000* (the latter – the maximum you mention – being what I should otherwise propose.) I can send you a 20,000 thing or a 30,000, in other words; but the latter would involve a better idea than the other & be, I think, the more addressed to circulation. And as both are things some time ago *begun* & lying by me, I should be able to finish & despatch them with promptitude. However, I don't mean that I shouldn't do my best for the 20,000 too.[2] Yours very truly

Henry James

**Notes**

1.  The present text is based upon a photocopy of the manuscript at NYPL.
2.  Pinker wrote Brett on 25 February (NYPL) that James would be 'very pleased to write a story for your series if we can arrange terms'. Length, as James suggests, is an important matter, so Pinker requests a cable from Brett specifying either 20,000 or 30,000 words. There is no record that James ever supplied the story.

## 266

S.J.L.                                                2nd March 1903.[1]
Henry James Esq.
Rye,
Sussex.
My dear James,

We have to-day heard from our people in New York that Messrs Scribner have offered them £10 for the right to include your essay on Turgénieff in the edition of Turgénieff's Works which they are just now publishing. For obvious reasons they wish not to print the copyright date, or the title of the book from which the essay is taken. Please let me know whether you consent to the arrangement. If so, we will accept the offer and put the money in question to your credit. We should offer no objection as far as we are concerned, and indeed if the essay was copyrighted in America it was probably before it came into our hands.[2]

I hope you were as much interested as we were in the play on Saturday night. I thought it was wonderfully acted, & very strong.[3]

I am,<br>Yours very truly<br>George A. Macmillan[4]

202 *The Correspondence of Henry James and Macmillan*

**Notes**

1. TLS. The typist's initials cannot be identified.
2. James's assent is given in letter 267.
3. The 'German play', as James characterises it, was Hermann Sudermann's *Es lebe das Leben* (1902) at the Great Queen-Street Theatre. See *The Times*, 25 February 1903, p. 8.
4. For George A. Macmillan, a partner in the firm, see letter 53. Macmillan penned in the last four words of the letter.

## 267

Reform Club,
Pall Mall. S.W.
March 4*th* 1903

Dear George Macmillan.

I am very glad to assent to Scribner's proposal to give £10 for the use of my Turgénieff article as an introduction to a collective translation or whatever. (There are really 2 articles; one in "French Poets & Novelists" & one in "Partial Portraits" – but he certainly means the former.) Kindly therefore consider my authorization given.[1]

I was much disposed to congratulate you both on your presence the other night at the German play. I thought the drama heavy & wanting in concentration, but the actress admirable & of the first order for artistic finish & sincerity.[2] I seem to gather that the Freds. are all in Rome.[3] But I am hoping to stay on here a couple of months more.

Yours very truly
Henry James

**Notes**

1. James's 'Ivan Turgénieff' had first appeared in the *North American Review* for April 1874 and been collected in *French Poets and Novelists* (1878). The second essay, also entitled 'Ivan Turgénieff', appeared in the *Atlantic Monthly* for January 1884 and was included in *Partial Portraits* (1888). James was wrong, however, about the choice of essay. Scribner's selected the second essay as an introduction to *The Novels and Stories of Ivan Turgénieff*, 16 volumes, 1903–4.
2. See letter 266, note 3. The actress presumably was Rosa Bertens, who had been 'specially engaged' for the play's run. See *The Times*, 25 February 1903, p. 8.
3. The Frederick Macmillans. For their return, see letter 268.

## 268

S.J.L.                                                                6th March 1903.[1]
Henry James Esq.
The Reform Club,
Pall Mall, S.W.

My dear James,

Many thanks for your letter of March 4 agreeing to Messrs Scribner's proposal in regard to your essay on Turgénieff. We will tell them what you say as to the two essays on the subject, and will also ask them to send the £10 to you direct.[2]

I am glad to find that you agree with us in thinking highly of the actress of Saturday night.[3]

Fred returned from Rome on Monday night, though his wife remains there for the present.[4]

I am,
Yours very truly
George A. Macmillan

**Notes**

1. TLS. The typist's initials cannot be identified.
2. See letter 267 and note 1.
3. See letter 267, note 2.
4. Frederick Macmillan returned to London Monday, 2 March.

## 269

Macmillan & Co. Ltd.
St. Martin's Street
London. W.C.
June 16/1903.[1]

My dear James,

I was delighted to hear from you yesterday that you are inclined to consider seriously the suggestion I made to you a short time ago that you should write a book on "Aspects of London" to be illustrated by J. Pennell.[2]

My idea is that it shall be a book of not less than 120,000 words & that it should form one of the series of books to which Crawford has contributed "Ave Roma" and "Rulers of the South" & for which he is now writing a book on Venice.[3] We would leave you to deal with the subject in any way that commended itself to you & Pennell should make his illustrations to suit your text. We should not ask you to tie yourself to finish it within any particular time, though we should like if possible to be able to publish it not later than 1906.

As to terms, we can offer you a royalty of twenty per cent on the respective English & American published prices with an advance of £1000 (one thousand pounds) on account.[4]

We should of course print the book both here & in the U.S. so as to secure copyright in both countries.

If these conditions are agreeable to you I will send you a formal memorandum of agreement for signature.[5]

I am<br>
Yours sincerely<br>
Frederick Macmillan

Henry James Esq

### Notes

1.  The present text is based upon the manuscript at L.C.; a file copy may be found in LB, MA.
2.  Joseph Pennell (1857–1926), the well-known American illustrator, had known James for years and in 1888 had illustrated James's 'London' for the *Century Magazine*, xxxvii (December), 219–39.
3.  Francis Marion Crawford (1854–1909), popular American novelist and nephew of Julia Ward Howe, published *Ave Roma Immortalis* in 1898, *The Rulers of the South* in 1900, and *Salve Venetia* in 1905. Joseph Pennell illustrated the volume on Venice.
4.  These terms are among the best ever offered by any firm to James for a book. The "advance", by the way, was to be paid "on publication". Ironically, he was never able to fulfil the contract. For his rueful comment on his efforts to work on the project, see letter 275.
5.  Macmillan enclosed the memorandum of agreement with his letter of 19 June 1903 (number 271) and James signed and returned it in a letter of 22 June (number 272).

## 270

Lamb House,<br>
Rye. Sussex.<br>
June 17<i>th</i> 1903

My dear Macmillan.

I am much obliged to you for your letter of the date of yesterday.[1]

I think I *am* ready to duly accept your proposal in respect to the book on London for the series containing Crawford's *Ave Roma* &c; so please consider that I hereby do so. The size & general character of Crawford's 4 volumes (in all) commend themselves to me, &, as the subject appeals to me, I am not without a confidence of being able, on the basis in question, to do something successful. I certainly shall not be able to treat my subject in *less* than 150,000 words – which as a maximum, I gather, you would even prefer to 120,000. And I will combine & arrange with Pennell for the best advantage of each of us. Last not least, I am obliged to you for your statement of terms – a royalty of 20 per cent. & an advance of one thousand pounds on account. The only shade on the picture, a little, for me is that a plan I have for next year may prevent my putting the book through as early, in time, as I should otherwise have been disposed to do. I am thinking, rather definitely, of going to America for 6 or 8 months (some time in 1904) & that won't contribute to a study of London – though it *may* (eventually) contribute to the subsequent leisure for dealing with it.[2] However, with the margin you mention, I don't think that need alarm me. I must do, as I reflect with pleasure, a good deal of fertilizing reading, besides other prowling & prying; but once these things get themselves adequately done, I think I shall be able to *write* the book in some eight months. And perhaps, after all, I shall be able to read – a little – even in America – even on a return there after 20 years of absence! Moreover I shall not start, even at the earliest, for a goodish many months. So on the whole, as I say, I am not afraid! Believe me, my dear Macmillan, yours always

Henry James

**Notes**

1.  See letter 269.
2.  James actually stayed in America almost a year. He left England 25 August 1904 and returned 13 July 1905. For the memorandum of agreement (LB, MA), see letter 269, note 5.

# 271

June 19 1903

My dear James,

    I am very glad to hear that you see your way to undertake the

"London" book. I have embodied the terms in the enclosed formal memorandum of agreement & if you will kindly sign & return it to me I will send you a duplicate signed by ourselves.[1] You will observe that nothing is said about the date of publication: we shall look forward to being able [to] bring the book out early in the autumn of 1906, but you are not tied in any way & in case circumstances render it impossible for you to get it finished by then you will not be breaking any contract.[2]

> Believe me
> Yours most sincerely
> Frederick Macmillan

Henry James Esq
Lamb House
Rye

### Notes

1. James returned the memorandum of agreement on 22 June.
2. As far as the manuscripts in the MA show, Macmillan never pressured James to complete the book, though he asked James about it on several occasions (see letter 274, for example), and they presumably discussed the work as late as 1909 (*CN*, p. 278n.). For James's notes on 'London Town', see *CN*, pp. 273–85.

## 272

> Reform Club,
> Pall Mall. S.W.
> June 22*d* 1903[1]

My dear Macmillan.

Your letter & form of agreement meet me here today, on my return hither from 3 days absence from Rye, to which I return on Wednesday. With thanks, after signing, I enclose herein the agreement for "London Town" – or whatever it seems (*shall* seem) best to call it in default of mere "London" rendered practically unavailable by W. Besant & by reason of one's wishing to mark that it isn't a question, exactly, of London *City* – alone.[2] But this is as yet a detail & I am yours always truly

> Henry James

**Notes**

1.  Previously printed in *HJL, IV,* 278. The present text differs in accidentals only.
2.  See letters 269–71 for discussion of 'London Town'. A copy of the agreement dated 19 June and signed by James is in LB, MA. Walter Besant (1836–1901) had published a volume on London (1892) in his series *Survey of London.*


## 273

W.B.                    (Enclo.)                    June 23rd, 1903.[1]
Henry James Esq.
Reform Club,
Pall Mall, S.W.
My dear James,

I am obliged to you for the signed agreement and return a duplicate with our signature attached to it.[2]

I think that "London Town" would be a charming title for the book.[3]

> I am,
> Yours ever,
> Frederick Macmillan


**Notes**

1.  TLS. The typist's initials cannot be identified.
2.  See letter 272, note 2; the original is in LB, MA.
3.  Though a final title was never adopted, the project was usually referred to as 'London Town'. Ironically enough, Edric Vredenburg published an illustrated quarto entitled *London Town* in 1905 and Frank Berkeley Smith's *In London Town* appeared the following year.


## 274

E.A.W.                                             April 3. 1908.[1]
Henry James, Esq.,
Lamb's House [*sic*],
Rye, Sussex.
My dear James,

A certain Mr. Alfred H. Hyatt says that he has in preparation a book on Venice to be published by Chatto & Windus, and asks for permission to print an extract consisting of four pages from

"Portraits of Places" and another of the same length from "Princess Casamassima". I do not suppose that you are likely to object to this, but I do not feel justified in giving Mr. Hyatt the permission he asks without referring to you. Please let me know your views.[2]

I take this opportunity of asking whether you have made any progress with the book on London. Pennell has produced an enormous mass of illustration and if we got the manuscript there would be nothing to prevent the book being published this Autumn. I suppose this is hardly likely to be the case, but I should be glad to know.[3]

I was very glad to hear from our friend Mrs Clifford that your play was a success in Glasgow last week. I hope it will not be long before we see it in London.[4]

> I am,
> Yours very sincerely,
> Frederick Macmillan.

### Notes

1. TLS. The typist's initials cannot be identified. The gap of almost five years between this letter and the previous one may be accounted for in part by James's association with other publishers – Methuen and Scribner's in particular; by the year he spent in America – 1904–5; and by the time he devoted to the preparation of the Edition de Luxe – 1906–8. The edition was issued in England by Macmillan & Co., but most of the details of publication were handled by James B. Pinker, his agent, and not by James himself, though it should be noted that James informed Pinker on 10 June 1908 that he was 'delighted with the M.'s proposal' covering the edition, and on 12 June he urged Pinker to proceed 'unreservedly with the Macmillans, from the moment they express themselves so favourably to the idea of undertaking the London issue of the Edition'. On 15 July 1908 James returned to Pinker 'the Macmillan Agreement signed and initial'd, with thanks' (Yale). The memorandum of agreement itself is printed below, pp. 212–13.
2. Hyatt had published selections from the work of Dickens, Emerson, and Hardy in pocket-sized editions in 1906 and was currently engaged in compiling anthologies of the *Charm of Paris* (1908) and the *Charm of Venice* (1908). For James's prompt, negative response to Hyatt's request, see letter 275.
3. This reminder about 'London Town' is typical of Macmillan's efforts to stimulate James to work on the book.
4. Johnston Forbes-Robertson (1853–1937), the well-known actor, produced James's *The High Bid* in Scotland (Edinburgh and Glasgow) in March 1908 and in London for a week in February 1909. Lucy Lane (Mrs W. K.) Clifford (?–1929), the author of fiction and plays, was one of James's oldest London friends. Several of her books, including *Anyhow Stories* (1882) and *The Last Touches and Other Stories* (1892), were published by Macmillan & Co.

**275**

Lamb House.
Rye. Sussex.
April 5th: 1908[1]

Frederick Macmillan Esq.,
St. Martin's St., W.C.
My dear Macmillan

Mr. A. H. Hyatt, of whom your letter of the 3rd: contains mention to me, has himself written me about his appropriating the three or four pages out of "The Princess Casamassima"; and I have answered him, but have had to do so in the negatively [*sic*]. Mrs Laurence Binyon many months ago appealed for my leave to include just the same morsel in a volume of specimen extracts of English Style, English Prose, or whatever; and I, having applied to your house for assent, wrote her she might do so – to which she proceeded with such effect that the book has been now for some time out. I don't therefore muddle the matter by renewing the license for a quite different publication; and this I have made Mr Hyatt duly understand – so there need be no further trouble for you.[2]

As for the other and much greater question, the "London" book, I don't wonder at your enquiry; only do wonder, rather, that some thunderbolt of reprobation hasn't descended on me long before this.[3] I have expected it very often, and crouched and grovelled, burying my head in the sand, whenever I could fancy the faintest distant mutter. How can I tell you coherently, or inspire you with any patience to hear, what a long train of fatality and difficulty and practical deterrence, has attended my connection with that (none the less cherished and unrelinquished) promise. Things kept going damnably against my performance of it, going practically, I mean, and perversely and pertinaciously, from very soon after my making it to you: this frustration and delay took the form of my having to keep as hard as possible at (more or less immediately productive) fiction, which I had near chances to serialise, and which with my lean ability to do but one good job at once, took all my weeks and months and – I blush red to write the word! – years, wretched years! Then came the immense distraction of my going for a year to America – which raised an enormous barrier, that of a different, an opposite association and interest; and from which I returned saddled, inevitably, with too portentous complications: very good in themselves, but awful from the point of view of buckling down to a book about

London and putting it through. One of these engagements was to begin immediately (immediately, that is, after I had written a great fat book of Impressions, the first of two vols. of such, the second of which will now, however, not appear)[4] the publication of an elaborately revised and retouched and embellished and copiously prefaced and introduced Collective, and *se*lective, Edition of my productions, in 24 Volumes – which I have been putting through, and which has proved a task of the most arduous sort, such as I can't but be glad of, but such as I at the same time wouldn't have had the courage to undertake had I measured all the job was to cost me. It is still going on, my own part of it, though I draw to a close. The beautiful vols. have begun successively to appear in New York – though arrangements for them here have been difficult, complicated and delayed.[5] I mention all this to account for my burdened and tied-up and apparently (in respect to "London") thankless and perfidious state. The worst is, however, that the Edition represents but half the burden I assumed in respect to New York: I came away pledged to supply two Novels for serialisation – and even the first of these (with which alone, perhaps, however, I shall be able to get off) has been most inconveniently and disgracefully delayed. The Edition has smothered me, in other words, like an enormous featherbed – and I have scarce breathed outside of it: indeed either outside or in! This is my sorry tale, and I scarce expect you to be able to take it for anything but a virtual, though deeply unintentional and most rueful, trifling with your honourable hopes! The case remains that, all the while, I haven't, for myself, "gone back" on the idea of the book at all, but have kept it constantly in view, making a great deal of preparation for it; I have been able fortunately to read a great deal (I've even bought a good many books) and roamed and poked and pried about in town when I have had leisure moments on being "up".[6] I feel still strongly, that I should like to do it; I feel that having known the subject, having sounded and cared for it, on certain sides, so well and so long, I shall quite have lost one of the opportunities of my life if I don't do it. But there remain [*sic*] the fact that I have absolutely to finish both my Edition and a longish Novel first; and that I am perfectly conscious of my little right to expect of you more waiting and postponing. If any other idea – by which I mean if any other image of "attractive" authorship – for getting the book done should hover before you, you certainly owe me no consideration; and I shouldn't look to you for any but definite notice! I hope still it won't come to that, and I feel that if I once clear away my Novel (the first to be done – I can manage for the time with that)[7] the ground will be more disencumbered than it has been for a long time, and a good deal of additional reading which I want to put in will have been managed. Don't answer this on the spot, but let me come to see you the next time I'm in town, when there are various other things I shall be able to say to you that may mitigate a little the disgrace, and still keep alive a little the hope,[8] of yours ever faithfully,

Henry James

P.S.    All thanks for your reference to the as yet but provincial, though apparently in spite of that definitely "successful", Play! It only needed a fresh plunge into the theatre – absolutely necessary at a time of long and laborious Editions with their fruit all in the future – to make my confusion worse confounded! It is a homely fact, however, that nothing can possibly conduce more to my having a real free and deliberate and leisurely hand for "London" than a definitely good and sustained success or two at the box-office! I haven't published a Novel, alas, since just before I went to America! The play Forbes Robertson has produced was *written* a dozen years ago; the re-preparation and rehearsing of it, however, has been a dire trap to one's weeks![9]

### Notes

1.    TLS. This letter has previously been published in part in *LM*, pp. 172–4.
2.    For Hyatt, see letter 274, note 2.
3.    For earlier references to 'London Town', see letters 269–74.
4.    *The American Scene* (1907).
5.    Ironically, the firm would shortly agree to issue this edition in England. (Several other English houses – John Murray and Archibald Constable, among them – had considered the project.) On 10 June James wrote Pinker to proceed 'unreservedly' with the Macmillan proposal to handle the edition in England, and he signed a Memorandum of Agreement dated 13 July 1908 (LB, MA); the first volume was published 29 September 1908 (*BHJ*, p. 138).
6.    For James's notes on the book, see *CN*, pp. 273–85.
7.    Possibly *The Ivory Tower*, one of two novels left incomplete by James.
8.    As late as September 1909 James was still discussing the project with Macmillan. See *CN*, p. 278. Nevertheless, he never completed the book on London, and Macmillan was also out £500 for the illustrations Pennell prepared. See Frederick Macmillan to Pennell, 10 April 1908 (LB, MA). In this letter Macmillan reports that James had 'declared' that he is 'very keen' about the book and 'will take it in hand on the first opportunity'.
9.    For *The High Bid*, see letter 274, note 4.

# Memorandum of Agreement

*Dated* July 13, 1908

BETWEEN

Henry James Esq.

AND

MACMILLAN. AND CO., LTD.

FOR THE PUBLICATION OF

a uniform collected edition of his works

───────────

Terms. Roy of 15%
S/o U.S.A. or Canadian rights
A/cs cheques to J. B. Pinker

MEMORANDUM OF AGREEMENT made this 13th day of July, 1908. Between HENRY JAMES ESQ. of Lamb House, Rye, Sussex (hereinafter termed the Author) of the one part and MACMILLAN AND COMPANY, LIMITED of St. Martin's Street, London, W.C. (hereinafter termed the Publishers) of the other part.

WHEREBY it is mutually agreed between the parties hereto for themselves and their respective executors, administrators, assigns or successors, as follows:-

1.  The Publishers shall at their own risk and expense and with due diligence produce and publish a uniform collected edition of the works of Henry James.

2.  The Publishers shall during the legal term of copyright have the exclusive right of producing and publishing in the United Kingdom and the British Colonies except in Canada the said uniform collected edition of the said works.

3. The Publishers shall pay the Author a royalty of Fifteen per cent (15%) of the advertised retail price of each and every copy of the works sold by them.

4. Accounts to be made up annually to June 30th. delivered on or before October 1st and settled by cash in the ensuing January.

5. If any difference shall arise between the Author and the Publishers the same shall be referred to the arbitration of two persons (one to be named by each party) or their umpire, in accordance with the provisions of the Arbitration Act 1889.

6. The Author guarantees that there is nothing in his contracts with other publishers to interfere with the appearance of this uniform edition and he hereby undertakes to indemnify Messrs. Macmillan against the cost of any legal proceedings in which they may be involved owing to negligence on his or his Agent's part in this respect.

7. The Author empowers the Publishers to pay to his Agent James B. Pinker of Talbot House, Arundel Street, Strand, W.C. all sums of money due under this agreement and declares that the said James B. Pinker's receipt shall be good and valid discharge to all persons paying such monies.

[James's signature]

## 276

> Lamb House.
> Rye. Sussex.
> 3rd: Aug: 1908

Messrs. The Macmillan Co.

Dear Sirs,

May I ask if you have still on hand and are able to send me a copy of an old volume of mine (1892) "The Lesson of the Master"? I possess one copy, but have rather an urgent use for a second; which, should you be able to find one, will greatly oblige yours very truly[1]

Henry James

**Note**

1. TLS. James presumably was working on copy for Volume xv of the New York Edition (Edition de Luxe in England). For the firm's lack of stock of the collection of stories, see letter 277.

## 277

G.B.M./E.A.W.[1]                                            August 5. 1908.

Henry James, Esq.
Lamb House,
Rye. Sussex.

Dear Sir,

We have your letter of the 3rd inst., and much regret that we are now not in possession of a single copy of your volume "The Lesson of the Master". Probably however we could obtain a second-hand copy by advertising, and we shall of course be happy to do this if such a copy will suit your purpose.[2]

> We are,
> Yours faithfully,
> Macmillan & Co. Ltd.[3]

### Notes

1. TLS. George B. Muir, the author of other company correspondence during this period but whose position with the firm cannot otherwise be clarified, apparently wrote this letter. The typist's initials cannot be identified. For another letter by Muir on James's work, see Introduction, p. xxiii and note 13.
2. See letters 276 and 278,
3. Initialled possibly by 'M' (presumably G.B.M.) though the letter (letters ?) is (are?) not perfectly legible.

## 278

> Lamb House.
> Rye. Sussex.
> 6th: Aug: 1908

Messrs. The Macmillan Company
Dear Sirs,

I am obliged to you for your letter about the irrecoverable "Lesson of the Master"; but I won't trouble you to institute a search for a copy, as I shall very possibly be able to make my single one serve.[1]

Believe me yours very truly

> Henry James

### Note

1. TLS. See letters 276–7.

**279**

Sept 4 1908

My dear James,

I enclose a specimen of the binding which – with your approval – we propose to adopt for the Edition de luxe of your novels.[1] Please let me know whether you like it,

I am just off to Overstrand,[2] but shall be in town again on Tuesday.

I am
Yours ever,
Frederick Macmillan

Henry James Esq
Lamb House
Rye

### Notes

1. James had signed a memorandum of agreement for the edition dated 13 July, and the first volume appeared on 29 September. See letter 275, note 5. Macmillan frequently checked with James about such aspects of his books as binding, paper, and type. For James's pleased response, see letter 280.
2. Macmillan's country home, Meadow Cottage, Overstrand, Norfolk was usually referred to as Overstrand.

**280**

Lamb House.
Rye. Sussex.
September 6th 1908.

My dear Macmillan.

A word to thank you for the pattern binding you send me for my Edition – which I greatly like. The colour particularly pleases me – it's charming & congruous, & though I find the gilding on a book perhaps a little heavy I reflect that the texture of the stuff probably demands – & approve the whole thing as it stands, in short, without any reserve.[1] I give the enterprise my heartiest best wishes & am most truly yours

Henry James

Frederic [*sic*] Macmillan Esq.

P.S.    I judge discreet to return the cover – separate from this.

**Note**

1.    The Macmillan issue was 'bound in green backram', with 'ornamental devices in gilt on front cover and spine', and 'lettered in gilt on spine' (*BHJ*, p. 138).


## 281

> Lamb House.
> Rye. Sussex.
> December 8*th* 1908.

My dear Macmillan.

I have happened – for reasons – to delay this considerable time acting, in respect to sending you a short list of names for the despatch of a few copies of my collective Edition, on our conversation of a month ago.[1] I am afraid the main reason has literally been that I haven't been able to bring my mind to the effort of making the particular reduced choice of recipients *most* designated by various considerations. But here it is, at any rate, the choice – of five persons including myself. Will you kindly direct that the copies be sent according to the list I enclose & that I be debited with the cost of the business according to what you told me of that? Unfortunately my delay has allowed the *first* volumes a little to multiply – but perhaps those sent to the two addresses in Paris can conveniently go by Book Post, two vols. at a time.[2] After that it will be simpler. Believe me yours ever

> Henry James


**Notes**

1.    The conversation alluded to had actually taken place in October, and in it Macmillan had informed James, as he, James, wrote Pinker on 13 October, that since the firm 'only bought [the text] from the Scribners they couldn't give me any [copies] – but would let me have what I wanted for a "very small" fragment! Thus it has been settled,' James added, 'I of course assenting – & I [am to] have from them what I want at the price they pay Scribners for them.' This was a shock to James, for Macmillan had hitherto always allowed him unlimited author's copies, and he observed to Pinker: 'It all adds to my sense of literature being for me somehow only an expensive job – but I won't go into that now. I shall "have" copies!' (Yale).
2.    Aside from himself, James's list included copies of each volume to Joseph Conrad, Edmund Gosse, Harriet Reubell, and Paul Bourget, the last two having Paris addresses at the time. The list is included with James's letter in LB, MA, as is also the firm's notation concerning the dates of posting of the volumes. James was charged 3/6d for each volume and the last copy was mailed 14 September 1909.

## 282

Dec 10 1908

My dear James,

Your letter of the 8[th] containing a list of the persons to whom you wish to give copies of your Collected Edition, has just reached me. All the volumes which have been published shall be despatched at once & the others shall go as they appear.[1]

I am

Yours ever sincerely

Frederick Macmillan

Henry James Esq

**Note**

1. See letter 281. Volumes 1–6 were dispatched 10 December except for *Roderick Hudson* to Gosse, who had already received a copy of the novel from James.

## 283

Lamb House.

Rye. Sussex.

March 17*th* 1909

My dear Macmillan.

Messrs. Nelsons, the publishers of a large cheap series of reprints of various distinguished works, have written to ask me if they may include *The American*, my novel of that name, in their collection, & I am disposed to assent on the basis of the text used being that of our Definitive Edition. My reason for this disposition is largely the result of the fact that the Edition has played for me, during the two or three years I have been busy with it, a terrible Dog-in-the Manger part; it has but just ceased to take (through my immense overworking of my books,) *all* my time, making every other remunerative labour impossible, & blocking my whole way, while up to this date it hasn't returned me a penny. It has been, in other words, & it will at the very least [be] if any future profits from it remain, the most expensive job of my life.[1] In these conditions – of my feeling in consequence of it rather high & dry – the Nelsons' offer of a substantial sum, on account, "down" for the use of "The American" comes to me, for the time, temptingly & helpfully; & I write to you to inquire as to the question of your assent in the matter. If you have no inexorable objection I should like to accept their proposal. It would suit me no more than you that the Edition at large should suffer the least real prejudice, but I think that this isn't to be feared from such an arrangement for one volume out of the twenty-four; & the book would be used without the preface now indefeasibly attached to the Edition presentation of it. Will you kindly let me hear from you as to this?[2] Believe me yours ever

Henry James

### Notes

1. James acknowledged his first royalty cheque for the edition – £7.14.2 – in a letter of 1 April 1909 (Yale). Six years later James was still bemoaning its 'complete failure', as he admitted to Gosse on 25 August 1915, 'from the point of view of profit either to the publishers or to myself' (*SLHJEG*, p. 313).
2. The 'Nelsons' offer' was for £135 'down'. See James to Pinker, 18 April 1909 (Yale). In letter 284 Macmillan agrees to James's request.

## 284

Macmillan & Co., Ltd.
St. Martin's Street
London, W.C.
Mch 18 1909[1]

My dear James,

I have your letter & write at once to say that we will raise no objection to the publication of *The American* in Nelsons Sevenpenny Library. If it has any effect on the sale of your 'Edition de Luxe' it will be a good one.[2]

I am
Yours ever,
Frederick Macmillan

Henry James Esq

### Notes

1. The text is based upon a collation of the photocopy of the original of this letter in NYPLB with the file copy in LB, MA.
2. The Nelson reprint of *The American* appeared later in the year without the preface, as James had prescribed in letter 283.

**285**

> Lamb House.
> Rye. Sussex.
> March 19*th* 1909.

My dear Macmillan

    I am obliged to you, much, for your letter about the Nelsons & "The American" – which improves the situation & leaves me yours very truly[1]

> Henry James

**Note**

1.    See letters 283 and 284.

**286**

> Lamb House.
> Rye. Sussex.
> March 22*d* 1909

Dear Sirs.

    Be so good as to send me a copy of the 2*d* volume of the Edition de Luxe of my Novels & Tales (containing *The American*,)[1] & oblige yours very truly

> Henry James

Messrs. the Macmillan Company
London

**Note**

1.    James apparently was supplying Nelson with copy for the reprint of the novel. See letters 283–5.

**287**

> Lamb House.
> Rye. Sussex.
> July 26*th* 1909[1]

My dear Macmillan.

    I am greatly interested in the fact that my accomplished & greatly valued friend of many years Morton Fullerton, is to do a book on Paris for you – which fact has after reflection made me think of *this* & decide to write to you. I know something – a good deal, of his personal & family situation, & especially of the financially depleting effect on him, lately aggravated, of the condition of his father, ill & helpless these many years in the U.S., & to whom he has had constantly to render assistance. It strikes me as not unlikely that he may have to write and ask you for some advance on the money he is to receive from you, for getting more clear & free for work at his book – & I should like to send you a cheque for £100, say, that he may profit by to that end, – *without his knowing it comes from me.* Would you be willing to send it to him, as a favour to me, *as* from yourselves (independently of anything you may yourselves send him?) & with no mention whatever, naturally, of my name in the matter? I ask you this frankly as the only way I can see to give him the advantage of the money, which I believe would be a great convenience to him – for I am far from sure of his not sending it (the £100) back to me were I to propose it to him straight. Pardon this slightly complicated proposition – I shall feel it a great service if you are able to act on it – & believe me yours always – [2]

Henry James

**Notes**

1.  This letter has previously been printed in *HJL*, IV, 529. My text differs in accidentals only.
2.  James was actually responding to a suggestion made by Edith Wharton (1862–1937), a good friend to both James and Fullerton (1865–1952), who planned to provide the money. Mrs Wharton and Fullerton, indeed, were in the midst of an affair. See *HJL*, IV, 527–32; *HJEW*, pp. 114–21; and letter 288.

**288**

Lamb House.<br>Rye. Sussex.<br>August 3d 1909[1]

My dear Macmillan.

Pardon my having had to delay a day or two thanking you for your letter about Morton Fullerton, the Paris book &c. Let me definitely say then that I will with pleasure become surety for such a sum in case of your advancing him, on the Book, & at his request, the

Hundred Pounds I wrote you of – in addition to the one I understand you already to have offered him. Should the book, in that case, not in due time be forthcoming, in other words, you are to call on me for the Hundred Pounds additionally supplied (advanced) & I will immediately respond to your call. But I greatly *believe* in the book.[2]
   Please say to Mrs. Macmillan that I should like nothing better than coming to pay you a little visit at Cromer – but that this month is unfavourable to me, always, through the frequency of small visitations of others to me here; which always leaves me much pressed with occupations between times. Will you kindly leave the question open to September, when I think I shall have a clearer field, & when I shall greatly enjoy proposing myself for a couple of days if I can grasp the right ones – & that shall suit you as well. Such a happy chance will have all the charm for me of a voyage of discovery & a first acquaintance with your so eminent part of the world.[3] And I risk & face with confidence the limits of your establishment! With kindest regards yours, my dear Macmillan, ever

Henry James

**Notes**

1.  This letter has previously been printed in *HJL*, *IV*, 531–2. My text differs chiefly in accidentals.
2.  Macmillan's letter is not in LB, MA. Although Fullerton never wrote the 'Paris book', Macmillan presumably did not call upon James for the £100.
3.  Despite James's less frequent appearances on the firm's list, the Macmillans continued to offer him hospitality in town and country, and, as he suggests, he visited them at Overstrand in Norfolk, a 'miniature English Newport' near Cromer, on 17–21 September (*CN*, pp. 178, 308–9).

## 289

Reform Club.<br>Sept. 25th 1909.

My dear Macmillan.
   Mrs. Wharton's address is:
   Hotel de Crillon
   Place de la Concorde
   Paris.[1]

Yours ever<br>Henry James

**Note**

1.  James had just returned from a weekend visit to Overstrand (letter 288, note 3), where he may have mentioned discreetly Mrs Wharton's general interest in the Fullerton book on Paris.

## 290

Lamb House.
Rye. Sussex.
October 19*th* 1909.

Messrs. Macmillan & Co. Ld.
Dear Sirs –
    Be so good as to send, for me, Vols. 5 & 6 (Princess Casamassima) & Vol. 10*th* (Spoils of Poynton,) of my Edition de Luxe to:-
    A Langdon Coburn Esq.
    9 Lower Mall
    Hammersmith W.[1]
& oblige yours very truly

Henry James

**Note**

1.  Alvin Langdon Coburn (1882–1966) had taken the photographs used as frontispieces for the edition. Volumes five and six contain 'The Dome of St Paul's' and 'Splendid Paris, Charming Paris' as frontispieces, and volume ten is illustrated by 'Some of the Spoils'.

## 291

95 Irving St
Cambridge, Mass.
U.S.A.
Dec: 12: 1910

Messrs The Macmillan Company
Dear Sirs.
    I beg to acknowledge with thanks the receipt from you a cheque for £4.18.11 – representing apparently the amount of certain royalties the statement of which has not, in my absence from England, reached me.[1]

Yours very truly
Henry James

**Note**

1.  The gap in correspondence between October 1909 and December 1910 may be partially explained by James's long illness and nervous breakdown in 1910, his brother William's concurrent illness in the same year and subsequent death on 26 August 1910. James had sailed for America with his brother and sister-in-law earlier in the month. The sum referred to, however, had not been sent by the London company. See letter 292. Since Brett in New York had of old dealt directly with James – long after James B. Pinker became his agent in 1898 – it seems likely that the cheque, even though in sterling and not dollars, was from that office.

## 292

Dec 22 1910

My dear James

We have this morning received a mysterious note from you thanking us for a cheque for £4.18.11 which we have certainly not sent you. I am at a loss to understand it unless perchance the cheque may have come from our New York house who may owe you something, but if it had I should have thought it would probably be drawn in dollars and cents rather than in sterling. In any case you owe *us* no thanks for it.[1]

I find that we do owe you a small sum of £14.10.11 which in the ordinary course of things would be paid next month: perhaps you will kindly let me know whether you would like it paid into your bank here (in which case please tell me the name of the bank) or whether you would prefer to have a draft for the equivalent in American money.[2]

There is also a sum of £73.6.3 due to you for royalties on the Edition de Luxe but this as arranged will be paid over to Mr. Pinker, in January.[3]

I hope that you are keeping well & that it will not be long before you return to England where your many friends are eager to welcome you. We have been having a very wet & not altogether agreeable winter but there has been a change for the better today & it looks as though we were to have a fine Christmas.

My wife is going to Rome in a weeks [*sic*] time & will stay there until the beginning of February when I hope to meet her on the Riviera. If she were here she would join me in sending you kind remembrances & the very best wishes for the New Year.

Believe me
Yours ever,
Frederick Macmillan

Henry James Esq
95 Irving St
Cambridge Mass.

**Notes**

1.  See letter 291 and note 1. There is no other explanation for this cheque in LB, MA.
2.  James presumably requested that this sum be deposited in his bank in Rye. See letter 293
3.  For the same period James received £80 from Scribner for the New York Edition. See his letter to Pinker of 2 January 1911 (Yale).

## 293

1*st* Feb. 1911

Dear Sir

We beg to inform you that we are paying to your credit at Lloyds Bank, Rye, the sum of £14.10–11 being the amount due to you as shown by the publishing account rendered to 30*th* June last.[1]

Yours truly
James Foster[2]

Henry James Esq.
95 Irving Street
Cambridge Mass.
U.S.A.

**Notes**

1.  See letter 292.
2.  James Foster had served the London firm since the 1860s. See Graves, p. 265. Foster also compiled *A Bibliographical Catalogue of Macmillan and Co.'s Publications from 1843 to 1889* (1891).

## 294

Lowland House,
Nahant P.O.,
Massachusetts.
June 16th, 1911[1]

Dear Lady Macmillan

All thanks for your letter of comprehension of my delayed return (for which all reports of the present condition of London quite console me,) & in respect to my coming to you at Overstrand on September 8*th*. Thanks to my still hanging rather on the fringe – the fringe of the fringe – of recovery (very difficult recovery) from a miserably long illness, I have just lately been rather unwell & unfit again, & that makes me a little nervous about committing myself to engagements far ahead. But on the other hand I think that what is the matter with me is mainly the desperate & temporarily frustrated desire to get back to dear old England again – so that I intensely *want* to believe that that is all that is needed for my steady re-establishment. I therefore insist on presuming that I shall be able to come to you on the said Friday *8th* Sept., as I shall certainly be delighted to do in the absence of any overwhelming disability. But I shall really be able, I fondly hold, to avert that, & should at the worst be able to notify you of it in sufficient time for your own convenience.[2] After all I have done nothing the last month but pay "country visits" – as I am paying one now & apparently do nothing else till I depart altogether. Norfolk isn't more difficult, to say the least, than Massachusetts – though this is a beautiful place too; a charming headland far out into a deep blue sea, & beautiful gardens (wondrous flowers) & lawns & trees – plus great breezy verandahs of the good old American sort of which I am fond.[3] But here one needs them more than in Norfolk, though we are having as yet, after a hot May, a charmingly cool June. I hope you won't have a hot coronation![4]

Yours all faithfully<br>Henry James

**Notes**

1. This letter is at Virginia. Mrs Macmillan became Lady Macmillan in 1909 when her husband was knighted by King Edward VII.
2. James reached Liverpool on 7 August 1911 and visited the Macmillans at Overstrand in Norfolk 8–12 September as planned. See *CN*, p. 342.
3. James spent most of June and July with George Abbott James, an old friend who was not related to him (*HJL*, IV, 597).
4. George V succeeded Edward VII in 1910 and was crowned in Westminster Abbey on 22 June 1911.

## 295

Jan. 22nd, 1913.

Henry James Esq.,
Lamb House,
Rye. Sussex.

Dear Sir,

We beg to advise you that we have this day paid into the credit of your a/c at Lloyd's Bank, Rye, the sum of £15-7-11 in settlement of publishing a/c to June 30 last.[1]

> We are, Yours faithfully,
> p.p. Macmillan & Co., Ltd.,
> G. J. Heath[2]

**Notes**

1.  TLS. Presumably for books contracted for before Pinker became his agent in 1898. For James's acknowledgement, see letter 296.
2.  G. J. Heath had joined the firm in 1877, came to know the 'whole financial aspect of publishing', and eventually became manager (Morgan, pp. 235–6).

## 296

> 21 Carlyle Mansions
> Cheyne Walk, S.W.
> February 5th., 1913[1]

Messrs. Macmillan and Co., Ltd.

Dear Sirs.

I am obliged to you for having paid into my account at Lloyd's Bank Ltd., Rye, the cheque – £15.7.11 – your letter of Jan. 22nd. informs me of. I have now a new London address, which kindly note, and your letter appears to have suffered some accidental delay in reaching me.

I am addressing you by this post, in another envelope, several sheets of Messrs. Ch. Scribner's Sons' paged Revise of my Book, "A Small Boy and Others", which you will be now setting up, I infer; as Messrs. Scribner tell me they are rapidly sending you this form of Copy.[2] I send the pages in question simply that you may take advantage of the few small corrections that I have marked on them. I will at once mark any others that are needful on receipt of the rest of the Revise, and let you have them so that you may kindly take advantage of the small rectifications. The Copy as a whole is so absolutely correct and right that I feel I shall not require to have Proof from you if you will see that it is followed carefully in every particular. Believe me yours very truly

> Henry James

P.S.   I am, after all, enclosing the few pages of the revise for setting up in this.[3]

**Notes**

1. TLS. James's new address is a flat in Chelsea he had examined the previous summer, as he indicated in correspondence with Gosse in the following October. See, for example, his letter of 7 October 1912 in *SLHJEG*, pp. 270–72. He had moved into Carlyle Mansions in January. For the cheque, see letter 295.
2. Scribner brought out the first volume of James's autobiography in New York on 29 March 1913, and Macmillan published the English edition 1 April. See *BHJ*, pp. 149–50. A memorandum of agreement with Macmillan, dated 20 November 1912, provided for the same terms for *A Small Boy* and *Notes of a Son and Brother*, viz. a 25% royalty with a down payment on the first 1,000 copies upon publication at 12/- (LB, MA).
3. The postscript is in James's own hand.

## 297

February 7th 1912 [1913][1]

Henry James, Esq.,
21, Carlyle Mansions,
Cheyne Walk, S.W.
My dear James,

I have your letter, and am glad to see that you are now settled in London; I hope in good health. I was away during the whole of January and only returned from Rome a fortnight ago.

I am much obliged to you for the corrected pages of your book, *A Small Boy and Others*. We shall take it for granted that the pages you have not sent to us are accurate and can be printed without further reference to you.

I suppose that the interesting daguerrotype [*sic*], of which we have just received a proof from Scribners, is the portrait the taking of which is described in the book itself.[2]

I am,
Yours ever,
Frederick Macmillan

**Notes**

1. TLS. Since James had moved into his flat in January 1913, the year in Macmillan's letter is incorrectly recorded as 1912. Moreover, the text of the letter is in response to James's of 5 February 1913.
2. The portrait referred to is the frontispiece to the book and is of Henry James and his father in 1854. See also letter 298.

**298**

Dictated.
21, Carlyle Mansions,
Cheyne Walk. S.W.
February 8th., 1913.[1]

My dear Macmillan.

All thanks for your letter of yesterday, this morning received. I am glad to learn by it of your own return, after much pleasure and profit I hope.[2]

You may take for granted that the Copy for A Small Boy etc. is exactly right, and has only to be scrupulously followed to the last comma etc. – by which I mean also to the last absence of the intrusive comma! – to serve perfectly. The Proof of the Photogravure of the Daguerreotype *is* from the picture spoken of in the text. Charles Scribner wrote me a day or two ago that he had sent it you, and that he can supply you with a Plate as frontispiece – but this he will have written to yourself. The Title to the frontispiece should be, please: "Henry James and his Father, from a daguerreotype taken in 1854." (The slip accompanying the proof sent to me had an error in date, 1855, which I have rectified.)[3]

I thank you for your good hopes for my health – which cannot, I assure you, after so dreadfully long an ordeal, exceed my own. I have pretty well emerged from my very latest visitation, a perfectly infernal attack of Herpes ("Shingles") followed by a fearful gastric and stomachic aggravation, of the most painful kind, and the most prolonged, over the whole ravaged Herpetic region; this being one of the sequent ills that Shingles at their worst produce; and this emergence is so much to the good. I have another trouble to reckon with – but I won't go into that, as I didn't at all mean to write you so "pathological" a letter; all the more that it will probably again prove manageable, as it has proved before, and as, above all, I have some such good elements still of strength and soundness.[4] But what will do me more good than anything else will be the getting back to a sustained and steady ability to work. I have for these now more than three years been in that respect damnably blighted. But on good days I really feel as if I had at last struggled quite *through*. I think of you as of the most consistent soundness, and I trust I am right. Believe me yours all faithfully

Henry James.

**Notes**

1. TLS.
2. The Macmillans had recently returned from Rome. See letter 297.
3. The title was printed as James directed.
4. James had contracted the 'atrocious affection known as "Shingles"' in September 1912, as he had written Gosse on 7 October (*SLHJEG*, pp. 270–72). The other 'trouble' referred to was presumably angina pectoris.

## 299

> 21, Carlyle Mansions,
> Cheyne Walk. S.W.
> February 19*th* 1913

My dear Macmillan.

This is a word to say that I am sending to St. Martin's Street, by this post, separately, correct Copy for the 2 last Chapters (XXVIII & XXIX) of "A Small Boy &c."[1] Yours all faithfully

> Henry James

**Notes**

1. The book appeared in London on 1 April 1913 (*BHJ*, p. 150).

## 300

> Feb 20 1913

My dear James,

Very many thanks for the corrected proof of Chapters 28 & 29 of your book. We can now go ahead with the printing. I am in correspondence with Scribners as to the date of publication which ought to be simultaneous in this country & in America.[1]

I hope that your health continues to mend. Believe me

> Yours ever,
> Frederick Macmillan

Henry James Esq
21 Carlyle Mansions
Cheyne Walk

**Note**

1.    See letter 299. Publication dates varied by only a few days – the American edition appearing on 29 March 1913 and the English issue a few days later on 1 April. *BHJ*, pp. 149–50.

## 301

March 3 1913

My dear James,

Scribners sent us proofs of the whole of your book except the Title page. Our printers here set up the enclosed, which of course can be altered to any extent if you will send the necessary instructions.[1]

Believe me
Yours ever,
Frederick Macmillan

Henry James Esq
21 Carlyle Mansions
Cheyne Walk

**Note**

1.    The reference is to *A Small Boy and Others*. See letters 299 and 300.

## 302

Dictated.

21, Carlyle Mansions,
Cheyne Walk. S.W.
March 31st., 1913.

Sir Frederick Macmillan.[1]
My dear Macmillan.

I am taking for granted that I shall have, on publication of the Volume, half a dozen copies of "A Small Boy etc." at my disposal, and am herewith enclosing you a list of certain friends to whom I should like a few sent. My list will at the best somewhat transcend my allowance of copies – and I shall be obliged if you will send me on this score a memorandum of what the extra ones will cost; as, instead of being debited with them on your account, I should prefer to send you a cheque for the sum at once. If I *am* entitled to six (let me premise) I shall be glad to have *two* of that number despatched to me here, while the others go to my list, which I put on a separate sheet.[2]

Yours all faithfully
Henry James

P.S.   I see that my Extra Copies, beyond the 6 that I hypothesise, will come to 12; for which I pay.[3]

### Notes

1. TLS. Frederick Macmillan had been knighted in 1909.
2. James's list is not included with his letter in LB, MA.
3. Despite James's instructions regarding extra copies, Macmillan, as of old, did not charge him for them. See letter 303.

## 303

April 1st 1913.[1]

Henry James, Esq.,
21, Carlyle Mansions,
Cheyne Walk, S.W.
My dear James,

   Your letter and mine crossed each other. We are sending you to-day one more copy of *A Small Boy and Others*, and are forwarding copies, with the author's compliments, to the persons whose names you give; there will be no charge for these.[2]

I am,
Yours ever,
Frederick Macmillan

### Notes

1. TLS.
2. As was his habit with James, Macmillan did not charge for extra presentation copies. See, for example, letter 149. The only exception to this practice was with the Edition de Luxe. See letter 281 and note 1.

**304**

Dictated.

21, Carlyle Mansions,
Cheyne Walk. S.W.
April 4th., 1913.[1]

My dear Macmillan.

I have had to delay a day or two to tell you (and am now obliged to do so in this form) that I am greatly obliged to you for your handsome allowance of Copies of A Small Boy etc., and that these will amply suffice – on the "free" basis, I mean.[2] I shall perhaps have to ask you to send out 3 or 4 more – such is the far range, alas, of really indicated propriety for me; but the charge for these I shall at the same time ask of you; without waiting for which, moreover, let me now beg that you be so good as to direct *that no reviews or notices of the Book be sent me.* This was anciently always my preference – I mean the not receiving them; but I forgot to mention it.[3]

There is another small matter – the result of my own obliviousness; which I refer to now on the chance that it isn't too late for something to be done about it. On the back of the Titlepage of the Book, or facing the reader on the left-hand side of some preliminary leaf, in the Scribners' issue, I look to find (when I see it) placed, by my request, the announcement of the complementary volume to this, as who should say: "In preparation; by the same Author: Notes of a Son and Brother." I meant to have asked you to have that inserted here, and stupidly forgot, though I saw it as rather important. Could anything still be done about it – for later impressions? If so will you kindly have it done?[4] If it isn't practicable no matter!

Yours all faithfully
Henry James

**Notes**

1. TLS.
2. For the 'free' copies of *A Small Boy*, see letter 303.
3. James's request concerning reviews of his books goes back to the late 1880s.
4. Macmillan accedes to the request in letter 305.

## 305

April 8th 1913.[1]

Henry James, Esq.,
21, Carlyle Mansions,
Cheyne Walk, S.W.

My dear James,

In reply to your letter of the 4th inst., I write to say that we can very easily print a leaf announcing *Notes of a Son and Brother* as 'in preparation', which leaf can be inserted in all unsold copies of *A Small Boy and Others*.[2]

> I am,
> Yours ever,
> Frederick Macmillan

**Notes**

1. TLS.
2. Macmillan immediately saw to it that a cancel leaf stating that *Notes of a Son and Brother* was 'in preparation' was inserted into all 'unsold copies'. See *BHJ*, p. 149.

## 306

Dictated.

21, Carlyle Mansions,
Cheyne Walk. S.W.
April 13th. 1913.[1]

My dear Macmillan.

It comes over me with sudden dismay that I might have before this positively rejoined to your good assent to the insertion of a leaf in all unsold copies of *A Small Boy* printedly announcing that Notes of a Son and Brother are "in preparation". My silence came but from my taking your understanding that I shall rejoice in this for granted; though I may mention that, now that I have a Scribners' copy of the Book, I see that for some reason or other, they *haven't* so proceeded. I took for granted they would – and your doing so will be much better.[2] Kindly act accordingly and believe me yours ever

Henry James

Sir Frederick Macmillan.

P.S.    Let me beseech you to find a convenient moment to cast your vote at the Athenaeum Ballot of to-morrow p.m. for the really admirable Guy du Maurier, the Candidate I second.[3]

**Notes**

1.    TLS.
2.    The Macmillan issue did indeed include the announcement. See letter 305, and note 2.
3.    In letter 307 Macmillan agrees to vote for Guy Du Maurier, the son of James's late friend George Du Maurier (1834–96).

### 307

April 14th 1913.[1]

Henry James, Esq.,
21, Carlyle Mansions,
Cheyne Walk, S.W.
My dear James,

It is all right. I took it for granted that as you did not object to our suggestion you would assent to the insertion of a leaf in *A Small Boy and Others*. This is being done.[2]

I will certainly vote for Guy du Maurier at the Atheneaum [*sic*] this afternoon.[3]

I am,
Yours ever,
Frederick Macmillan

**Notes**

1.    TLS.
2.    See letters 305 and 306.
3.    See letter 306, note 3.

### 308

Lamb House
Rye [,] Sussex
October 16*th* 1913.

My dear Macmillan.

I should have finished my Volume "Notes of a Son & Brother" 2 or 3 weeks ago if I had not been held up by the temporary defection of my amanuensis, on whom the end of book – its ending – had, for reasons, led me particularly to depend.[1] However, that goal is in near view, & I desire very much in this case to send you the MS. (very *good* MS. *as* MS.) straight, & not in the form, this time, of the American sheets – as was the case with the *Small Boy*. But what I should like to ask you is whether in this case you should be able to set it up with rather earnest *rapidity* for me, so that I may be able to post off the sheets to the Scribners in N. Y., for *their* production of the volume, with the minimum of delay.[2] I feel a good bit belated all round, & desire to shake off the consciousness; so that a word of good assurance from you as to promptitude of printing here will enable me to write to New York about the matter with a high confidence. (I can't *conveniently* send them copious duplicate MS.) I hope not to come up to London for the winter till about Dec: 10*th* – but I imagine you as already back there perhaps – & I hope in "good shape." Yours all faithfully

Henry James

**Notes**

1. Theodora Bosanquet (1880–1961), James's typist since 1907, returned to work on 28 October 'after several weeks absence' (*CN*, p. 381).
2. Macmillan responded favourable to this request in letter 309.

# 309

October 17th 1913.[1]

Henry James, Esq.,
Lamb House,
Rye, Sussex.
My dear James,

I had a note from Mr. Pinker the other day to say that you would probably ask us to set up the plates of *A Son and Brother* first in this country, and I told him of course that we should be very glad to do so. If you will send us the manuscript I will see that it is put through with all speed.[2]

I hope you are keeping well. We shall look forward to seeing you in London early in December.[3]

With kindest regards,

> I am,
> Yours ever,
> Frederick Macmillan

### Notes

1. TLS.
2. Pinker, James's agent, had anticipated his client's request made in letter 308, and Macmillan had written him on 15 October (LB, MA) that the book would be 'set up' in London.
3. James returned to London earlier than anticipated – on 19 November (see letter 310) – and dined with the Macmillans on 4 December (*CN*, pp. 382, 383).

## 310

> Lamb House
> Rye [,] Sussex
> November 6th. 1913.[1]

My dear Macmillan.

I have greatly regretted the inevitable delay in my sending you my great lump of a Manuscript (Notes of a Son and Brother;) but it goes to you by post definitely to-day – and the extraneous reasons which have during these last days complicated my getting it off don't now matter.[2] Of course I shall greatly rejoice in swiftness of setting-up, as my promptitude with proof-reading will vividly testify. The Book is slightly longer, as to number of pages, than A Small Boy; but not so much so, if I am not mistaken, as to require any reduction of the beautiful page in which the S.B. was cast. There are a great many cited letters, but as these are all of necessity in small type, the page taking thus twice as many lines, the question of space will come to about the same thing.[3] I am sending your proof-sheets to Charles Scribner for setting up of the New York volume, and shall thus be very glad of course of an *extra* Revise (which is what I shall transmit to him) for the purpose. And the Book is much Better than the Other! I come up to town for the winter about the 20th.[4]

> Yours all faithfully
> Henry James

P.S. Scribner is having a few drawings and photographs reproduced for illustration, but I fear I can't be definite about this matter
for some little time yet. There will probably be a frontispiece, but the
number of the other things will fall short, I think, of a dozen; and as
none of them will be in the text, but all separate, I judge there will be
no difficulty as to Scribner's sending you plates for your own use as
soon as these are ready. You shall in this case have plenty of time.[5]

**Notes**

1. TLS.
2. In his pocket-diary entry for 6 November, James notes: 'I took down and posted
   to the Macmillans complete copy of Notes of a Son and Brother' (*CN* p. 381).
3. In the Macmillan texts, the *Small Boy* contained 440 pages and *Notes* had 482
   pages (*BHJ*, pp. 149, 151).
4. James actually arrived in town on the night of 19 November (*CN*, p. 382).
5. A frontispiece and five illustrations were eventually included (*BHJ*, p. 151).

# 311

November 10th 1913.[1]

Henry James, Esq.,
Lamb House,
Rye, Sussex.
My dear James,

I write to acknowledge your letter of the 6th and the manuscript
of *Notes of a Son and Brother*. The latter has already gone to the
printers, and proofs will be sent to you with as little delay as possible. I shall certainly try to use exactly the same type as for 'A Small
Boy'; unless the book is very much longer than the former one we
shall be able to do so.[2]

I am,
Ever yours,
Frederick Macmillan

**Notes**

1. TLS.
2. Though *Notes* contained forty-two pages more than *A Small Boy*, Macmillan
   retained the same type and page size of the first volume. See *BHJ*, pp. 149–51.

**312**

21 Carlyle Mansions
Cheyne Walk [,] S.W.
December 18*th* 1913.

Messrs. Macmillan Co. Ld.[1]
Dear Sirs.

There has been an accidental delay of a day or two in my returning you the enclosed Proof – or rather there has been a slight *intentional*! I have kept it over a little to see if I should get used to the *&* in the Title instead of an *and*.[2] I find I have done so, & now I prefer it & think it handsome & right. Only please note that I have marked the importance of a reference, as nearly face to face with Title as possible, to the former Vol. of which this is the Sequel & Complement. This mention of *A Small Boy & Others* as preceding & leading up to the present ought to be very much in evidence.[3]

Further, may I have a word from you as to whether you are yourselves sending a complete set of the Revise to Messrs. Charles Scribner's Sons, 597 Fifth Avenue, New York, as I seem to gather from a letter of theirs just received? I myself have sent them my duplicate paged Proofs as coming-in, but should be glad if they might now have the whole Set from yourselves.

The question of some 6 or 8 photogravure *illustrations* is under consideration with them (at the least a Frontispiece) – but I understand from them that they are communicating with you about this.[4] Believe me yours very truly

Henry James

**Notes**

1.  James addressed this letter to the firm because he apparently thought Frederick Macmillan had left the office for the Christmas holiday. See letter 313.
2.  For emphasis, James put the underscored words in boxes.
3.  For James's concern about relating the two volumes, see letters 304–7.
4.  James had already mentioned the page proofs in letter 310 and the illustrations in the postscript to that letter.

**313**

December 19th 1913.[1]

Henry James, Esq.,
21, Carlyle Mansions,
Cheyne Walk, S.W.

My dear James,

I reply to your letter of yesterday addressed to the firm, although this is my last day here.[2]

I write to say that we will certainly add an advertisement of *A Small Boy and Others* exactly opposite the title-page of *Notes of a Son and Brother*; it undoubtedly ought to be there.

We have not hitherto sent any proofs to Scribners, but I will arrange now to send them a complete set of the sheets as finally revised by yourself. We are already in correspondence with them about the photogravures.[3]

I am off to-morrow, as I say, for four weeks, and expect to be back here on January 25th. Meanwhile, with all best wishes for Christmas and the New Year,

I am,
Yours ever,
Frederick Macmillan

**Notes**

1. TLS.
2. See letter 312, note 1.
3. These are Macmillan's favourable responses to James's requests in letter 312.

**314**

January 9th. 1914.[1]

Henry James, Esq.,
21, Carlyle Mansions,
Cheyne Walk, S.W.

Dear Mr. Henry James,

I am writing to acknowledge your letter of January 7th., addressed to my father, who is in India till the end of February.[2]

We will do all we can to help Mr. Coburn in putting him in touch with Lewis Carroll's representatives, who will probably know more about the photographs than we do.[3]

> I am,
> Yours truly,
> Daniel Macmillan

### Notes

1. TLS.
2. Since Frederick Macmillan was away from his office temporarily (see letter 313), James had written to Maurice Macmillan, Daniel's father, only to learn that he, too, was out of town. Maurice had been in charge of the firm's business in India since the 1880s.
3. The reference is to Alvin Langdon Coburn (1882–1966), James's friend and the photographer who provided the photographic frontispieces for the Edition de Luxe (New York Edition) of James's work. The late Lewis Carroll (C.L. Dodgson, 1832–98) had also published with Macmillan. The photographs referred to have not been identified.

## 315

> Feb 3 1914

My dear James,

I find on looking up Scribner's letter that I was mistaken about the number of illustrations they are doing for your new book [.] The number is *six*.[1]

> I am
> Yours ever,
> Frederick Macmillan

Henry James Esq

### Note

1. The total includes the frontispiece. See letter 310, note 5.

# 316

21 Carlyle Mansions
Cheyne Walk, S.W.
3rd. March 1914[1]

My dear Macmillan.

As I understand that Notes of a Son and Brother is to be very immediately out I am addressing to you a list of the names of a few friends to whom I should like Author's Copies sent – and this in particular because I have given such an assurance in respect of one of them at the earliest possible day that I beg you to let me call your attention to it. It is the first name on the list – the Hugh Bells sailing for America on Saturday and I having promised Lady B. that she shall if possible have the book on this Friday 6th., in order to take it with her and read it on the ship. I shall be very glad therefore if you can see that she receives it as soon as possible at 95 Sloane Street, as indicated. I dare say my list transcends my allowance of Author's Copies; if so please debit me for the amount by which it exceeds.[2] Of course I shall greatly appreciate one Copy for myself *here*. I languish in particular to see what has become of the illustrations – I mean of the so too much reduced (I fear) reproductions of my Brother's drawings. My Nephew writes me, alas, from New York that they have lost much by belittlement, but I have as yet seen nothing.[3] May nothing and nobody, however, belittle the Text! Yours all faithfully

Henry James

### Notes

1.  TLS. The stationery has the Reform Club's address imprinted on it, but the Carlyle Mansions address is typed in.
2.  The list is not available with James's letter in LB, MA, but a note in pencil on the letter indicates that James's request regarding Lady Bell is to be honoured. Though the book came out on 13 March (*BHJ*, p. 151), it is likely that Lady Bell received an advance copy in time. James had known Sir Hugh (1844–1931) and Lady Florence Bell (1851–1930) for years, had visited them in Yorkshire, and had exchanged many letters with Lady Bell (see *HJL*, III, 310–11, for example). For Macmillan's practice with regard to presentation copies, see letters 44, 149 and 303.
3.  The illustrations for both American and English editions are 'smaller than text page size' (*BHJ*, p. 151). The nephew is presumably Henry James III, William's eldest son.

**317**

Mch 16 1914

My dear James,

Very appreciative reviews of your book are coming in every day, but we are not forwarding them to you as I fancy you do not care to read newspaper criticism of your work.[1] They are of course at your service if you care to see them. There is every sign that the book is going to "do".[2]

Believe me<br>Yours ever,<br>Frederick Macmillan.

Henry James Esq

**Notes**

1. James, as he reported in letter 304, had 'anciently' requested that notices and reviews not be sent him. See also letter 318.
2. According to *BHJ*, 'the first (and only) printing' in England consisted of '1250 copies' (p. 151).

**318**

Dictated.

21 Carlyle Mansions<br>Cheyne Walk, S.W.<br>March 17th 1914[1]

My dear Macmillan.

Kindly permit me to thank you with this lurid legibility, under excaptional [sic] pressure, for your interesting note about reviews etc. of my book just out. I am glad to hear of such friendly symptoms, but shall not trouble you to have them passed on – not from indifference to the reception of the work, but from preferring, on the whole, to take the friendliness for granted and perhaps even hug a little the illusion of its being even more splendid than in fact.[2] May it at any rate be splendid enough to give the book a lift; I am delighted to hear that there is such an appearance, and am yours all faithfully

Henry James

Sir Frederick Macmillan.
St. Martin's Street, W.C.

**Notes**

1.   TLS. Although this is James's last letter in LB, MA, he continued to visit the Macmillans from time to time until May 1915, only six months before his final illness (*CN*, 395–98, 403, 404, 422).
2.   This had been James's habit with the firm since the late 1880s. See letter 304, for example.

# Index

'Abasement of the Northmores,
  The', 195n2
Abbey, Edwin A., 129n2
Adams, Clover (Marian Hooper),
  76n4
Adams, Henry, 76n4
Albemarle, George Thomas Keppel,
  Earl of, 5, 6n2
Aldrich, T. B., 121n1
*American Scene, The*, xxii, 210,
  211n4
*American, The*
  American edition of, 3, 4n2
  author's copies of, 34
  changes by James for, 23
  in *Collective Edition*, 79
  English edition of, xviii, 4n2,
    14n1, 21–2, 21n1, 21n4, 22n1,
    25n4, 48
  financial arrangements for, 15n1,
    25–6
  French translation of, 91n1
  Grove's reservations about, 14,
    14n1, 15n4
  Nelson reprint of, 217–19, 218n2,
    219n1
  piracy of, 6n1, 14, 14n1, 48
  plates for, 21, 22
  proofs, of, 25, 26
  sales of, xviii, 6n1, 52, 52n1, 64,
    65n1
  six-shilling edition of, 52, 52n1,
    65n1, 91n2
Anesko, Michael, xiii, xxv
Arnold, Matthew, 33, 34n3, 75n6,
  129n2
*Aspern Papers, The*
  author's copies of, 147–8
  financial arrangements for,
    141n5, 160n2
  length of, 150
  publication of, 140, 141n3, 142n2,
    145, 146, 146n4, 147n2, 148,
    148n1, 156

*Atlantic Monthly*
  dramatised *Daisy Miller* in, 81n4
  *The Europeans* in, 10–11, 10n3,
    11n2, 15n2, 16n4
  'The Old Things' in, 177, 178n2
  *Portrait of a Lady* in, 38–40, 38n2,
    39n2, 40n2, 42, 43, 57–8, 57n1
  *The Princess Casamassima* in, 124n1
  *The Tragic Muse* in, 145, 156, 157,
    158n3
  Turgénieff article in, 202n1
*Author of Beltraffio, The*, xviii, 75n6,
  82n5, 91, 91n3, 93, 94n1, 104n5
*Awkward Age, The*, 177, 177n1,
  177n2, 187n3, 188n2

'Beldonald Holbein, The', 19–20,
  20n1
Bell, Lady Florence, 241, 241n2
Bell, Sir Hugh, 241, 241n2
Bertens, Rosa, 202n2
Besant, Walter, 206, 207n2
Binyon, Mrs Laurence, 209
Boer War, 196, 196n3
*Bohemian, The* (De Kay), 24–5, 24n1,
  26
Booth, Edwin, 62, 63n6
Bosanquet, Theodora, 235n1
*Bostonians, The*
  American reception of, 122, 122n2
  author's copies of, 120–1, 121n1,
    122
  Brett's view of, xix
  contract with Osgood for, 100–1,
    115–17, 117nn2–4
  financial arrangements for,
    105–6, 105n1, 110, 110n1,
    123, 124, 124n2, 142n3, 158n1
  James's work on, 92–3
  length of, 77, 78n5
  number of copies printed, 122,
    122n1
  one-volume edition of, 121,

121nn1–2, 122n1
plates of, 110–13, 111n1
proofs of, 119
publications of, xx, 101, 102n2,
    103n3, 105
serialisation of, 99–104,
    104nn2–3, 105–6, 106n1, 107,
    113n2, 119n1
three-volume edition of, 120–1,
    121nn1–2, 122n1
Bourget, Paul, 216n2
Brett, George E., xviii, 103n3,
    111n2, 174n2
Brett, George P.
contact with Macmillan for
    assistance in dealing with
    James, 188n1
and delay in publication of *The
    Two Magics,* 191, 191n2
direct dealings with James rather
    than his agent, 223n1
and *Embarrassments,* xxi, 177n2,
    180
in England, 176, 186–7, 190n4,
    192, 192n4
James's plans with, 186–92,
    187n2, 188nn2–3
James's unhappiness with, xxii,
    184n1, 195–6n2
and *John Delavoy,* 189–90
and *The Other House,* xxi, 177n2,
    178–81, 179n1, 179n3, 180n3,
    183, 187, 187n4
as president of Macmillan
    Company of New York,
    xviii, 111–12n2, 174n2, 175n1
request of short story from
    James, 200–1, 201n2
and *The Soft Side,* 194–7,
    195–6nn2–3, 197n2
Bronson, Katherine De Kay, 24n2
Broughton, Rhoda, 128, 128n1
'Bundle of Letters, A', 52, 52n2,
    59n2
Burnett, Frances Hodgson, 68, 69n4


Carlyle, Thomas, 129n2
Carr, J. W. Comyns, xviii, 74, 75n4,
    140

Carroll, Lewis, 240, 240n3
*Century*
article on 'Robert Louis
    Stevenson' in, 130, 130n3,
    131n1
*The Bostonians* in, 99–104,
    104nn2–3, 105n1, 107, 113n2,
    119n1
'The Liar' in, 145, 146n5, 150
Chapman, Mrs John Jay, 121n1
Charles Scribner's Sons, *see*
    Scribner's
Chatto and Windus
ending of rights to *Confidence,*
    80n2, 81, 84, 84n2
publication of *Confidence* by, xix,
    47n2, 77, 79, 80n2
*Choice of Books and Other Literary
    Pieces, The* (Harrison), 129,
    129n2, 130
Clifford, Lucy Lane (Mrs W. K.),
    208, 208n3
Coburn, Alvin Langdon, 222n1,
    240, 240n3
*Collective Edition*
appearance of, 77
contents of, 77–9, 78nn5–6, 80–1,
    80nn2–3
Macmillan's interest in, 48, 50n3,
    77, 78n2
plans for, 79–81, 80nn2–3
publication of, xviii, xxiv, 75n7,
    78n2, 90n4
type sample for, 79
*Collier's Weekly,* 189, 190n3
Collins, Arthur, 122, 123, 123n3
*Confidence*
in *Collective Edition,* 50n3, 77, 79,
    80n2, 81, 84, 84n1
ending of rights of Chatto and
    Windus to, 80n2, 81, 84, 84n2
financial arrangements for, 47n2
Macmillan's interest in, 47, 49
Macmillan's response to
    publication by Chatto and
    Windus, xix, 48
publication of, by Chatto and
    Windus, xix, 47n2
questions about proper names in,
    84, 85

Conrad, Joseph, 216n2
Cook, Thomas W., 72
Copyright, 140, 141n2, 171, 172n1
Coquelin, Benoit Constant, 129n2
*Cornhill Magazine, The*, 146n3
*Cosmopolis*, 194, 194n3
'Cousin Maria' (*see also* 'Mrs
   Temperly'), 141n4, 144n1
'Covering End, The', 190n3
Craig, Gibson, 135
Craik, George Lillie, xviii, 50–1,
   50n1, 53
Crawford, Francis Marion, 112n2,
   172, 172n1, 203–5, 204n3
Curtis, Ariana, 163n3
Curtis, Daniel, 163n3

*Daisy Miller*
   American edition of, 70n2
   author's copies of, 30–4, 33n1,
      34n2, 51, 51n1
   in *Collective Edition*, 77, 78n3
   English edition of, 30, 30n3, 33n1,
      70, 70n2
   financial arrangements for, 15n1,
      25–6
   one-volume edition of, 51
   plates of, 71, 71n1
   publication in the *Cornhill*, 146n2
   six-shilling edition of, 52n1, 91n2
   two-shilling edition of, 143
*Daisy Miller: A Comedy*, 70–1, 70n2,
   71n1, 72n3, 81, 81n4, 82n5,
   104n5
Dana, Charles A., 121n1
Daudet, Alphonse, 78n7, 81, 82n5,
   129n2, 155, 156n2, 157–8,
   158n4
'Diary of a Man of Fifty, The',
   28–31, 29nn1–2, 30n6
Dilke, Sir Charles W., 18, 19n1
Du Maurier, George, 78n7, 81,
   82n5, 129n2, 234n3
Du Maurier, Guy, 234, 234n3
Duckworth and Company, 177n1

Edel, Leon, xiii, xiv, xxv
Edition de Luxe (*see also* New York

Edition under Scribner's)
   author's copies of, 216–17,
      216nn1–2, 217n1, 222
   binding for, 215, 216n1
   charges for author's copies of,
      35n2, 216n2
   financial arrangements for, 213
   financial failure of, xxii–xxiii,
      217, 218n1
   frontispiece for, 240n3
   James's work on, 208n1, 210, 217
   memorandum of agreement
      concerning, 211n5, 212–13
   publication of, xxiv, 211n5
Edward VII, 225n1, 225n4
Eliot, George, 129n2
*Embarrassments*, xxi, 179–84, 177n2,
   180nn1–2, 182n1
Emerson, Ralph Waldo, 129n2, 130,
   130n3
*English Illustrated Magazine*
   'The Author of Beltraffio' in,
      xviii, 91, 91n3
   editors of, xviii, 75n4
   Fullerton's article on Cairo in,
      165, 165n1
   James's contributions to, 75,
      75n6
   James's interest in contributing
      to, 77, 78n6
   'The Patagonia', in, 141–2, 141n6
   proposed titles for, 74–5, 75n5
English Men of Letters series,
   17–18, 18nn3–4, 28, 28n4, 32n3,
   41, 41n3
*Esmeralda* (Burnett), 69n4
'Europe', 195n2
*Europeans, The*
   American edition of, 15n2
   author's copies of, 16, 18–19,
      19n1, 34
   in *Collective Edition*, 80n2
   English edition of, xviii, 10n3, 15,
      15n2
   financial arrangements for, 15,
      15n1, 25–6
   interest in serialisation in
      *Macmillan's Magazine*, 10–11,
      10n3, 11n2

Pater's praise for, 21, 21n2
printings of, 16n3
profit from, 16
promotion of, 19
reviews of, 20, 20n2
serialisation of, 10–11, 10n3,
 11n2, 15n2, 16n4
six-shilling edition of, 52n1, 91n2

Fawcett, Edgar, 121n1
*Finer Grain, The*, xxiii
Forbes-Robertson, Johnston, 208n4,
 211
'Fortune's Fool' (J. Hawthorne),
 79n10
Foster, James, 224, 224n2
*French Poets and Novelists*
 author's copies of, 34
 consultation with James on cover
  of, 12
 contents of, 202n1
 financial arrangements for, 6n1,
  15n1, 25–6
 James's inquiry letter to
  Macmillan on, xvii, 3–4
 lack of American edition of, 5–6,
  6n3
 length of, xvii, 6, 6n2
 Macmillan's consideration of, for
  publication, xvii, 4–5
 Macmillan's decision to publish,
  xvii, 5–7, 6n1
 printing of, 7
 proofs for, 8–11
 publication of, xviii, 4n3, 10n1
 reviews of, 12–13, 12n1
 Tauchnitz edition of, 73, 74n2,
  87–8, 87n2, 88n2
 unfavourable reading by Morley,
  6n1
Fullerton, Morton, 165, 165nn1–2,
 220–1, 220n2, 221n3

Gabillard, Mme, 153
Gardner, Mrs J. L. (Isabella
 Stewart), 121n1
Garnaut, Phoebe, 4n2
Garrison, W. P., 13, 13n2
Gates, Lewis E., 192, 192n4

George V, 225n4
'Georgina's Reasons', 93
Gilder, Richard Watson, 24, 24n2
'Given Case, The', 195n2
Godkin, Edwin Lawrence, 67, 68n3,
 82, 84n2, 109n1
Godkin, Katherine (Mrs E. L.),
 109n1, 121n1
*Golden Bowl, The*, xxii
Gosse, Edmund, xxii, 120n1, 144n2,
 216n2, 217n1, 218n1
Grädener, Karl, 54–5
Graves, Charles L., xiii
'Great Condition, The', 195n2
'Great Good Place, The', 195n2
Green, Alice Stopford, 76, 76n1, 78
Green, John Richard, 76, 76n1
Grove, George
 and 'The Diary of a Man of
  Fifty', 28–31, 29nn1–2, 30n6
 as editor of *Dictionary of Music
  and Musicians*, 46, 46n3
 as editor of *Macmillan's Magazine*,
  xviii, 24n3, 75n3
 James's meeting with, 15n2
 relationship with James, 24, 24n3
 reservations about *The American*,
  14, 14n1, 15n4
 and serialisation of *Portrait of a
  Lady*, 44, 46, 46n2, 52
Gurney, Mrs E. W. (Ellen Hooper),
 121n1

Harper and Brothers
 *The Awkward Age* published by,
  177, 177n1, 177n2
 *Hawthorne* published by, 27–8,
  27n1, 28n3, 46, 47n1
 as James's publisher, xxi, 177n1
*Harper's Magazine*, and James's
 translation of Daudet's *Port
 Tarascon*, 157–8
*Harper's Weekly*, 131–2, 132n2, 145,
 177n1
Harrison, Frederic, 129, 129n2
*Hawthorne*
 American edition of, 18n3
 completed work sent to Morley,
  41, 42

*Hawthorne* — *continued*
  English edition of, 18n3, 36, 37n2,
    48, 49n5
  financial arrangements for, 27–8,
    27n1, 28n3, 36, 43, 47n1
  James's decision to write, 21,
    21n1, 21n3
  Julian Hawthorne's help with,
    28, 28n4, 32n3
  memorandum of agreement with
    Harper and Brothers, 46,
    47n1
  Morley's reaction to, 43
  Morley's request for James to
    write book on, 17–18
  sales of, in America, 28n3, 47n1
Hawthorne, Julian, 28, 28n4, 32n3,
  51, 51n2, 69n5, 78, 79n10
Hawthorne, May Albertina
  Amelung, 68–9, 69n5
Hay, John, 68n5
*He That Will Not When He May*
  (Oliphant), 39n4
Heath, G. J., 226, 226n2
Heinemann, William, xxi, 176–81,
  177n1, 178n2, 180n1, 183, 185,
  190n3, 191, 191n2
Henley, William Ernest, 30, 30n5,
  33, 34n2
Herbert S. Stone and Co., 177n1
*High Bid, The*, 208, 208n3, 211
Hodgson, Francis, memoirs of, 23,
  23n1
Houghton, Richard Monckton
  Milnes, Lord, 17, 18n2
Houghton, Mifflin and Co.
  complaint about timing of
    *Macmillan's Magazine* in US,
    57–8
  as James's publisher, 177n1
  *The Old Things* published by,
    178n2
  *The Tragic Muse*, xx, 155–7,
    155n1, 157nn2–3, 158n3
Howard, George James, 34n1, 108n2
Howard, Rosalind Frances, 34,
  34n1, 108, 108n2, 109
Howe, Julia Ward, 19–20, 20n1,
  21n1

Howells, William Dean, 38, 38n3,
  40, 121n1
Hunt, William Morris, 62, 63n5
Hutton, R. H., 20n2
Hyatt, Alfred H., 207–9, 208n2

*Illustrated London News*, 178, 178n2,
  180, 180n3
'Impressions of a Cousin, The',
  78n5, 84n5, 92, 93n5
*In Cairo* (Fullerton), 165, 165n2
'International Episode, An', 146n3
Irving, Henry, 62, 63n6
*Ivory Tower, The*, 211, 211n7

James, Alice, 33–4, 72, 72n2, 73,
  74n3, 83
James, Garth Wilkinson (Wilky),
  28n4, 74n6
James, Henry
  advances for, 53, 65, 65n1, 90,
    90n3, 145–6
  in America, 64–9, 65n2, 69n1,
    71–83, 72n1, 72n4, 74n5,
    75n8, 76n3, 79n8, 84n6, 205,
    205n2, 208n1, 209, 223n1,
    224–5
  American reputation of, 6n1
  and bankruptcy of James R.
    Osgood, xix–xx, 99–104,
    110–11
  Bolton Street flat of, 11, 11n1,
    17n1, 57, 57n2
  Chelsea flat of, 120n1, 227n1
  consultation with, about binding,
    paper and type of books, 12,
    12n1, 56–7, 215, 215n1
  contract with James R. Osgood,
    115–17
  and copyright, 140
  in Cornwall, 57
  death of, xxiv
  debt to father, 35n2
  in Dover, 92–3, 114, 115n3
  drama by, 147n2, 177n1, 208,
    208n4, 211
  dropping use of 'Junior' in name,
    66n4, 73n5, 78, 79n11, 81,
    82n7

'farewell' letter to Macmillan, xx–xxi, 160–1, 161n2

and father's death, 71–2, 72nn1–2

financial arrangements with Chatto and Windus, 47n2

financial arrangements with Harpers, 27–8, 27n1, 28n3, 47n1

financial arrangements with Macmillan, xx–xxi, 6n1, 15, 15n1, 25–6, 49, 50n2, 94–5, 94n3, 147n1, 158–61, 158n1, 159n2, 160n2, 161n2, 168n1

financial arrangements with Osgood, 90n3

financial contribution to Fullerton's book, 220–1

first letter to Macmillan, 3–4

in France, 9, 41, 60, 114, 114n2, 115n3, 154–5, 192, 192n2

French translations of works of, 91, 91n1, 118–19, 119n1, 152–3, 153n1

friendship with A. Macmillan, xviii, 39–40, 39n3, 45, 45n2

friendship with F. Macmillan, xviii, xxiii, xxiv, 10n2, 15n2, 47, 53, 64, 70, 76, 76n2, 89, 90n1, 125, 125n4, 134, 134n1, 137–8, 147, 147n2, 152, 170–1, 170n2, 221, 221n3, 236, 236n3, 243n1

friendship with Mrs F. Macmillan, xviii, xxiii, xxiv, 10n3, 38, 39n5, 47, 48, 49n4, 53, 76, 82, 83, 93, 148, 148n1, 221, 224–5

generosity of Macmillan with author's copies to, 32n2, 34, 34n2, 51n1, 121, 121n2, 152n1, 168, 168n1, 216n1, 231n3

and home in St John's Wood, 84, 84n3, 88, 88n3, 93, 93n4

homesickness for London, 68, 69n3, 73, 83, 162

illnesses and injuries of, 181n1, 223n1, 224–5, 228, 229n4

in Italy, 45, 48, 49n2, 54, 54n2, 60,

128, 128n2, 162–4, 163n3, 164n2

on De Kay's *The Bohemian*, 24–6, 24n1

Kensington flat of, 120, 120n1, 122n1, 122n3

at Lamb House, 192, 193n3

literary agents of, xxi–xxii, 161n2, 187n2, 193n2, 194, 195n2

Macmillan's suggestion that James consider a more 'general' audience, xvii, 6, 6n4

meeting with Grove, 15n2

memorandum of agreement on the Edition de Luxe, 212–13

memorandum of agreement with Macmillan and Company, 25–6

payments from Macmillan, 22, 22n1, 30–1, 30n7, 35–6, 35n2, 36n1, 43–4, 44n5, 50–3, 50n1, 53n1, 54n1, 56, 56n1, 60, 60n1, 64, 65n1, 72–3, 91, 94, 98n1, 110, 110n1, 124–6, 125n1, 125n3, 126n1, 133, 134n2, 142, 146, 147, 156, 157n4, 162, 162n1, 168–9, 168n1, 173, 173n1, 182, 186, 186n1, 197, 199, 222–6, 226n1

pets of, 73, 74n4

publishers of, xxi–xxii, 177n1, 208n1

relationships with Macmillan staff, xviii

review of J. Hawthorne's *Saxon Studies*, 28n4

review of *Memoir of the Revd Francis Hodgson, B. D.*, 23, 23n1

review of *Pensées of Joubert*, 13, 13n2; *see also* Joubert

reviews of works not wanted by, 13n1, 162, 163n2, 184–5, 185n2, 232, 232n3, 242, 242n1, 243n2

in Scotland, 16–17, 17n3

on supper parties, 144n2

Sussex retreat of, 181–2, 181n2, 182n2

James, Henry — *continued*
  in Switzerland, 148, 148n1
  translation of Daudet's *Port
      Tarascon*, 155, 156n2, 157–8,
      158n4
  Turgénieff article by, 201–3,
      202n1
  typist for, 69, 69n2, 235, 235n1
  unhappiness with Brett, xxii,
      195–6n2
  unhappiness with sales of works,
      xix, 42, 44n5, 89, 90, 146
  *see also* titles of works
James, Henry, Sr
  death of, 71–2, 72nn1–2
  friendships of, 33n1
  James's debt to, 35n2
  and sales of *Hawthorne*, 28n3,
      47n1
James, Robertson (Bob), 28n4
James, William, 63n5, 74n5, 106n1,
      121n1, 122n2, 193, 194n2,
      223n1
*John Delavoy*, 189, 189n2, 190n2,
      194, 195nn3–4
Joubert's *Thoughts*, review by James
      of, 13, 13n2

Kay, Charles De, 24–5, 24n1, 26
Keppel, George Thomas, *see*
      Albemarle, George Thomas
      Keppel, Earl of

'Lady Barberina' (later 'Lady
      Barbarina'), 77, 78n5, 84n5
LaFarge, Mrs John, 121n1
Lang, Andrew, 84n7
Lang, Mrs Andrew, 83, 84n7
Lazarus, Emma, 82, 84n4
*Lesson of the Master, The*
  American editor of, 166, 166n1,
      167n1
  author's copies of, 168, 168n1
  contents of, 154, 154n2
  English edition of, 166n1, 167n1,
      168n1
  financial arrangements for,
      141n5, 173, 173n1
  inclusion in Macmillan's

Colonial Library, 170, 171
  lack of stock of, 213–14
  proofs for, 166–7, 166n1, 167n1
  publication of, 146, 146n6, 147n2,
      156–7, 157n4, 170n1
  registration of title of, 146
  serialisation of, 145
  type used for, 172–3
Lewis, Elizabeth, 108, 108n1
Lewis, George Henry, 108n1
'Liar, The', 140, 145, 146nn5–6,
      150n2
'Light Man, A', 94
*Little Tour of France, A*, 104n5
Lodge, Mrs Henry Cabot, 121n1
*London Life, A*
  author's copies of, 150–2,
      151–2n1
  contents of, 140, 149–50, 150n2
  financial arrangements for, 141n5
  miscalculations in, 149–50, 150n1
  number of copies published, 152,
      152n2
  one-volume edition of, 152, 152n2
  publication of, 141n4, 146, 146n6,
      147n2, 151n1, 156
  sales of, 151, 152, 152n1
  in *Scribner's Magazine*, 145, 146n5
'London Town'
  agreement for, 206–7
  financial arrangements for, xxiv,
      204, 204n4, 205
  James's delays in writing,
      xxii–xxiii, 209–11, 211n8
  James's interest in, 205–6
  Macmillan's inquiries about, 208,
      208n3
  Macmillan's proposal to James,
      xxii, 203–4
Lord, Samuel, 37
'Lord Beauprey' (later 'Lord
      Beaupré'), 168–9, 168n1
'Louisa Pallant', 146n4, 150n2
Lubbock, Percy, xiii

Macmillan, Alexander
  friendship with James, xviii,
      39–40, 39n3, 45, 45n2
  interest in branch of Macmillan

in New York, 38–9n4
and Pater's praise for *The
    Europeans*, 21n2
and *Portrait of a Lady*, 39–40,
    39n2, 42, 42n1
request from James for payment,
    43–4, 44n5
wife of, 41, 41n4
Macmillan, Mrs Alexander (Emma
    Pignatel), 41, 41n4, 82
Macmillan, Daniel, 239, 240n2
Macmillan, Frederick O.
    in America, 38, 38–9n4, 40, 40n3,
        41, 41n2, 44, 44n6, 45,
        45nn1–2, 47, 52, 86n3, 87, 92,
        93n1, 164–5, 165n3
    in Bournemouth, 126n2, 127–8,
        127n2
    in Brighton, 115, 120, 120n2, 125,
        125n4, 154–5, 154n4
    consultation with James about
        binding, paper and type of
        books, 12, 12n1, 56–7, 215,
        215n1
    country retreat at Temple
        Dinsley, 181–2, 181n2
    driving tour to Cheshire by, 147
    first letter to James, 4–5
    in France, 7, 8, 9n2
    friendship with James, xviii,
        xxiii, xxiv, 10n2, 15n2, 47, 53,
        64, 70, 76, 76n2, 89, 90n1,
        125, 125n4, 134, 134n1,
        137–8, 147, 147n2, 152,
        170–1, 170n2, 221, 221n2,
        236, 236n3, 243n1
    generosity in author's copies to
        James, 32n2, 34, 34n2, 51n1,
        121, 121n1, 152n1, 168,
        168n1, 216n1, 231n3
    home in Walton-on-Thames, 63,
        63n4
    illness of, 24, 126
    in Italy, 202, 202n3, 203, 203n4,
        223, 227, 229n2
    marriage of, 10n10, 42n3
    in Normandy, 52
    Northwick Terrace home of, 92,
        92n3, 93, 93n4, 170, 170n2

    Overstrand country home of,
        215, 215n2
    on promotion of six-shilling
        editions of James, 64
    as reference for James, 120
    as representative of Macmillan in
        New York, 21n1, 42n3
    in St Moritz, 94n4, 95
    suggestion that James consider a
        more 'general' audience,
        xvii, 6, 6n4
    on supper parties, 143, 144n2
    in Switzerland, 92
    Weybridge home of, 169, 170n2
Macmillan, George A.
    business relationship with James,
        xviii, 42n4
    on *French Poets and Novelists*, 7–8
    on *Madonna of the Future*, 41
    and *Portraits of Places*, 88, 88n1
    and Turgénieff article by James,
        201–3
Macmillan, Georgiana Elizabeth
    Warrin
    in America, 38n4, 40–1, 40n3,
        41n2, 45n1, 47, 92–3, 93n1,
        164–5, 165n3, 181
    in Bournemouth, 126n2, 127–8,
        127n2
    in Brighton, 115, 120, 120n2, 125,
        125n4, 154–5, 154n4
    driving tour to Cheshire by, 147
    friendship with James, xviii,
        xxiii, xxiv, 10n3, 47, 48, 49n4,
        82, 148, 148n1, 221, 224–5
    health of, 47, 48n3, 92–5, 107,
        125, 125n4, 126, 127n2
    in Italy, 202–3, 202n3, 223
    marriage of, 10n3
    in St Mortiz, 94n4, 95, 97, 97n3
Macmillan, Malcolm Kingsley,
    97n2
Macmillan, Maurice Crawford,
    xviii, 85–6, 239, 240n2
Macmillan and Company
    advances for James's works, 65,
        65n1, 90, 90n3, 145–6
    as American corporation,
        111–12n2

Macmillan and Co. — *continued*
  financial arrangements with
    James, xx–xxi, 6n1, 15, 15n1,
    25–6, 49, 50n2, 94–5, 94n3,
    147n1, 158–61, 158n1, 159n2
  financial losses of, xxiv
  headquarters of, 90n2
  memorandum of agreement
    concerning the Edition de
    Luxe, 212–13
  memorandum of agreement with
    James, 25–6
  payments to James, 22, 22n1,
    30–1, 30n7, 35–6, 35n2, 36n1,
    43–4, 44n5, 50–3, 50n1, 53n1,
    54n1, 56, 56n1, 60, 60n1, 64,
    65n1, 72–3, 91, 94, 98n1, 110,
    110n1, 124–6, 125n1, 125n3,
    126n1, 133, 134n2, 142, 146,
    147, 156, 157n4, 162, 162n1,
    168–9, 168n1, 173, 173n1,
    182, 186, 186n1, 197, 199,
    222–6, 226n1
  staff of, xviii
  titles of James's works published
    by, xviii, xxiv
  *see also* titles of James's works
*Macmillan's Magazine*
  'The Diary of a Man of Fifty' in,
    28–31, 29nn1–2, 30n6
  editors of, xviii, 74, 75n3
  Grove as editor of, xviii, 24n3,
    75n3
  J. Hawthorne's 'Fortune's Fool'
    in, 79n10
  interest in serialisation of *The
    Europeans*, 10–11, 10n3, 11n2
  'The Life of Emerson' in, 130,
    130n3
  'Lord Beauprey' (later 'Lord
    Beaupré') in, 168–9, 168n1
  Morley as editor of, xviii, 74, 75n3
  Morris as editor of, 109n1
  *The Portrait of a Lady* in, xviii,
    37–40, 37n1, 38n2, 39n2,
    40n2, 42–4, 43n2, 46, 46n2,
    52, 52n3, 57–8, 57n1
  'The Reverberator' in, xviii,
    131–2, 132n1, 136

'Madame de Mauves', 75n7
*Madonna of the Future and other
    Tales, The*
  author's copies of, 40–1, 41n1,
    42n1, 43
  contents of, 35, 35n3
  in *Collective Edition*, 77, 78n3
  publication of, 35n3, 41n1, 44n1,
    47n2
  reviews of, 48, 49n2
  sales of, 47, 54, 62, 62n3
  six-shilling edition of, 52n1
  Tauchnitz publication in multi-
    volume set, 54n2
  two-shilling edition of, 143
Mathews, Mrs Frank, 33, 33n1
'Maud-Evelyn', 195n2
McClure, S. S., 140–3, 141n1, 142n1,
    143n2
*Memoir of the Revd Francis Hodgson,
    B.D.*, James's review of, 23,
    23n1
Methuen and Company, 177n1,
    194, 196, 196n3, 198, 208n1
Milnes, Richard Monckton, *see*
    Houghton, Richard Monckton
    Milnes, Lord
'Miss Gunton of Poughkeepsie',
    195n2
'Mrs Temperly' (first published as
    'Cousin Maria'), 141n4, 144n1,
    145, 146n6, 149–50, 150nn1–2
*Mr Isaacs* (Crawford), 112n2, 113
'Modern Warning, The', 146n4,
    150n2
Moore, Rayburn S., xiv
Morgan, Charles, xiv
Morley, John
  as author and editor, 18n2
  as editor of *Macmillan's Magazine*,
    xviii, 74, 75n3
  *Hawthorne* volume sent to, 41, 42
  and James's decision to write
    volume on Hawthorne, 21
  reaction to *Hawthorne*, 43
  request to James for book on
    Hawthorne, 6n1, 17–18
  unfavourable reading of *French
    Poets and Novelists*, 6n1

Morris, Mowbray, xviii, 109, 109n1, 114, 122–3, 131–2, 132n1
Mudie's Circulating Library, 59, 59n1
Muir, George B., xxiii, 214n1
Myers, Frederick, 151, 151–2n1

Nadal, Ehrman Syme, 5, 5n2, 9
Nelson, Thomas, and Sons, 217–19, 218n2, 219n1
'New England Winter, A', 78n5, 84n5
Norris, Frank, 192n4
*North American Review*, 23n1
Norton, Grace, 121n1
*Notes of a Son and Brother*
  announcement of, 232–4, 232n2, 233n2
  announcement of *A Small Boy and Others* in, 238–9
  author's copies for, 241, 241n2
  delay in work on, 234–5, 236
  illustrations in, 237–8, 237n5, 240, 241, 241n3
  length of, 236, 237n2
  number of copies printed, 242n2
  plates for, 235
  proofs of, 237–9
  publication of, xxiv
  reviews of, xxiii–xxiv, 242
Nowell-Smith, Simon, xiii, xxv, 15n3

'Old Things, The' (*see also The Spoils of Poynton*), 177, 178n2
Oliphant, Margaret, 37, 39, 39n4
Osgood, James R. and Co.
  *The American* published by, 3
  *The Author of Beltraffio* published by, 93, 94n1
  bankruptcy of, xix–xx, 77n5, 82n5, 90n3, 99–104, 108n3, 110–11
  and *Collective Edition*, 77, 81
  contract with James, 115–17
  *Daisy Miller* published by, 70n2, 71n1
  financial arrangements with, 90n3

plates for *The American*, 21, 22
  *Portraits of Places* published by, 86–8, 86n2
  publication of James's works by, 77, 81, 82n5, 83
Osgood, McIlvaine and Co., xxi, 177n1
*Othello* production, 62, 63n6
*Other House, The*
  American edition of, 177n2, 186, 186n2
  American serial rights for, 178–80, 179n3, 180n3
  author's copies of, 185
  English edition of, 185n3
  financial arrangements for, 178, 181–6, 184n1, 186n1
  number of copies printed, 187n4
  publication of, xxi, 178, 178n2
  serialisation of, 178, 178n2, 180–1, 188n1

Paget, Violet, 151, 152n1
'Pandora', 93
Parkman, Francis, 121n1
*Partial Portraits*
  author's copies of, 139
  change in title of, 129n2, 131, 131n2, 135
  contents of, 78n7, 82n5, 202n1
  essays in, 130, 130n3
  financial arrangements for, 129–30, 129n1, 139n2, 141n5, 142
  format for, 128–30
  James's proposal for, 128, 129n2
  length of, 134–5, 135n1, 136, 136n4
  proofs of, 138, 138n1
  proposed titles of, 135, 135n3, 136, 136n1
  publication of, 133, 134n3, 139, 139n1
'Passionate Pilgrim, A', 93
'Paste', 195n2
'Patagonia, The', 140–2, 141n1, 141n6, 142n3, 145, 146n6, 150, 150n2
Pater, Walter, 21, 21n2

'Path of Duty, The', 75n6, 93
Pawling, Syndey S., 191n2
Pennell, Joseph, xxii, 203, 204, 204n2, 211n8
*Pensées of Joubert*, James's review of, 13, 13n2
'Pension Beaurepas, The', 52n2, 59, 59n2, 75n7
Perry, T. S., 121n1
Phillips, Wendell, 4n2
Pillon, François, 119n1
Pillon, Mme F., 119n1
Pinker, James B.
  and Brett's interest in story by James, 200, 201n2
  and Edition de Luxe, 208n1, 211n5, 213, 216n1
  and *The Finer Grain*, xxiii
  and *The Great Good Place*, 194, 195n2
  and *Notes of a Son and Brother*, 235, 236n2
  payments to, 193n2, 223, 223n1
  and *The Soft Side*, 195–6, 195–6nn2–3, 198, 198n2
*Point of View, The*, 70, 70n1, 75, 76, 77n6, 83, 84n9, 89, 90n5
'Poor Richard', 95, 96n2
*Port Tarascon* (Daudet), James's translation of, 155, 156n2
*Portrait of a Lady, The*
  advance for, 65, 65n1
  American edition of, 68n4
  in *Atlantic Monthly*, 38–40, 38n2, 39n2, 40n2, 42, 43, 57–8, 57n1
  author's copies of, 66, 67n1, 68
    in *Collective Edition*, 79
  copyright of, 58
  English edition of, 37n1
  financial arrangements for, 39, 39n2, 40, 40n3, 43n2, 53, 54n1, 56, 56n1, 60, 60n1, 64, 65n2
  French translation of, 152–3, 153n1
  Grädener's interest in publication of, 54–5
  James to Grove on, 14, 15n3
  in *Macmillan's Magazine*, xviii, 37–40, 37n1, 38n2, 39nn2–3,
    40n2, 42–4, 43n2, 46, 46n2, 52, 52n3, 57–8, 57n1
  reviews of, 67, 68n5
  revisions for book form of, 63–4, 63n1
  sales of, 67, 68n4
  three-volume edition of, 52n2
*Portraits of Places*, 82n5, 83, 84n8, 85–9, 85n1, 86n2, 88n1, 90n4, 207–9
Powers, Lyall H., xiii
*Princess Casamassima, The*
  American edition of, 125n2, 126, 126–7n1
  author's copies of, 126, 128, 128n1
  design of, 123
  English edition of, 125n2, 126, 126–7n1
  financial arrangements for, 105n1, 123–4, 124n1, 125n1, 126, 126n1, 141n5, 142n3, 158n1
  number of copies printed, 142n4
  one-volume edition of, 125n2, 126, 126–7n1, 198, 199n2
  proofs of, 125
  request to reprint pages from, 207–9
  revised copy for, 123, 124
  three-volume edition of, 125n2, 126, 126–7n1
  two-shilling edition of, 137, 137n1, 142–3
Procter, Anne Benson Skepper, 61, 62n1, 84n4, 106–7, 107n3
Procter, Bryan Waller, 62n1, 107n3

'Real Right Thing, The', 195n2
*Real Thing and other Tales, The*
  copyright and, 171
  financial arrangements for, 170–1
  inclusion in Macmillan's Colonial Library, 170, 171
  James's proposal of, 169
  length of, 169
  proofs of, 171–6, 174n1, 175n1
  publication of, 176n1
Reinhart, Charles S., 144, 144n1, 145, 149

Renan, Ernest, 129n2
Reubell, Harriet, 216n2
*Reverberator, The*
  author's copies of, 143, 144, 146
  financial arrangements for, 133,
    133n1, 139, 139n2, 141n5, 142
  length of, 150, 151
  publication of, 133n3, 146n3
  and publication of *The Aspern
    Papers*, 142, 142n2
  sales of, 143, 144n1
  serialisation of, xviii, 131, 132n1,
    136, 138, 139n1
Rhodes, James Ford, 200, 200n2
Ritchie, Anne Isabella Thackeray,
  131, 132n2, 151, 151n1
*Roderick Hudson*
  author's copies of, 33–4, 216n2
  in *Collective Edition*, 79
  English edition of, xviii, 33, 33n1,
    35n3
  French translation of, 91n1
  one-volume edition of, 198,
    199n2
  review of, 30, 30n5, 34, 35n3
  sales of American edition in
    England, xviii, 6n1
  six-shilling edition of, 91n2
  two-shilling edition of, 137,
    137n1, 138n1
Rosebery, Countess of, 66, 67n1, 68,
  151, 151n1
Rosebery, Earl of (Archibald Philip
  Primose), 67n1, 151n1
Rothschild, Hannah de, *see*
  Rosebery, Countess of

Sainte-Beuve, Charles Augustin,
  129n2
Sands, Mahlon, 109n1
Sands, Mary Hartpence, 109, 109n1
Sargent, John Singer, 114, 114n4,
  129n2
*Saxon Studies* (J. Hawthorne),
  James's review of, 28n4
Schlesinger, Max, 61, 61n2, 62
Scribner's, Charles, Sons
  as James's publisher, 208n1
  'A Light Man' published by, 94

New York edition, xxiii, xxiv,
  210, 213n1, 216n1, 217, 218n1
*Notes of a Son and Brother*
  published by, 235–40
  purchase of Edition de Luxe
    from, 35n2, 216n1
*A Small Boy and Others* published
  by, 226, 227, 227n2, 228, 232
*Scribner's Magazine*, 145, 146n5, 150
*Siege of London, The*, 75–6, 75n7,
  77n6, 83, 84n9, 104n5
*Small Boy and Others, A*
  announcement of forthcoming
    volume in, 232–4, 232n2,
    233n2
  author's copies of, 230–2,
    231nn2–3
  frontispiece of, 227, 227n2, 228
  length of, 236, 237n2
  proofs of, 226–30
  publication of, xxiii, 227n2, 230n1
Smalley, Evelyn Garnaut, 199,
  199n2
Smalley, George Washburn, 3, 4n2,
  79n10, 125, 125n4, 199n2
Smalley, Phoebe Garnaut, 82, 199n2
Smith, Frank Berkeley, 207n3
Smith, W. H., and Sons, 59, 59n1,
  142, 142n4
*Soft Side, The*
  agreement for, 196
  author's copies of, 199, 199n2
  contents of, 190n2, 195n4, 197,
    197n2
  financial arrangements for,
    195n2, 196n3, 197
  James's proposal for, 189, 189n2,
    190n4, 192, 192n4, 194–5,
    195n4
  proofs of, 198
  publication of, xxii, 198n2
'Solution, The', 154–5, 154nn1–2,
  155n1
*Spoils of Poynton, The* (*see also* 'The
  Old Thing'), xxi, 178n2
Stephen, Leslie, 144, 146, 146n3
Stevenson, Robert Louis, 30, 30n5,
  100, 127, 127n2, 129n2, 130,
  130n3, 131n1, 147n2

*Stories Revived*, 93n2, 95–8, 96nn1–2, 97n4, 98n1, 105n5, 106–9, 107n1, 113–15, 113n1, 114n1
Sudermann, Hermann, 202n3
Symonds, John Addington, 18n4

*Tales of Three Cities*, 77, 78n5, 82n5, 92n1, 93n5, 104, 104–5nn5–6
Tauchnitz, 54–5, 54n2, 55n2, 73, 74n2, 87–8, 87n2, 88n2, 93
Tauchnitz, Baron Christian Bernhard von, 19, 19n1
'Third Person, The', 194, 195n4
Ticknor, Benjamin, 117n3
Ticknor and Co., 110–12, 115–18, 116n1, 117n3
Tilton, Caroline, 121n1
*Tragic Muse, The*
American edition of, xx, 155–6, 155n1, 157, 157nn2–3, 158n3
author's copies of, 162, 163
English edition of, xviii, 157n3, 162n1, 163, 163n1, 164n1
financial arrangements for, xx–xxi, xxiv, 156–61, 158n1, 159n2, 160n2, 161n2
inquiry by Macmillan about, 155
proofs of, 161, 161n1, 162
sales of, 147n2
serialisation of, 156, 157, 158n3
writing of, 145–6, 146n7, 148n1
'Tree of Knowledge, The', 195n2
Trollope, Anthony, 78n7, 81, 82n5, 129n2
Trübner and Company, 6n1
Turgénieff, Ivan, James's article on, 129n2, 201–3, 202n1
'Turn of the Screw, The', xxii, 189, 190nn3–4
Tweedy, Edmund, 121n1
*Two Magics, The*, xxii, 188n3, 190n3, 191, 191n2, 193

*Undiscovered Country, The* (W. D. Howells), 38, 38n3

Unwin, Fisher, 153

*Varieties of Religious Experience, The* (W. James), 194n2
Vredenburg, Edric, 207n3

Walsh, Catherine, 121n1
Ward, Lock and Co., 6n1, 14, 14n1
Warner, Joseph Bangs, 108n2, 111, 111n1, 112n1
Warrin, Georgiana Elizabeth, *see* Macmillan, Georgiana Elizabeth Warrin
Warrin, Miss, 20, 21n2, 69
*Washington Square*
author's copies of, 59
in *Collective Edition*, 79
English edition of, 59n1
James's discussion with Macmillan about, 53
misprint in, 56, 56n1
number of copies printed, 59, 59n1, 62–3n3
publication in the *Cornhill*, 146n3
publication of, 52n2, 55n1
receipt by Macmillan from James, 55
reviews of, 30, 30n5, 61, 61n3, 62
sales of, 59, 62, 62n3
section headings in, 56–7
two-shilling edition of, 138n1, 143
Watt, Alexander Pollack, xxi, 161n2, 162
Wharton, Edith, 220n2, 221, 222n1
*What Maisie Knew*, xxi, 187n3, 188n2
Wilkinson, J. J. Garth, 33n1
William Heinemann, *see* Heinemann, William
Woolson, Constance Fenimore, 125, 129n2, 148n1
Wormeley, Katherine Prescott, 121n1

Zola, Émile, 129n2